Operations Management

MGTS 352

Custom Edition

MacEwan University

| PEARSON COLLECTIONS |

PEARSON

Attention bookstores: For permission to return any unsold stock, contact us at pe-uscustomreturns@pearson.com

Pearson Learning Solutions, 501 Boylston Street, Suite 900, Boston, MA 02116

A Pearson Education Company
www.pearsoned.com

ISBN 10: 1323962689

ISBN 13: 9781323962688

Printed in the USA

Table of Contents

FORECASTING

KIMBERLY-CLARK

Annette M. Drowlette/ZUMAPRESS/Newscom

Accurate forecasting is crucial to maintaining the proper amount of product in the supply chain. Kimberly-Clark recently incorporated demand-signal data—information on actual consumer sales—into its forecasting system and greatly increased the accuracy of the forecasts. Here a worker moves pallets of paper products at a Kimberly-Clark warehouse in Beech Island, South Carolina.

What do Kleenex tissues, Huggies diapers, and Scott paper towels all have in common? They are all produced by Kimberly-Clark, a $18 billion multinational company based in Irving, Texas. With 91 production and warehouse facilities worldwide, one can only imagine the complexity of ensuring that retail customers located in 175 countries receive their orders on time.

From Chapter 8 of *Operations Management: Processes and Supply Chains*, Twelfth Edition. Lee J. Krajewski, Manoj K. Malhotra, Larry P. Ritzman. Copyright © 2019 by Pearson Education, Inc. All rights reserved.

Any time the retailer's inventories are out of sync with production forecasts, it can have a dramatic effect on Kimberly-Clark's bottom line: Empty shelves at the retail level force consumers to seek out competitors' products; too much inventory, on the other hand, is very costly for the company. For example, during the high-volume flu season, a one-day reduction in safety stock inventories translates into a $10 million savings across the supply chain network. It is no wonder that forecast accuracy is a top priority at Kimberly-Clark. Forecast errors drive the need for safety stocks (greater forecast errors equate to greater uncertainty in demands) and result in inefficient operations and higher costs. Consequently, Kimberly-Clark undertook a major project to improve its forecasting performance.

Prior to the onset of the project, forecasts were based on historical shipment data. The shipments were geared to satisfy actual customer orders. Intuitively, those data should be good for making forecasts of future orders. However, actual shipments may be subject to all sorts of anomalies such as supply disruptions, factory or transportation capacity limits, or severe weather, all of which could delay the shipments and miss the dates when the customer actually wanted the product. Perhaps the biggest problem with using past shipment data for making forecasts is that it is backward looking; forecasts assume that what happened in the past will happen in the future. Such an approach will miss spikes in consumer demand. For example, Hurricane Sandy pummeled the East Coast in 2012 and caused a drop in the sales of paper products in the northeast region. Estimating weekly sales on the basis of historical shipment data when there was no storm will be fraught with errors; even managerial judgment to temper the forecasts will not provide much relief. When would consumers in the northeast turn their attention from buying generators and portable lighting products to paper towels and diapers again?

The project to improve forecasting performance was a major part of a larger project to create a demand-driven supply chain. Kimberly-Clark reduced the number of production facilities and warehouses, opened new larger facilities, and repurposed others to handle a smaller set of customers or to ship only promotional items. All told, this design not only improved logistical efficiency but also simplified the forecasting effort. The key, however, to creating a demand-driven supply chain was to incorporate demand-signal data—information about actual consumer purchases—into its plans to resupply retailers with product. In close collaboration with Terra Technology, whose Multienterprise Demand Sensing (MDS) system was chosen for the forecasting tool, Kimberly-Clark incorporated the point-of-sale (POS) data from three of its largest retail customers in North America. The software uses that data along with inventory in the distribution channel, shipments from warehouses, and the retailer's own forecasts to create a daily operational forecast. These inputs are reevaluated weekly for their influence on the forecast. For example, POS might be the best predictor of a shipment forecast on a 3-week horizon, but actual orders could be the best predictor for the current week. A new metric for evaluating forecast performance was created; it was defined as the absolute difference between shipments and forecast and reported as a percentage of shipments. Using that metric and the new forecasting system, Kimberly-Clark observed forecast error reductions as high as 35 percent in the first week of the horizon and 20 percent on a 2-week horizon. These forecast error reductions can translate into a 1- to 3-week reduction in safety stocks.

Sources: James A. Cooke, "Kimberly-Clark Connects Its Supply Chain to the Store Shelf," *DC Velocity,* April 10, 2013; Paul Taylor, "Demand Forecasting Pays Off for Kimberly-Clark," *Financial Times,* September 10, 2011; Heather Clancy, "Kimberly-Clark Makes Sense of Demand," *CGT,* **http://consumergoods.edgl.com**; Kimberly-Clark Annual Report, 2013, **http://www.Kimberly-Clark.com**.

LEARNING GOALS *After reading this text, you should be able to:*

1 Explain how managers can change demand patterns.

2 Describe the two key decisions on making forecasts.

3 Calculate the five basic measures of forecast errors.

4 Compare and contrast the four approaches to judgmental forecasting.

5 Use regression to make forecasts with one or more independent variables.

6 Make forecasts using the five most common statistical approaches for time-series analysis.

7 Describe the big-data approach and the six steps in a typical forecasting process.

Balancing supply and demand begins with making accurate forecasts, and then reconciling them across the supply chain as shown by Kimberly-Clark. A **forecast** is a prediction of future events used for planning purposes. Planning, on the other hand, is the process of making management decisions on how to deploy resources to best respond to the demand forecasts. Forecasting methods may be based on mathematical models that use available historical data, or on qualitative methods that draw on managerial experience and judgments, or on a combination of both.

In this text our focus is on demand forecasts. We begin with different types of demand patterns. We examine forecasting methods in three basic categories: (1) judgment, (2) causal, and (3) time-series methods. Forecast errors are defined, providing important clues for making better forecasts. We next consider the forecasting techniques themselves, and then how they can be combined to bring together insights from several sources. We conclude with a discussion of new advanced forecasting methods that make use of the vast amounts of data available from cellular devices and the Internet, along with an overall process for making forecasts and designing the forecasting system.

Forecasts are useful for both managing processes and managing supply chains. At the supply chain level, a firm needs forecasts to coordinate with its customers and suppliers. At the process

forecast

A prediction of future events used for planning purposes.

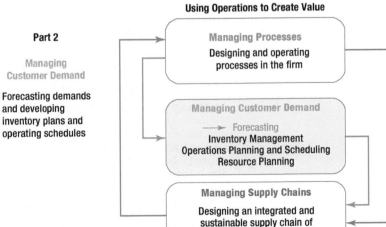

Using Operations to Create Value

Part 2

Managing Customer Demand

Forecasting demands and developing inventory plans and operating schedules

Managing Processes
Designing and operating processes in the firm

Managing Customer Demand
→ Forecasting
Inventory Management
Operations Planning and Scheduling
Resource Planning

Managing Supply Chains
Designing an integrated and sustainable supply chain of connected processes between firms

level, output forecasts are needed to design the various processes throughout the organization, including identifying and dealing with in-house bottlenecks.

As you might imagine, the organization-wide forecasting process cuts across functional areas. Forecasting overall demand typically originates with marketing, but internal customers throughout the organization depend on forecasts to formulate and execute their plans as well. Forecasts are critical inputs to business plans, annual plans, and budgets. Finance needs forecasts to project cash flows and capital requirements. Human resources will use forecasts to anticipate hiring and training needs. Marketing is an important source for sales forecast information because it is closest to external customers. Operations and supply chain managers need forecasts to plan output levels, purchases of services and materials, workforce and output schedules, inventories, and long-term capacities. Managers at all levels need estimates of future demands, so that they can plan activities that are consistent with the firm's competitive priorities.

Managing Demand

Before we get into the tools and techniques for forecasting demands, it is important to understand that the timing and sizing of customer demand can often be manipulated. Accurately forecasting customer demand is a difficult task because the demand for services and goods can vary greatly. For example, demand for lawn fertilizer predictably increases in the spring and summer months; however, the particular weekends when demand is heaviest may depend on uncontrollable factors such as the weather. These demand swings are costly to satisfy for any process, even if they are predictable. However, managers can often do two things to alleviate the pains of demand swings: First, understand the demand pattern they are facing; second, employ one or more options to alleviate any avoidable swings.

Demand Patterns

time series

The repeated observations of demand for a service or product in their order of occurrence.

Forecasting demand requires uncovering the underlying patterns from available information. The repeated observations of demand for a service or product in their order of occurrence form a pattern known as a **time series**. There are five basic patterns of most demand time series:

1. *Horizontal.* The fluctuation of data around a constant mean.
2. *Trend.* The systematic increase or decrease in the mean of the series over time.
3. *Seasonal.* A repeatable pattern of increases or decreases in demand, depending on the time of day, week, month, or season.
4. *Cyclical.* The less predictable gradual increases or decreases in demand over longer periods of time (years or decades).
5. *Random.* The unforecastable variation in demand.

Cyclical patterns arise from two influences. The first is the business cycle, which includes factors that cause the economy to go from recession to expansion over a number of years. The other influence is the service or product life cycle, which reflects the stages of demand from development through decline. Business cycle demand is difficult to predict because it is affected by national or international events.

The four patterns of demand—horizontal, trend, seasonal, and cyclical—combine in varying degrees to define the underlying time pattern of demand for a service or product. The fifth pattern, random variation, results from chance causes and thus cannot be predicted. Random variation is an aspect of demand that makes every forecast ultimately inaccurate. Figure 1 shows the first four patterns of a demand time series, all of which contain random variations.

Demand Management Options

demand management

The process of changing demand patterns using one or more demand options.

Matching supply with demand becomes a challenge when forecasts call for uneven demand patterns—and uneven demand is more the rule than the exception. Demand swings can be from one month to the next, one week to the next, or even one hour to the next. Peaks and valleys in demand are costly or can cause poor customer service. Air New Zealand can lose sales because capacity is exceeded for one of its flights, while another of its flights to the same destination at about the same time has many empty seats. If nothing is done to even out demand, sales are lost or greater capacity cushions might be needed. All come at an extra cost. Here we deal with **demand management**, the process of changing demand patterns using one or more demand options.

Various options are available in managing demand, including complementary products, promotional pricing, prescheduled appointments, reservations, revenue management, backlogs, backorders, and stockouts. The manager may select one or more of them, as we illustrate next.

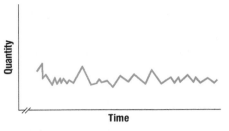

(a) Horizontal: Data cluster about a horizontal line.

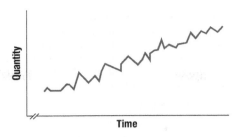

(b) Trend: Data consistently increase or decrease.

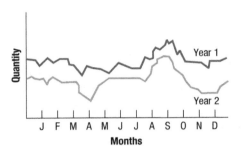

(c) Seasonal: Data consistently show peaks and valleys.

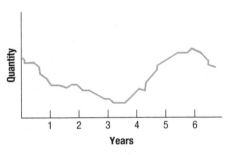

(d) Cyclical: Data reveal gradual increases and decreases over extended periods of time.

◄ **FIGURE 1**
Patterns of Demand
MyLab Operations Management Animation

Complementary Products One demand option for a company to even out the load on resources is to produce **complementary products**, or services that have similar resource requirements but different demand cycles. For example, manufacturers of matzoh balls for the Jewish Passover holiday are in a seasonal business. The B. Manischewitz Company, a kosher foods manufacturer in Jersey City, New Jersey, previously experienced 40 percent of its annual sales for the 8-day Passover holiday alone. It expanded toward markets with yearround appeal such as low-carb, low-fat foods, including canned soups and crackers, borscht, cake mixes, dressing and spreads, juices, and condiments.

For service providers, a city parks and recreation department can counterbalance seasonal staffing requirements for summer activities by offering ice skating, tobogganing, or indoor activities during the winter months. The key is to find services and products that can be produced with the existing resources and can level off the need for resources over the year.

complementary products

Services or products that have similar resource requirements but different demand cycles.

Promotional Pricing Promotional campaigns are designed to increase sales with creative pricing. Examples include automobile rebate programs, price reductions for winter clothing in the late summer months, reduced prices for hotel rooms during off-peak periods, and "two-for-the-price-of-one" automobile tire sales. Lower prices can increase demand for the product or service from new and existing customers during traditional slack periods or encourage customers to move up future buying.

Prescheduled Appointments Service providers often can schedule customers for definite periods of order fulfillment. With this approach, demand is leveled to not exceed supply capacity. An appointment system assigns specific times for service to customers. The advantages of this method are timely customer service and the high utilization of service personnel.

Retailers can manage demand for certain products with promotional pricing through the use of apps such as the new Amazon Windowshop for iPad tablet computers.

Doctors, dentists, lawyers, and automobile repair shops are examples of service providers that use appointment systems. Doctors can use the system to schedule parts of their day to visit hospital patients, and lawyers can set aside time to prepare cases. Care must be taken to tailor the length of appointments to individual customer needs rather than merely scheduling customers at equal time intervals.

Reservations Reservation systems, although quite similar to appointment systems, are used when the customer actually occupies or uses facilities associated with the service. For example, customers reserve hotel rooms, automobiles, airline seats, and concert seats. The major advantage of reservation systems is the lead time they give service managers and the ability to level demand. Managers can deal with no-shows with a blend of overbooking, deposits, and cancellation penalties. Sometimes overbooking means that a customer with reservations cannot be served as promised. In such cases, bonuses can be offered for compensation. For example, an airline passenger might not only get on the next available flight, but also may be given a free ticket for a second flight sometime in the future.

Revenue Management   A specialized combination of the pricing and reservation options for service providers is revenue management. **Revenue management** (sometimes called *yield management*) is the process of varying price at the right time for different customer segments to maximize revenues generated from existing supply capacity. It works best if customers can be segmented, prices can be varied by segment, fixed costs are high, variable costs are low, service duration is predictable, and capacity is lost if not used (sometimes called *perishable capacity*). Airlines, hotels, cruise lines, restaurants (early-bird specials), and rental cars are good examples. Computerized reservation systems can make hour-by-hour updates, using decision rules for opening or closing price classes depending on the difference between supply and continually updated demand forecasts. In the airlines industry, prices are lowered if a particular airline flight is not selling as fast as expected, until more seats are booked. Alternately, if larger than expected demand is developing, prices for the remaining seats may be increased. Last-minute business travelers pay the higher prices, whereas leisure travelers making reservations well in advance and staying over the weekend get the bargain prices. Southwest Airlines now segments its customers by creating a "Business Select" ticket class that rewards more perks to frequent fliers willing to pay higher prices.

Backlogs   Much like the appointments or reservations of service providers, a **backlog** is an accumulation of customer orders that a manufacturer has promised for delivery at some future date. Manufacturers in the supply chain that maintain a backlog of orders as a normal business practice can allow the backlog to grow during periods of high demand and then reduce it during periods of low demand. Airplane manufacturers do not promise instantaneous delivery, as do wholesalers or retailers farther forward in the supply chain. Instead, they impose a lead time between when the order is placed and when it is delivered. For example, an automotive parts manufacturer may agree to deliver to the repair department of a car dealership a batch of 100 door latches for a particular car model next Tuesday. The parts manufacturer uses that due date to plan its production of door latches within its capacity limits. Firms that are most likely to use backlogs—and increase the size of them during periods of heavy demand—make customized products and tend to have a make-to-order strategy. Backlogs reduce the uncertainty of future production requirements and also can be used to level demand. However, they become a competitive disadvantage if they get too big.

Backorders and Stockouts   A last resort in demand management is to set lower standards for customer service, either in the form of backorders or stockouts. Not to be confused with a backlog, a **backorder** is a customer order that cannot be filled when promised or demanded but is filled later. Demand may be too unpredictable or the item may be too costly to hold it in inventory. Although the customer is not pleased with the delay, the customer order is not lost and it is filled at a later date. In contrast, a **stockout** is an order that cannot be satisfied, resulting in a loss of the sale. A backorder adds to the next period's demand requirement, whereas a stockout does not. Backorders and stockouts can lead dissatisfied customers to do their future business with another firm. Generally, backorders and stockouts are to be avoided.

Combinations of demand options can also be used. For example, a manufacturer of lighting equipment had several products characterized as "slow movers with spikes," where only 2 or 3 units were sold for several weeks, and then suddenly there was a huge order for 10,000 units the next week. The reason is that their product was purchased by commercial property managers who might be upgrading the lighting in a large office building. The result was a forecasting nightmare and having to resort to high-cost supply options to meet the demand spikes. The breakthrough in solving this problem was to combine the pricing and backlog options. Contractors are now offered a 3 percent discount (the pricing option) on any order in excess of 10,000 units that are placed 5+ weeks before they are needed (the backlog option). The advanced warning allows the manufacturer to smooth out its production processes, saving millions of dollars annually.

Key Decisions on Making Forecasts

Before using forecasting techniques, a manager must make two decisions: (1) what to forecast, and (2) what type of forecasting technique to select for different items.

Deciding What to Forecast

Although some sort of demand estimate is needed for the individual services or goods produced by a company, forecasting total demand for groups or clusters and then deriving individual service or product forecasts may be easiest. Also, selecting the correct unit of measurement (e.g., units, customers, or machine-hours) for forecasting may be as important as choosing the best method.

---

revenue management

Varying price at the right time for different customer segments to maximize revenues yielded by existing supply capacity.

backlog

An accumulation of customer orders that a manufacturer has promised for delivery at some future date.

backorder

A customer order that cannot be filled when promised or demanded but is filled later.

stockout

An order that cannot be satisfied, resulting in a loss of the sale.

Level of Aggregation   Few companies err by more than 5 percent when forecasting the annual total demand for all their services or products. However, errors in forecasts for individual items and shorter time periods may be much higher. Recognizing this reality, many companies use a two-tier forecasting system. They first cluster (or "roll up") several similar services or products in a process called **aggregation**, making forecasts for families of services or goods that have similar demand requirements and common processing, labor, and materials requirements. Next, they derive forecasts for individual items, which are sometimes called stock-keeping units. A *stock-keeping unit (SKU)* is an individual item or product that has an identifying code and is held in inventory somewhere along the supply chain, such as in a distribution center.

aggregation

The act of clustering several similar services or products so that forecasts and plans can be made for whole families.

Units of Measurement   Rather than using dollars as the initial unit of measurement, forecasts often begin with service or product units, such as individual products, express packages to deliver, or customers needing maintenance service or repairs for their cars. Forecasted units can then be translated to dollars by multiplying them by the unit price. If accurately forecasting demand for a service or product is not possible in terms of number of units, forecast the standard labor or machine-hours required of each of the critical resources.

Choosing the Type of Forecasting Technique

Forecasting systems offer a variety of techniques, and no one of them is best for all items and situations. The forecaster's objective is to develop a useful forecast from the information at hand with the technique that is appropriate for the different patterns of demand. Two general types of forecasting techniques are used: judgment methods and quantitative methods. **Judgment methods** translate the opinions of managers, expert opinions, consumer surveys, and salesforce estimates into quantitative estimates. Quantitative methods include causal methods, time-series analysis, and trend projection with regression. **Causal methods** use historical data on independent variables, such as promotional campaigns, economic conditions, and competitors' actions, to predict demand. **Time-series analysis** is a statistical approach that relies heavily on historical demand data to project the future size of demand and recognizes trends and seasonal patterns. **Trend projection with regression** is a hybrid between a time-series technique and the causal method.

judgment methods

A forecasting method that translates the opinions of managers, expert opinions, consumer surveys, and salesforce estimates into quantitative estimates.

causal methods

A quantitative forecasting method that uses historical data on independent variables, such as promotional campaigns, economic conditions, and competitors' actions, to predict demand.

time-series analysis

A statistical approach that relies heavily on historical demand data to project the future size of demand and recognizes trends and seasonal patterns.

trend projection with regression

A forecasting model that is a hybrid between a time-series technique and the causal method.

Forecast Error

For any forecasting technique, it is important to measure the accuracy of its forecasts. Forecasts almost always contain errors. Random error results from unpredictable factors that cause the forecast to deviate from the actual demand. Forecasting analysts try to minimize forecast errors by selecting appropriate forecasting models, but eliminating all forms of errors is impossible.

Forecast error for a given period t is simply the difference found by subtracting the forecast from actual demand, or

$$E_t = D_t - F_t$$

where

$$E_t = \text{forecast error for period } t$$

$$D_t = \text{actual demand for period } t$$

$$F_t = \text{forecast for period } t$$

This equation (notice the alphabetical order with D_t coming before F_t) is the starting point for creating several measures of forecast error that cover longer periods of time.

There are five basic measures of forecast error: CFE, MSE, (σ), MAD, and MAPE. Figure 2 shows the output from the *Error Analysis* routine in Forecasting's dropdown menu of POM for Windows. Part (a) gives a big-picture view of how well the forecast has been tracking the actual demand. Part (b) shows the detailed calculations needed to obtain the summary error terms; and Part (c) gives the summary error measures summarized across all 10 time periods, as derived from Part (b).

forecast error

The difference found by subtracting the forecast from actual demand for a given period.

Cumulative Sum of Forecast Errors

The **cumulative sum of forecast errors (CFE)** measures the total forecast error:

$$\text{CFE} = \Sigma E_t$$

CFE is a cumulative sum. Figure 2(b) shows that it is the sum of the errors for all 10 periods. For any given period, it would be the sum of errors up through that period. For example, it would be -8 (or $2 - 6$) for period 2. CFE is also called the *bias error* and results from consistent mistakes—the forecast is always too high or too low. This type of error typically causes the greatest disruption to planning efforts. For example, if a forecast is consistently lower than actual demand,

cumulative sum of forecast errors (CFE)

A measurement of the total forecast error that assesses the bias in a forecast.

FIGURE 2(A) ▶

Graph of Actual and Forecast Demand Using *Error Analysis* of Forecasting in POM for Windows

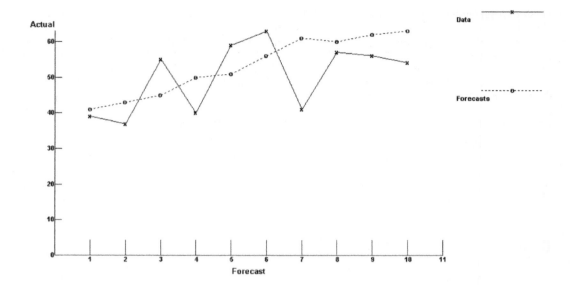

then the value of CFE will gradually get larger and larger. This increasingly large error indicates some systematic deficiency in the forecasting approach. The average forecast error, sometimes called the *mean bias*, is simply

$$\overline{E} = \frac{\text{CFE}}{n}$$

mean squared error (MSE)

A measurement of the dispersion of forecast errors.

standard deviation of the errors (σ)

A measurement of the dispersion of forecast errors.

mean absolute deviation (MAD)

A measurement of the dispersion of forecast errors.

Dispersion of Forecast Errors

The **mean squared error (MSE)**, **standard deviation of the errors (σ)**, and **mean absolute deviation (MAD)** measure the dispersion of forecast errors attributed to trend, seasonal, cyclical, or random effects:

$$\text{MSE} = \frac{\Sigma E_t^2}{n}$$

$$\sigma = \frac{\Sigma (E_t - \overline{E})^2}{n - 1}$$

$$\text{MAD} = \frac{\Sigma |E_t|}{n}$$

Figure 2(b) shows the squared error in period 1 is 4, and MSE is 87.9 for the whole sample. The standard deviation of the errors, shown as 9.883 in Figure 2(b), is calculated using a separate

FIGURE 2(B) ▶

Detailed Calculations of Forecast Errors

	Actual	Forecast	Error	|Error|	Error^2	|Pct Error|
Past period 1	39	41	-2	2	4	5.128%
Past period 2	37	43	-6	6	36	16.216%
Past period 3	55	45	10	10	100	18.182%
Past period 4	40	50	-10	10	100	25%
Past period 5	59	51	8	8	64	13.559%
Past period 6	63	56	7	7	49	11.111%
Past period 7	41	61	-20	20	400	48.78%
Past period 8	57	60	-3	3	9	5.263%
Past period 9	56	62	-6	6	36	10.714%
Past period 10	54	63	-9	9	81	16.667%
TOTALS	501		-31	81	879	170.621%
AVERAGE	50.1		-3.1	8.1	87.9	17.062%
Next period forecast			0	(Bias)	(MAD)	(MSE)	(MAPE)
				Std err	9.883	

function available in Excel. The absolute value of the error in period 2 is 6, and MAD is 8.1 across the whole sample.

The mathematical symbol | | is used to indicate the absolute value—that is, it tells you to disregard positive or negative signs. If MSE, σ, or MAD is small, then the forecast is typically close to actual demand; by contrast, a large value indicates the possibility of large forecast errors. The measures do differ in the way they emphasize errors. Large errors get far more weight in MSE and σ because the errors are squared. MAD is a widely used measure of forecast error and is easily understood; it is merely the mean of the absolute forecast errors over a series of time periods, without regard to whether the error was an overestimate or an underestimate.

Mean Absolute Percent Error

The **mean absolute percent error (MAPE)** relates the forecast error to the level of demand and is useful for putting forecast performance in the proper perspective:

$$\text{MAPE} = \frac{(\Sigma |E_t|/D_t)(100)}{n} \text{ (expressed as a percentage)}$$

For example, an absolute forecast error of 100 results in a larger percentage error when the demand is 200 units than when the demand is 10,000 units. MAPE is the best error measure to use when making comparisons between time series for different SKUs. Looking again at Figure 2(b), the percent error in period 2 is 16.22 percent, and MAPE, the average over all 10 periods, is 17.062 percent.

Finally, Figure 2(c) summarizes the key error terms across all 10 time periods. They are actually found in selected portions of Figure 2(b). For example, CFE is −31, which is in the error column of Figure 2(b) in the TOTALS row. MAD is 8.1, found in the |Error| column and AVERAGE row. Finally, MAPE is 17.062 percent, which is in the |Pct Error| column and AVERAGE row.

mean absolute percent error (MAPE)

A measurement that relates the forecast error to the level of demand and is useful for putting forecast performance in the proper perspective.

◀ **FIGURE 2(C)**
Error Measures
Source: Howard J. Weiss, POM for Windows, Pearson Prentice Hall

Measure	Value
Error Measures	
CFE (Cumulative Forecast Error)	-31
MAD (Mean Absolute Deviation)	8.1
MSE (Mean Squared Error)	87.9
Standard Deviation of Errors	9.883
MAPE (Mean Absolute Percent Error)	17.062%

EXAMPLE 1 | **Calculating Forecast Error Measures**

The following table shows the actual sales of upholstered chairs for a furniture manufacturer and the forecasts made for each of the last 8 months. Calculate CFE, MSE, σ, MAD, and MAPE for this product.

Month, t	Demand, D_t	Forecast, F_t	Error, E_t	Error, Squared, E_t^2	Absolute Error, $|E_t|$	Absolute Percent Error, $(|E_t|/D_t)(100)$
1	200	225	−25	625	25	12.5%
2	240	220	20	400	20	8.3
3	300	285	15	225	15	5.0
4	270	290	−20	400	20	7.4
5	230	250	−20	400	20	8.7
6	260	240	20	400	20	7.7
7	210	250	−40	1,600	40	19.0
8	275	240	35	1,225	35	12.7
		Total	−15	5,275	195	81.3%

SOLUTION
Using the formulas for the measures, we get

Cumulative forecast error (bias):

CFE = −15 (the bias, or the sum of the errors for all time periods in the time series)

Average forecast error (mean bias):

$$\bar{E} = \frac{CFE}{n} = \frac{-15}{8} = -1.875$$

Mean squared error:

$$MSE = \frac{\Sigma E_t^2}{n} = \frac{5{,}275}{8} = 659.4$$

Standard deviation of the errors:

$$\sigma = \sqrt{\frac{\Sigma[E_t - (-1.875)]^2}{7}} = 27.4$$

Mean absolute deviation:

$$MAD = \frac{\Sigma|E_t|}{n} = \frac{195}{8} = 24.4$$

Mean absolute percent error:

$$MAPE = \frac{[\Sigma|E_t|/D_t]\,100}{n} = \frac{81.3\%}{8} = 10.2\%$$

A CFE of −15 indicates that the forecast has a slight bias to overestimate demand. The MSE, σ, and MAD statistics provide measures of forecast error variability. A MAD of 24.4 means that the average forecast error was 24.4 units in absolute value. The value of σ, 27.4, indicates that the sample distribution of forecast errors has a standard deviation of 27.4 units. A MAPE of 10.2 percent implies that, on average, the forecast error was within about 10 percent of actual demand. These measures become more reliable as the number of periods of data increases.

DECISION POINT
Although reasonably satisfied with these forecast performance results, the analyst decided to test out a few more forecasting methods before reaching a final forecasting method to use for the future.

Computer Support

Computer support, such as from OM Explorer or POM for Windows, makes error calculations easy when evaluating how well forecasting models fit with past data. Errors are measured across past data, often called the *history file* in practice. They show the various error measures across the entire history file for each forecasting method evaluated. They also make forecasts into the future, based on the method selected.

Judgment Methods

Forecasts from quantitative methods are possible only when there is adequate historical data (i.e., the *history file*). However, the history file may be nonexistent when a new product is introduced or when technology is expected to change. The history file might exist but be less useful when certain events (such as rollouts or special packages) are reflected in the past data, or when certain events are expected to occur in the future. In some cases, judgment methods are the only practical way to make a forecast. In other cases, judgment methods can also be used to modify forecasts that are generated by quantitative methods. They may recognize that one or two quantitative models have been performing particularly well in recent periods. Adjustments certainly would be called for if the forecaster has important contextual knowledge. *Contextual knowledge* is knowledge that practitioners gain through experience, such as cause-and-effect relationships, environmental cues, and organizational information that may have an effect on the variable being forecast. Adjustments also could account for unusual circumstances, such as a new sales promotion or unexpected international events. They could also have been used to remove the effect of special one-time events in the history file before quantitative methods are applied. Four of the more successful judgment methods are (1) salesforce estimates, (2) executive opinion, (3) market research, and (4) the Delphi method.

Salesforce estimates are forecasts compiled from estimates made periodically by members of a company's salesforce. The salesforce is the group most likely to know which services or products customers will be buying in the near future and in what quantities. Forecasts of individual salesforce members can be combined easily to get regional or national sales estimates. However, individual biases of the salespeople may taint the forecast. For example, some people are naturally optimistic, whereas others are more cautious. Adjustments in forecasts may need to be made to account for these individual biases.

Executive opinion is a forecasting method in which the opinions, experience, and technical knowledge of one or more managers or customers are summarized to arrive at a single forecast. All of the factors going into judgmental forecasts would fall into the category of executive opinion. Executive opinion can also be used for **technological forecasting**. The quick pace of technological change makes keeping abreast of the latest advances difficult.

Market research is a systematic approach to determine external consumer interest in a service or product by creating and testing hypotheses through data-gathering surveys. Conducting a market research study includes designing a questionnaire, deciding how to administer it, selecting a representative sample, and analyzing the information using judgment and statistical tools to interpret the responses. Although market research yields important information, it typically includes numerous qualifications and hedges in the findings.

The **Delphi method** is a process of gaining consensus from a group of experts while maintaining their anonymity. This form of forecasting is useful when no historical data are available from which to develop statistical models and when managers inside the firm have no experience on which to base informed projections. A coordinator sends questions to each member of the group of outside experts, who may not even know who else is participating. The coordinator prepares a statistical summary of the responses along with a summary of arguments for particular responses. The report is sent to the same group for another round, and the participants may choose to modify their previous responses. These rounds continue until consensus is obtained.

In the remainder of this text, we turn to the commonly used quantitative forecasting approaches.

Causal Methods: Linear Regression

Causal methods are used when historical data are available and the relationship between the factor to be forecasted and other external or internal factors (e.g., government actions or advertising promotions) can be identified. These relationships are expressed in mathematical terms and can be complex. Causal methods are good for predicting turning points in demand and for preparing long-range forecasts. We focus on linear regression, one of the best known and most commonly used causal methods.

In **linear regression**, one variable, called a dependent variable, is related to one or more independent variables by a linear equation. The **dependent variable** (such as demand for door hinges) is the one the manager wants to forecast. The **independent variables** (such as advertising expenditures and new housing starts) are assumed to affect the dependent variable and thereby "cause" the results observed in the past. Figure 3 shows how a linear regression line relates to the data. In technical terms, the regression line minimizes the squared deviations from the actual data.

In the simplest linear regression models, the dependent variable is a function of only one independent variable and, therefore, the theoretical relationship is a straight line:

$$Y = a + bX$$

where

$$Y = \text{dependent variable}$$
$$X = \text{independent variable}$$
$$a = Y\text{-intercept of the line}$$
$$b = \text{slope of the line}$$

The objective of linear regression analysis is to find values of a and b that minimize the sum of the squared deviations of the actual data points from the graphed line. Computer programs are used for this purpose. For any set of matched observations for Y and X, the program computes the values of a and b and provides measures of forecast accuracy. Three measures commonly reported are (1) the sample correlation coefficient, (2) the sample coefficient of determination, and (3) the standard error of the estimate.

The *sample correlation coefficient, r,* measures the direction and strength of the relationship between the independent variable and the dependent variable. The value of r can range from -1.00 to $+1.00$. A correlation coefficient of $+1.00$ implies that period-by-period changes in

salesforce estimates

The forecasts that are compiled from estimates of future demands made periodically by members of a company's salesforce.

executive opinion

A forecasting method in which the opinions, experience, and technical knowledge of one or more managers are summarized to arrive at a single forecast.

technological forecasting

An application of executive opinion to keep abreast of the latest advances in technology.

market research

A systematic approach to determine external consumer interest in a service or product by creating and testing hypotheses through data-gathering surveys.

Delphi method

A process of gaining consensus from a group of experts while maintaining their anonymity.

linear regression

A causal method in which one variable (the dependent variable) is related to one or more independent variables by a linear equation.

dependent variable

The variable that one wants to forecast.

▼ **FIGURE 3**
Linear Regression Line Relative to Actual Demand

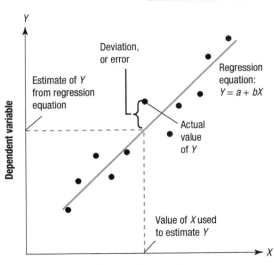

independent variables

Variables that are assumed to affect the dependent variable and thereby "cause" the results observed in the past.

direction (increases or decreases) of the independent variable are always accompanied by changes in the same direction by the dependent variable. An r of -1.00 means that decreases in the independent variable are always accompanied by increases in the dependent variable, and vice versa. A zero value of r means no linear relationship exists between the variables. The closer the value of r is to ± 1.00, the better the regression line fits the points.

The *sample coefficient of determination* measures the amount of variation in the dependent variable about its mean that is explained by the regression line. The coefficient of determination is the square of the correlation coefficient, or r^2. The value of r^2 ranges from 0.00 to 1.00. Regression equations with a value of r^2 close to 1.00 mean a close fit.

The *standard error of the estimate*, s_{xy}, measures how closely the data on the dependent variable cluster around the regression line. Although it is similar to the sample standard deviation, it measures the error from the dependent variable, Y, to the regression line, rather than to the mean. Thus, it is the standard deviation of the difference between the actual demand and the estimate provided by the regression equation.

EXAMPLE 2	**Using Linear Regression to Forecast Product Demand**

MyLab Operations Management

Active Model 1 in MyLab Operations Management provides insight on varying the intercept and slope of the model.

The supply chain manager seeks a better way to forecast the demand for door hinges and believes that the demand is related to advertising expenditures. The following are sales and advertising data for the past 5 months:

Month	Sales (in 1000s of units)	Advertising (in $1000s)
1	264	2.5
2	116	1.3
3	165	1.4
4	101	1.0
5	209	2.0

The company will spend $1,750 next month on advertising for the product. Use linear regression to develop an equation and a forecast for this product.

SOLUTION

We used POM for Windows to determine the best values of a, b, the correlation coefficient, the coefficient of determination, and the standard error of the estimate.

$$a = -8.135$$
$$b = 109.229$$
$$r = 0.980$$
$$r^2 = 0.960$$
$$s_{yx} = 15.603$$

The regression equation is

$$Y = -8.135 + 109.229X$$

and the regression line is shown in Figure 4. The sample correlation coefficient, r, is 0.98, which is unusually close to 1.00 and suggests an unusually strong positive relationship exists between sales and advertising expenditures. The sample coefficient of determination, r^2, implies that 96 percent of the variation in sales is explained by advertising expenditures.

DECISION POINT

The supply chain manager decided to use the regression model as input to planning production levels for month 6. As the advertising expenditure will be $1,750, the forecast for month 6 is $Y = -8.135 + 109.229 (1.75) = 183.016$, or 183,016 units.

Often several independent variables may affect the dependent variable. For example, advertising expenditures, new corporation startups, and residential building contracts all may be important for estimating the demand for door hinges. In such cases, *multiple regression analysis* is helpful in determining a forecasting equation for the dependent variable as a function of several independent variables. Such models can be analyzed with POM for Windows or OM Explorer and can be quite useful for predicting turning points and solving many planning problems.

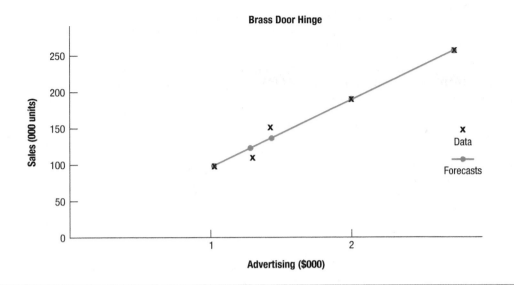

Time-Series Methods

Rather than using independent variables for the forecast as regression models do, time-series methods use historical information regarding only the dependent variable. These methods are based on the assumption that the dependent variable's past pattern will continue in the future. Time-series analysis identifies the underlying patterns of demand that combine to produce an observed historical pattern of the dependent variable and then develops a model to replicate it. In this section, we focus on five statistical time-series methods that address the horizontal, trend, and seasonal patterns of demand: simple moving averages, weighted moving averages, exponential smoothing, trend projection with regression, and multiplicative seasonal method. Before we discuss statistical methods, let us take a look at the simplest time-series method for addressing all patterns of demand—the naïve forecast.

Naïve Forecast

A method often used in practice is the **naïve forecast**, whereby the forecast for the next period (F_{t+1}) equals the demand for the current period (D_t). So if the actual demand for Wednesday is 35 customers, the forecasted demand for Thursday is 35 customers. Despite its name, the naïve forecast can perform well.

The naïve forecast method may be adapted to take into account a demand trend. The increase (or decrease) in demand observed between the last two periods is used to adjust the current demand to arrive at a forecast. Suppose that last week the demand was 120 units and the week before it was 108 units. Demand increased 12 units in 1 week, so the forecast for next week would be 120 + 12 = 132 units. The naïve forecast method also may be used to account for seasonal patterns. If the demand last July was 50,000 units, and assuming no underlying trend from one year to the next, the forecast for this July would be 50,000 units. The method works best when the horizontal, trend, or seasonal patterns are stable and random variation is small.

naïve forecast

A time-series method whereby the forecast for the next period equals the demand for the current period, or Forecast $= D_t$.

Horizontal Patterns: Estimating the Average

We begin our discussion of statistical methods of time-series forecasting with demand that has no apparent trend, seasonal, or cyclical patterns. The horizontal pattern in a time series is based on the mean of the demands, so we focus on forecasting methods that estimate the average of a time series of data. The forecast of demand for *any* period in the future is the average of the time series computed in the current period. For example, if the average of past demand calculated on Tuesday is 65 customers, the forecasts for Wednesday, Thursday, and Friday are 65 customers each day.

Consider Figure 5, which shows patient arrivals at a medical clinic over the past 28 weeks. Assuming that the time series has only a horizontal and random pattern, one approach is simply to calculate the average of the data. However, this approach has no adaptive quality if there is a

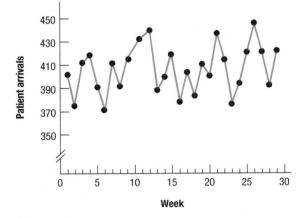

▲ FIGURE 5
Weekly Patient Arrivals at a Medical Clinic

trend, seasonal, or cyclical pattern. The statistical techniques that do have an adaptive quality in estimating the average in a time series are (1) simple moving averages, (2) weighted moving averages, and (3) exponential smoothing.

Simple Moving Averages The **simple moving average method** simply involves calculating the average demand for the n most recent time periods and using it as the forecast for future time periods. For the next period, after the demand is known, the oldest demand from the previous average is replaced with the most recent demand and the average is recalculated. In this way, the n most recent demands are used, and the average "moves" from period to period.

Specifically, the forecast for period $t + 1$ can be calculated at the end of period t (after the actual demand for period t is known) as

$$F_{t+1} = \frac{\text{Sum of last } n \text{ demands}}{n} = \frac{D_t + D_{t-1} + D_{t-2} + \cdots + D_{t-n+1}}{n}$$

where

$$D_t = \text{actual demand in period } t$$
$$n = \text{total number of periods in the average}$$
$$F_{t+1} = \text{forecast for period } t + 1$$

simple moving average method

A time-series method used to estimate the average of a demand time series by averaging the demand for the n most recent time periods.

| EXAMPLE 3 | Using the Moving Average Method to Estimate Average Demand |

MyLab Operations Management

Active Model 2 in MyLab Operations Management provides insight on the impact of varying n using the example in Figure 5.

MyLab Operations Management

Tutor 1 in MyLab Operations Management provides another example to practice making forecasts with the moving average method.

a. Compute a 3-week moving average forecast for the arrival of medical clinic patients in week 4. The numbers of arrivals for the past 3 weeks were as follows:

Week	Patient Arrivals
1	400
2	380
3	411

b. If the actual number of patient arrivals in week 4 is 415, what is the forecast error for week 4?

c. What is the forecast for week 5?

SOLUTION

a. The moving average forecast at the end of week 3 is

$$F_4 = \frac{411 + 380 + 400}{3} = 397.0$$

b. The forecast error for week 4 is

$$E_4 = D_4 - F_4 = 415 - 397 = 18$$

c. The forecast for week 5 requires the actual arrivals from weeks 2 through 4, the three most recent weeks of data.

$$F_5 = \frac{415 + 411 + 380}{3} = 402.0$$

DECISION POINT

Thus, the forecast at the end of week 3 would have been 397 patients for week 4, which fell short of actual demand by 18 patients. The forecast for week 5, made at the end of week 4, would be 402 patients. If a forecast is needed now for week 6 and beyond, it would also be for 402 patients.

The moving average method may involve the use of as many periods of past demand as desired. Large values of n should be used for demand series that are stable, and small values of n should be used for those that are susceptible to changes in the underlying average. If n is set to its lowest level (i.e., 1), it becomes the naïve method.

Weighted Moving Averages In the simple moving average method, each demand has the same weight in the average—namely, $1/n$. In the **weighted moving average method**, each historical demand in the average can have its own weight. The sum of the weights equals 1.0. For example, in a *three-period* weighted moving average model, the most recent period might be assigned a weight of 0.50, the second most recent might be weighted 0.30, and the third most recent might be weighted 0.20. The average is obtained by multiplying the weight of each period by the value for that period and adding the products together:

$$F_{t+1} = 0.50D_t + 0.30D_{t-1} + 0.20D_{t-2}$$

weighted moving average method

A time-series method in which each historical demand in the average can have its own weight; the sum of the weights equals 1.0.

For a numerical example of using the weighted moving average method to estimate average demand, see Solved Problem 2 and Tutor 2 of OM Explorer in MyLab Operations Management.

The advantage of a weighted moving average method is that it allows you to emphasize recent demand over earlier demand. (It can even handle seasonal effects by putting higher weights on prior years in the same season.) The forecast will be more responsive to changes in the underlying average of the demand series than the simple moving average forecast.

Exponential Smoothing The **exponential smoothing method** is a sophisticated weighted moving average method that calculates the average of a time series by implicitly giving recent demands more weight than earlier demands, all the way back to the first period in the history file. It is the most frequently used formal forecasting method because of its simplicity and the small amount of data needed to support it. Unlike the weighted moving average method, which requires n periods of past demand and n weights, exponential smoothing requires only three items of data: (1) the last period's forecast; (2) the actual demand for this period; and (3) a smoothing parameter, alpha (α), which has a value between 0 and 1.0. The equation for the exponentially smoothed forecast for period $t + 1$ is calculated

$$F_{t+1} = \alpha D_t + (1 - \alpha)F_t$$

exponential smoothing method

A weighted moving average method that calculates the average of a time series by implicitly giving recent demands more weight than earlier demands.

The emphasis given to the most recent demand levels can be adjusted by changing the smoothing parameter. Larger α values emphasize recent levels of demand and result in forecasts more responsive to changes in the underlying average. Smaller α values treat past demand more uniformly and result in more stable forecasts. Smaller α values are analogous to increasing the value of n in the moving average method and giving greater weight to past demand. In practice, various values of α are tried and the one producing the best forecasts is chosen.

Exponential smoothing requires an initial forecast to get started. There are several ways to get this initial forecast. OM Explorer and POM for Windows use the actual demand in the first period as a default setting, which becomes the forecast for the second period. Forecasts and forecast errors then are calculated beginning with period 2. If some historical data are available, the initial forecast can be found by calculating the average of several recent periods of demand. The effect of the initial estimate of the average on successive estimates of the average diminishes over time.

| EXAMPLE 4 | Using Exponential Smoothing to Estimate Average Demand |

a. Reconsider the patient arrival data in Example 3. It is now the end of week 3, so the actual number of arrivals is known to be 411 patients. Using $\alpha = 0.10$, calculate the exponential smoothing forecast for week 4.

b. What was the forecast error for week 4 if the actual demand turned out to be 415?

c. What is the forecast for week 5?

MyLab Operations Management

Active Model 3 in MyLab Operations Management provides insight on the impact of varying α in Figure 5.

SOLUTION

a. The exponential smoothing method requires an initial forecast. Suppose that we take the demand data for the first 2 weeks and average them, obtaining $(400 + 380)/2 = 390$ as an initial forecast. (POM for Windows and OM Explorer simply use the actual demand for the first week as a default setting for the initial forecast for period 1, and do not begin tracking forecast errors until the second period.) To obtain the forecast for week 4, using exponential smoothing with $D_3 = 411$, $\alpha = 0.10$, and $F_3 = 390$, we calculate the forecast for week 4 as

$$F_4 = 0.10(411) + 0.90(390) = 392.1$$

MyLab Operations Management

Tutor 3 in MyLab Operations Management provides a new practice example of how to make forecasts with the exponential smoothing method.

Thus, the forecast for week 4 would be 392 patients.

b. The forecast error for week 4 is

$$E_4 = 415 - 392 = 23$$

c. The new forecast for week 5 would be

$$F_5 = 0.10(415) + 0.90(392.1) = 394.4$$

or 394 patients. Note that we used F_4, not the integer-value forecast for week 4, in the computation for F_5. In general, we round off (when it is appropriate) only the final result to maintain as much accuracy as possible in the calculations.

DECISION POINT

Using this exponential smoothing model, the analyst's forecasts would have been 392 patients for week 4 and then 394 patients for week 5 and beyond. As soon as the actual demand for week 5 is known, then the forecast for week 6 will be updated.

Because exponential smoothing is simple and requires minimal data, it is inexpensive and attractive to firms that make thousands of forecasts for each time period. However, its simplicity also is a disadvantage when the underlying average is changing, as in the case of a demand series with a trend. Like any method geared solely to the assumption of a stable average, exponential smoothing results will lag behind changes in the underlying average of demand. Higher α values may help reduce forecast errors when there is a change in the average; however, the lags will still occur if the average is changing systematically. Typically, if large α values (e.g., larger than 0.50) are required for an exponential smoothing application, chances are good that another model is needed because of a significant trend or seasonal influence in the demand series.

Trend Patterns: Using Regression

Let us now consider a demand time series that has a trend. A *trend* in a time series is a systematic increase or decrease in the average of the series over time. Where a significant trend is present, forecasts from naïve, moving average, and exponential smoothing approaches are adaptive, but still lag behind actual demand and tend to be below or above the actual demand.

Trend projection with regression is a forecasting model that accounts for the trend with simple regression analysis. To develop a regression model for forecasting the trend, let the dependent variable, Y, be a period's demand and the independent variable, t, be the time period. For the first period, let $t = 1$; for the second period, let $t = 2$; and so on. The regression equation is

$$F_t = a + bt$$

One advantage of the trend projection with regression model is that it can forecast demand well into the future. The previous models project demand just one period ahead, and assume that demand beyond that will remain at that same level. Of course, all of the models (including the trend projection with regression model) can be updated each period to stay current. One *apparent* disadvantage of the trend with regression model is that it is not adaptive. The solution to this problem comes when you answer the following question: If you had the past sales of Ford automobiles since 1920, would you include each year in your regression analysis, giving equal weight to each year's sales, or include just the sales for more recent years? You most likely would decide to include just the more recent years, making your regression model more adaptive. The trend projection with regression model can thus be made more or less adaptive by the selection of historical data periods to include in the same way as moving average (changing n) or exponential smoothing (changing α) models do.

The trend projection with regression model can be solved with either the *Trend Projection with Regression* Solver or the *Time Series Forecasting* Solver in OM Explorer. Both solvers provide the regression coefficients, coefficient of determination r^2, error measures, and forecasts into the future. POM for Windows has an alternative model (a description is provided in MyLab Operations Management) that includes the trend, called the *Trend-Adjusted Smoothing* model.

The *Trend Projection with Regression* Solver focuses exclusively on trend analysis. Its graph gives a big-picture view of how well the model fits the actual demand. Its sliders allow you to control when the regression begins, how many periods are included in the regression analysis, and how many periods you want forecasted into the future. The *Time Series Forecasting* Solver, on the other hand, covers all time series models, including the trend projection with regression. It also computes a combination forecast, which we cover in a subsequent section on using multiple techniques.

MyLab Operations Management

| EXAMPLE 5 | Using Trend Projection with Regression to Forecast a Demand Series with a Trend |

Medanalysis, Inc., provides medical laboratory services to patients of Health Providers, a group of 10 family-practice doctors associated with a new health maintenance program. Managers are interested in forecasting the number of blood analysis requests per week. Recent publicity about the damaging effects of cholesterol on the heart has caused a national increase in requests for standard blood tests. The arrivals over the last 16 weeks are given in Table 1. What is the forecasted demand for the next three periods?

TABLE 1 | ARRIVALS AT MEDANALYSIS FOR LAST 16 WEEKS

Week	Arrivals	Week	Arrivals
1	28	9	61
2	27	10	39
3	44	11	55
4	37	12	54
5	35	13	52
6	53	14	60
7	38	15	60
8	57	16	75

SOLUTION

Figure 6(a) shows the results using the *Trend Projection with Regression* Solver when all 16 weeks are included in the regression analysis, with Figure 6(b) showing the worksheet that goes with it.

Looking at the Results sheet of Figure 6(a), we see that the Y-intercept of the trend line (a) is 28.50 and the slope of the line (b) is 2.35. Thus, the trend equation is $F_t = a + bt$, where t is the time period for which you are forecasting. The forecast for period 19 is $28.5 + 2.35(19) = 73$. The error terms are

Solver - Trend Projection with Regression

◀ **FIGURE 6(A)**
Trend Projection with Regression Results

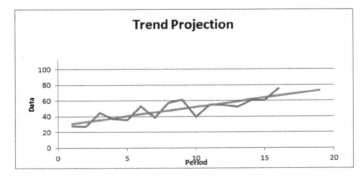

Regression begins in period	1
Error analysis begins in period	1
Number of future forecasts	3

Trend Projection

a (Y intercept)	28.50
b (slope or trend)	2.35
r2	0.69
CFE	0.00
MAD	6.21
MSE	52.96
MAPE	13.53%
Forecast for period 17	68.375
Forecast for period 18	70.72059
Forecast for period 19	73.06618

CFE = 0 (which is to be expected when the regression begins at the same time that error analysis begins), MAD = 6.21, MSE = 52.96, and MAPE = 13.53 percent. The coefficient of determination r^2 is decent at 0.69. The trend line is rising gently and reaches 73 for period 19. Each period, the forecast predicts an increase of 2.35 arrivals per week.

FIGURE 6(B) ▶
Detailed Calculations of
Forecast Errors

						Averages	
			CFE	MSE	MAD	MAPE
				0.000	52.958	6.210	13.53%
Period #	Actual Demand	Forecast	Error	Running CFE	Error Squared	Absolute Error	Abs % error
1	28	31	-2.846	-2.846	8.097	2.846	10.16%
2	27	33	-6.191	-9.037	38.331	6.191	22.93%
3	44	36	8.463	-0.574	71.626	8.463	19.23%
4	37	38	-0.882	-1.456	0.779	0.882	2.38%
5	35	40	-5.228	-6.684	27.331	5.228	14.94%
6	53	43	10.426	3.743	108.711	10.426	19.67%
7	38	45	-6.919	-3.176	47.874	6.919	18.21%
8	57	47	9.735	6.559	94.776	9.735	17.08%
9	61	50	11.390	17.949	129.725	11.390	18.67%
10	39	52	-12.956	4.993	167.855	12.956	33.22%
11	55	54	0.699	5.691	0.488	0.699	1.27%
12	54	57	-2.647	3.044	7.007	2.647	4.90%
13	52	59	-6.993	-3.949	48.897	6.993	13.45%
14	60	61	-1.338	-5.287	1.791	1.338	2.23%
15	60	64	-3.684	-8.971	13.571	3.684	6.14%
16	75	66	8.971	0.000	80.471	8.971	11.96%

Seasonal Patterns: Using Seasonal Factors

Seasonal patterns are regularly repeating upward or downward movements in demand measured in periods of less than 1 year (hours, days, weeks, months, or quarters). In this context, the time periods are called *seasons*. For example, customer arrivals at a fast-food shop on any day may peak between 11 A.M. and 1 P.M. and again from 5 P.M. to 7 P.M.

An easy way to account for seasonal effects is to use one of the techniques already described, but to limit the data in the time series to those time periods in the same season. For example, for a day-of-the-week seasonal effect, one time series would be for Mondays, one for Tuesdays, and so on. Such an approach accounts for seasonal effects, but has the disadvantage of discarding considerable information on past demand.

multiplicative seasonal method

A method whereby seasonal factors are multiplied by an estimate of average demand to arrive at a seasonal forecast.

Other methods are available that analyze all past data, using one model to forecast demand for all of the seasons. We describe only the **multiplicative seasonal method**, whereby an estimate of average demand is multiplied by seasonal factors to arrive at a seasonal forecast. The four-step procedure presented here involves the use of simple averages of past demand, although more sophisticated methods for calculating averages, such as a moving average or exponential smoothing approach, could be used. The following description is based on a seasonal pattern lasting 1 year and seasons of 1 month, although the procedure can be used for any seasonal pattern and season of any length.

1. For each year, calculate the average demand per season by dividing annual demand by the number of seasons per year.

2. For each year, divide the actual demand for a season by the average demand per season. The result is a *seasonal factor* for each season in the year, which indicates the level of demand relative to the average demand. For example, a seasonal factor of 1.14 calculated for April implies that April's demand is 14 percent greater than the average demand per month.

3. Calculate the average seasonal factor for each season, using the results from step 2. Add the seasonal factors for a season and divide by the number of years of data.

4. Calculate each season's forecast for next year. Begin by forecasting next year's annual demand using the naïve method, moving averages, exponential smoothing, or trend projection with regression. Then, divide annual demand by the number of seasons per year to get the average demand per season. Finally, make the seasonal forecast by multiplying the average demand per season by the appropriate seasonal factor found in step 3.

| EXAMPLE 6 | Using the Multiplicative Seasonal Method to Forecast the Number of Customers |

The manager of the Stanley Steemer carpet cleaning company needs a quarterly forecast of the number of customers expected next year. The carpet cleaning business is seasonal, with a peak in the third quarter and a trough in the first quarter. The manager wants to forecast customer demand for each quarter of year 5, based on an estimate of total year 5 demand of 2,600 customers.

SOLUTION

The following table calculates the seasonal factor for each week.

It shows the quarterly demand data from the past 4 years, as well as the calculations performed to get the average seasonal factor for each quarter.

	YEAR 1		YEAR 2		YEAR 3		YEAR 4		
Quarter	Demand	Seasonal Factor (1)	Demand	Seasonal Factor (2)	Demand	Seasonal Factor (3)	Demand	Seasonal Factor (4)	Average Seasonal Factor [(1+2+3+4+)/4]
1	45	45/250 = 0.18	70	70/300 = 0.23333	100	100/450 = 0.22222	100	100/550 = 0.18182	0.2043
2	335	335/250 = 1.34	370	370/300 = 1.23333	585	585/450 = 1.30	725	725/550 = 1.31818	1.2979
3	520	520/250 = 2.08	590	590/300 = 1.96667	830	830/450 = 1.84444	1160	1160/550 = 2.10909	2.0001
4	100	100/250 = 0.40	170	170/300 = 0.56667	285	285/450 = 0.63333	215	215/550 = 0.39091	0.4977
Total	1,000		1,200		1,800		2,200		
Average	1,000/4 = 250		1,200/4 = 300		1,800/4 = 450		2,200/4 = 550		

For example, the seasonal factor for quarter 1 in year 1 is calculated by dividing the actual demand (45) by the average demand for the whole year (1000/4 = 250). When this is done for all 4 years, we then can average the seasonal factors for quarter 1 over all 4 years. The result is a seasonal factor of 0.2043 for quarter 1.

Once seasonal factors are calculated for all four seasons (see last column in the previous table), we then turn to making the forecasts for year 5. The manager suggests a forecast of 2,600 customers for the whole year, which seems reasonable given that the annual demand has been increasing by an average of 400 customers each year (from 1,000 in year 1 to 2,200 in year 4, or 1,200/3 = 400). The computed forecast demand is found by extending that trend, and projecting an annual demand in year 5 of 2,200 + 400 = 2,600 customers. (This same result is confirmed using the *Trend Projection with Regression* Solver of OM Explorer.) The quarterly forecasts are straightforward. First, find the average demand forecast for year 5, which is 2,600/4 = 650. Then multiply this average demand by the average seasonal index, giving us

Quarter	Forecast
1	650 × 0.2043 = 132.795
2	650 × 1.2979 = 843.635
3	650 × 2.0001 = 1,300.065
4	650 × 0.4977 = 323.505

Figure 7 shows the computer solution using the *Seasonal Forecasting* Solver in OM Explorer. Figure 7(b), the results, confirms all of the calculations we've made in this example. Notice in Figure 7(a), the inputs sheet, that a computer demand forecast is provided as a default for year 5. However, there is an option for user-supplied demand forecast that overrides the computer-supplied forecast if the manager wishes to make a judgmental forecast based on additional information.

DECISION POINT

Using this seasonal method, the analyst makes a demand forecast as low as 133 customers in the first quarter and as high as 1,300 customers in the third quarter. The season of the year clearly makes a difference.

FIGURE 7 ▶
Demand Forecasts Using the
Seasonal Forecasting
Solver of OM Explorer

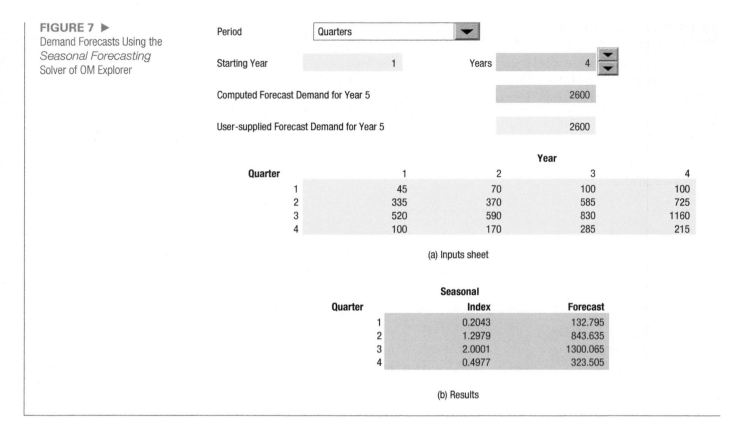

(a) Inputs sheet

Quarter	Seasonal Index	Forecast
1	0.2043	132.795
2	1.2979	843.635
3	2.0001	1300.065
4	0.4977	323.505

(b) Results

additive seasonal method

A method in which seasonal forecasts are generated by adding or subtracting a constant to the estimate of average demand per season.

An alternative to the multiplicative seasonal method is the **additive seasonal method**, whereby seasonal forecasts are generated by adding or subtracting a seasonal constant (say, 50 units) to the estimate of average demand per season. This approach is based on the assumption that the seasonal pattern is constant, regardless of average demand. The amplitude of the seasonal adjustment remains the same regardless of the level of demand.

Criteria for Selecting Time-Series Methods

Of all the time-series forecasting methods available, which should be chosen? Forecast error measures provide important information for choosing the best forecasting method for a service or product. They also guide managers in selecting the best values for the parameters needed for the method: n for the moving average method, the weights for the weighted moving average method, α for the exponential smoothing method, and when regression data begin for the trend projection with regression method. The criteria to use in making forecast method and parameter choices include (1) minimizing bias (CFE); (2) minimizing MAPE, MAD, or MSE; (3) maximizing r^2 for trend projections using regression; (4) using a holdout sample analysis; (5) using a tracking signal; (6) meeting managerial expectations of changes in the components of demand; and (7) minimizing the forecast errors in recent periods. The first three criteria relate to statistical measures based on historical performance, the fourth is a test under realistic conditions, the fifth evaluates forecast performance and the potential need to change the method, the sixth reflects expectations of the future that may not be rooted in the past, and the seventh is a way to use whatever method seems to be working best at the time a forecast must be made.

Using Statistical Criteria Statistical performance measures can be used in the selection of which forecasting method to use. The following guidelines will help when searching for the best time-series models:

1. For projections of more stable demand patterns, use lower α values or larger n values to emphasize historical experience.

2. For projections of more dynamic demand patterns using the models covered in this text, try higher α values or smaller n values. When historical demand patterns are changing, recent history should be emphasized.

Using a Holdout Sample Often, the forecaster must make tradeoffs between bias (CFE) and the measures of forecast error dispersion (MAPE, MAD, and MSE). Managers also must recognize that the best technique in explaining the past data is not necessarily the best technique to predict the future, and that "overfitting" past data can be deceptive. A forecasting method may have small errors relative to the history file, but may generate high errors for future time periods. For this reason, some analysts prefer to use a **holdout sample** as a final test (see Experiential Learning Exercise 1 at the end of this text). To do so, they set aside some of the more recent periods from the time series and use only the earlier time periods to develop and test different models. Once the final models have been selected in the first phase, they are tested again with the holdout sample. Performance measures, such as MAD and CFE, would still be used but they would be applied to the holdout sample. Whether this idea is used or not, managers should monitor future forecast errors, and modify their forecasting approaches as needed. Maintaining data on forecast performance is the ultimate test of forecasting power—rather than how well a model fits past data or holdout samples.

holdout sample

Actual demands from the more recent time periods in the time series that are set aside to test different models developed from the earlier time periods.

Using a Tracking Signal   A **tracking signal** is a measure that indicates whether a method of forecasting is accurately predicting actual changes in demand. The tracking signal measures the number of MADs represented by the cumulative sum of forecast errors, the CFE. The CFE tends to be close to 0 when a correct forecasting system is being used. At any time, however, random errors can cause the CFE to be a nonzero number. The tracking signal formula is

tracking signal

A measure that indicates whether a method of forecasting is accurately predicting actual changes in demand.

$$\text{Tracking signal} = \frac{\text{CFE}}{\text{MAD}} \text{ or } \frac{\text{CFE}}{\text{MAD}_t}$$

Each period, the CFE and MAD are updated to reflect current error, and the tracking signal is compared to some predetermined limits. The MAD can be calculated in one of two ways: (1) as the simple average of all absolute errors (as demonstrated in Example 1) or (2) as a weighted average determined by the exponential smoothing method:

$$\text{MAD}_t = \alpha \, |E_t| + (1 - \alpha)\text{MAD}_{t-1}$$

If forecast errors are normally distributed with a mean of 0, the relationship between σ and MAD is simple:

$$\sigma = (\sqrt{\pi/2})(\text{MAD}) \cong 1.25(\text{MAD})$$

$$\text{MAD} = 0.7978\sigma \cong 0.8\sigma$$

where

$$\pi = 3.1416$$

This relationship allows use of the normal probability tables to specify limits for the tracking signal. If the tracking signal falls outside those limits, the forecasting model no longer is tracking demand adequately. A tracking system is useful when forecasting systems are computerized because it alerts analysts when forecasts are getting far from desirable limits. Figure 8 shows tracking signal results for 23 periods plotted on a *control chart*. The control chart is useful for determining whether any action needs to be taken to improve the forecasting model. In the example, the first 20 points cluster around 0, as we would expect if the forecasts are not biased. The CFE will tend toward 0. When the underlying characteristics of demand change but the forecasting model does not, the tracking signal eventually goes out of control. The steady increase after the 20th point in Figure 8 indicates that the process is going out of control. The 21st and 22nd points are acceptable, but the 23rd point is not.

▼ **FIGURE 8**
Tracking Signal

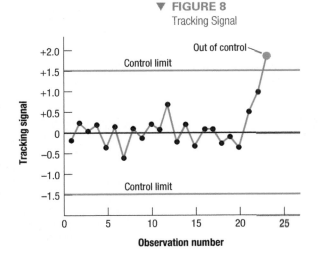

Insights into Effective Demand Forecasting

Often companies must prepare forecasts for hundreds or even thousands of services or products repeatedly. For example, a large network of health care facilities must calculate demand forecasts for each of its services for every department. This undertaking involves voluminous data that must be manipulated frequently. However, software can ease the burden of making these forecasts and coordinating the forecasts between customers and suppliers. Many forecasting software packages are available, including Manugistics, Forecast Pro, and SAS. The forecasting routines in OM Explorer and POM for Windows give some hint of their capabilities. In the hope of garnering improved insights into the demands for their products and services, a growing number of organizations are, however, going beyond these traditional forecasting capabilities and delving into the vast amounts of data that are being generated daily using advanced analytical methods. They realize that forecasting is not just a set of techniques, but instead a process that must be designed and managed. While there is no one approach to effective demand forecasting that works for everyone, here we describe the challenges and benefits of harnessing vast amounts of relevant data for demand forecasting and a comprehensive forecasting process that can be quite effective in managing operations and the supply chain.

Big Data

In this text thus far we have discussed two general types of statistical forecasting models. First, causal models use data on a set of independent variables to predict an independent variable, such as demand. The independent variables have been shown historically to have an influence on the dependent variable. The second type is time-series models, which use only data on past demands to predict the future. The assumption is that the demand pattern of the past will repeat itself in the future. Now, suppose that you have detailed data on every one of your organization's sales transactions on a given day, not only the type and quantity of the purchased product, but also other products or services customers looked at, how long they looked, and how many products were temporarily placed in the shopping cart. Suppose you also have data on how much they were influenced by promotions and product recommendations, and how they navigated your website by looking at the sequence of mouse clicks. You can also accumulate data on what the weather was like, or even whether the Cleveland Indians had a home game that day. This could amount to a lot of data. For example, it is estimated that Walmart collects more than 2.5 petabytes of data every *hour* from its customer transactions. A petabyte is 1 quadrillion bytes, or the equivalent of about 20 million filing cabinets worth of text.[1] Walmart uses this data to estimate demand for its more than 16 million online products. Imagine the enormity of the data files for Amazon.com, which sells more than 405 million products online.

To describe this phenomenon, information technologists have coined the term **big data**, which refers to data sets that are so large or complex that traditional data processing applications are inadequate to deal with them. Big data is a collection of data from traditional and digital sources that represent a source for discovery and analysis. It is characterized by three Vs: volume, variety, and velocity.

big data

Data sets that are so large or complex that traditional data processing applications are inadequate to deal with them.

Volume   More data cross the Internet every second than were stored in the entire Internet just 20 years ago. Where does it come from? It comes from a myriad of sources, such as business sales records, smartphones, or real-time sensors used in the *Internet of Things (IoT)*. We have already noted how much data online retailers such as Walmart and Amazon collect. Fortunately, the cost of collecting and storing this amount of data has dramatically declined over time.

Variety   Data useful for forecasting can come from a variety of sources. Mobile phones, online shopping, social networks, electronic communication, GPS, and instrumented machinery all produce data that can be used to predict future demands for products or services. For example, customer reviews of their experiences at a hotel on Travelocity can affect the demand for the services of that hotel. Data may exist in a wide variety of file types, including structured data (such as traditional database stores), unstructured data (such as twitter communication), or streaming data (such as data from sensors in the IoT).

Velocity   Often it is the speed, or velocity, at which the data are created and analyzed that is critical. Every big-data analytics project will ingest, correlate, and analyze data sources in response to a particular query or need. Real-time or nearly real-time information makes it possible for a company to be more agile—an important competitive priority.

Big data seems to hold a lot of promise for predicting the demand for products and services. However, there are serious considerations for managers who want to tap its powers. First, the computing power to quickly process high volumes and varieties of data can swamp a single server or cluster of servers. In some cases, it can take hundreds or thousands of servers to handle the load, which may only be used occasionally. Consequently, public cloud providers have emerged to host big-data projects. Companies are only charged for the storage and compute time actually used. An example is Amazon's Web Services (AWS), which is (as of 2015) a $7.3 billion business, and is one of the fastest growing cloud services. Well-known companies such as Adobe Systems, Airbnb, BMW, Canon, and GE have moved their online customer service applications to the Amazon cloud service where customer behavioral data are being accumulated and analyzed.[2]

Second, many companies do not have the skills needed to execute a big-data project. Critical to success are data scientists and other professionals skilled at working with large quantities of information. Skills in cleaning and organizing large data sets that rarely come in structured

---

[1]For an overview of big data and its benefits, see Andrew McAfee and Erik Brynjolfsson, "Big Data: The Management Revolution," *Harvard Business Review* (October 2012), 60–68; Lisa Arthur, "What Is Big Data?" *Forbes* (August 15, 2013), **http://onforb.es/127cyYm**; Margaret Rouse, "Big Data," **SearchCloudComputing.com** (accessed January 13, 2017).

[2]See **https://aws.amazon.com/solutions/case-studies/all/** for detailed cases of AWS clients (accessed January 20, 2107).

formats are very important. Finally, management must develop a culture that allows for the acceptance of findings from a big-data project. Starting at the top, managers who have been making decisions based on their past experiences and intuition must be amenable to accepting results that counter that judgment. Further, managers, and not technicians, must be the ones to identify the problems to tackle using big-data methods, because they have the deepest knowledge of the problem domains. Cultural change in an organization is not an overnight process and takes total managerial commitment. Nonetheless, companies employing data-driven decisions tend to be more successful than others. Managerial Practice 1 shows how big-data approaches are being used in the health care industry.

MANAGERIAL PRACTICE 1 — Big Data and Health Care Forecasting

Reliable health forecasts are important for a number of reasons. They can enhance efforts of preventive health care services, predict major life-threatening events, and estimate the demand for health care services. Big-data approaches are being used by health care facilities worldwide to improve the quality of life.

Preventive Health Care

Health care providers are being pressured by insurers and employers to find ways to prevent two critical health conditions: diabetes and heart disease. If hospitals could forecast a patient's medical future, preemptive actions could reduce the chances of hospitalization and even premature death. Some hospitals are collecting new information from patients directly, while others have sought data from companies that sell consumer and financial information, or federal agencies that provide statistics on poverty, housing density, and unemployment under the assumption that how a person lives is important for predicting future medical intervention. For example, Fairview Health Services asks primary-care patients to complete a survey of their self-confidence to manage their illness. An analysis of responses over 1 year showed that patients without confidence to manage their diabetes were 56 percent more likely to be readmitted to the hospital than the most assured and knowledgeable patients. The analysis enables Fairview to identify the high-risk patients, set up a program to help them, and plan for the necessary resources.

Predicting Cardiac Arrests

Each year, approximately 209,000 patients suffer from an in-hospital cardiac arrest in the United States, with less than a quarter living long enough to be discharged. Big-data researchers are taking advantage of the vast availability of electronic medical records to develop prediction models that would pick out the high-risk patients so that medical personnel can treat them accordingly. To facilitate this effort, the Center for Research at the University of Chicago has created a massive data warehouse of 10 years of medical records. Researchers have created a model based on 60,000 records that produces a score for each patient, based on data such as the patient's medical record, respiratory rate, blood pressure, and recent lab results. The score is monitored in real time and if it gets above a certain threshold, a response team is sent to intervene.

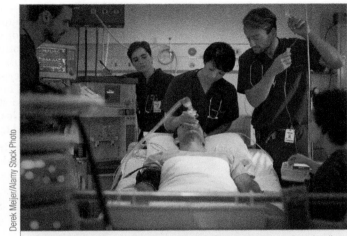

Big data is useful for forecasting demands for healthcare services in all facets of hospital operations. Here doctors treat a patient in an intensive care unit.

Demand Forecasting

Reliable demand forecasting is critical for determining staff sizes as well as capacity requirements. Such was the case when New York's Long Beach Medical Center was destroyed by Hurricane Sandy in 2012. Declaring bankruptcy after the disaster, it never reopened as a full-service hospital. The question arose as to whether another hospital should be built to replace it. Demand forecasts using data such as the size of the expected population in the coming years, the market share of the old hospital, out-of-area draw, the percentage of the population that would use the facility for inpatient care or surgery, and demographic information on the surrounding area were used to estimate the required number of physicians, assistants, rooms, and beds. The conclusion was to use freestanding emergency rooms with ambulatory care, a solution many hospitals favor over expanding of traditional hospital facilities.

Sources: Evans, Melanie. "Doctors Dig for More Data about Patients," *Wall Street Journal,* (September 25, 2016); Landro Laura. "Hospitals See Data-Crunching as a Key to a Better ICU," *Wall Street Journal,* (June 29, 2105); Kim, Meeri. ""A Netflix-Like Predictive Model: Hospital Systems Could Pinpoint Which Patients are Most Likely to Code on Their Watch," *The Washington Post* (December 4, 2015); Worth, Tammy. "Healthcare Providers Increase Reliance on Demand Forecasting," *Healthcare Finance* (December 4, 2014). pp. 1-9.

A Typical Forecasting Process

There are many inputs to the forecasting process. A key input to the database is a history file on past demand, which is kept up to date with the actual demands as they occur. Clarifying notes and adjustments are made to the database to explain unusual demand behavior, such as the impact of special promotions and closeouts. Final forecasts just made at the end of the prior cycle are entered in the history file so as to track forecast errors. Other information sources in the database are from salesforce estimates, outstanding bids on new orders, booked orders, market research studies, competitor behavior, economic outlook, new product introductions, pricing, and promotions. If point-of-sale (POS) data are used, as is done by Kimberly-Clark in the opening vignette, then considerable information sharing will take place with retail customers. For new products, a history database is constructed based on the firm's experience with prior products and the judgment of personnel.

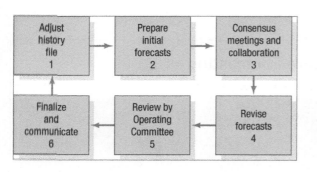

Outputs of the process are forecasts for multiple time periods into the future. Typically, they are on a monthly basis and are projected out from 6 months to 2 years or, as in the case of some big-data applications, the time horizon may be measured in hours. Most software packages have the ability to "roll up" or "aggregate" forecasts for individual stock-keeping units (SKUs) into forecasts for whole product families. Forecasts can also be "blown down" or "disaggregated" into smaller pieces. In a make-to-stock environment, forecasts tend to be more detailed and can get down to specific individual products. In a make-to-order environment, the forecasts tend to be for groups of products or services, or may actually be focused on the resources needed to produce them. Similarly, if the lead times to buy raw materials and manufacture a product or provide a service are long, the forecasts go farther out into the future.

The typical forecast process, predicated on a monthly forecast cycle, consists of six structured steps, facilitated by a demand manager and assisted by forecast analysts as needed. Shorter cycles, and a different process, are needed when forecast horizons are less than a month as in some of the health care examples in Managerial Practice 1.

Step 1. The cycle begins midmonth just after the forecasts have been finalized and communicated to the stakeholders. Now is the time to update the history file and review forecast accuracy. At the end of the month, enter actual demand and review forecast accuracy.

The demand forecasting process for the Moto Z Droid smartphone was considerably improved by closely collaborating with major retailers, obtaining point-of-sale data from them.

Step 2. Prepare initial forecasts using some forecasting software package and judgment. Adjust the parameters of the software to find models that fit the past demand well and yet reflect the demand manager's judgment on irregular events and information about future sales pulled from various sources and business units.

Step 3. Hold consensus meetings with the stakeholders, such as marketing, sales, supply chain planners, and finance. Make it easy for business unit and field sales personnel to make inputs. Use the Internet to get collaborative information from key customers and suppliers. The goal is to arrive at consensus forecasts from all important players.

Step 4. Revise the forecasts using judgment, considering the inputs from the consensus meetings and collaborative sources.

Step 5. Present the forecasts to the operating committee for review and to reach a final set of forecasts. It is important to have a set of forecasts that everybody agrees upon and will work to support.

Step 6. Finalize the forecasts based on the decisions of the operating committee and communicate them to the important stakeholders. Supply chain planners are usually the biggest users.

As with all work activity, forecasting is a process and should be continually reviewed for improvements. A better process will foster better relationships between departments such as marketing, sales, and operations. It will also produce better forecasts. This principle is the first one in Table 2 to guide process improvements.

Using Multiple Forecasting Methods

Step 2 of the forecasting process relates to preparing an initial forecast. However, we need not rely on a single forecasting method. Several different forecasts can be used to arrive at a final forecast. Initial statistical forecasts using several time-series methods and regression are distributed to knowledgeable individuals, such as marketing directors and sales teams (and sometimes even suppliers and customers) for their adjustments. They can account for current

TABLE 2 | SOME PRINCIPLES FOR THE FORECASTING PROCESS

- Better processes yield better forecasts.
- Demand forecasting is being done in virtually every company, either formally or informally. The challenge is to do it well—better than the competition.
- Better forecasts result in better customer service and lower costs, as well as better relationships with suppliers and customers.
- The forecast can and must make sense based on the big picture, economic outlook, market share, and so on.
- The best way to improve forecast accuracy is to focus on reducing forecast error.
- Bias is the worst kind of forecast error; strive for zero bias.
- Whenever possible, forecast at more aggregate levels. Forecast in detail only where necessary.
- Far more can be gained by people collaborating and communicating well than by using the most advanced forecasting technique or model.

Source: From Thomas F. Wallace and Robert A. Stahl, *Sales Forecasting: A New Approach* (Cincinnati, OH: T. E. Wallace & Company, 2002), p. 112. Copyright © 2002 T.E. Wallace & Company. Used with permission.

market and customer conditions that are not necessarily reflected in past data. Multiple forecasts may come from different sales teams, and some teams may have a better record on forecast errors than others.

Research during the last two decades suggests that combining forecasts from multiple sources often produces more accurate forecasts. **Combination forecasts** are produced by averaging independent forecasts based on different methods, different sources, or different data. It is intriguing that combination forecasts often perform better over time than even the *best* single forecasting procedure. For example, suppose that the forecast for the next period is 100 units from technique 1 and 120 units from technique 2. Technique 1, which uses different information than technique 2, has generally provided more accurate forecasts to date; however, technique 2 occasionally beats it. A combination forecast for next period, giving equal weight to each technique, is 110 units (or $0.5 \times 100 + 0.5 \times 120$). Other weighting schemes could be used, such as 60–40 in favor of technique 1. It is possible that an averaging technique used consistently into the future will be much more accurate than those of any single best forecasting technique (in this example, technique 1). Combining is most effective when the individual forecasts bring different kinds of information into the forecasting process. Forecasters have achieved excellent results by weighting such forecasts equally, and this is a good starting point. However, unequal weights may provide better results under some conditions. OM Explorer and POM for Windows allow you to evaluate several forecasting models and create combination forecasts from them. In fact, the *Time-Series Forecasting* Solver of OM Explorer automatically computes a combination forecast as a weighted average, using the weights that you supply for the various models that it evaluates. The models include the naïve, moving average, exponential smoothing, and regression trend projector methods. Alternately, you can create a simple Excel spreadsheet that combines forecasts generated by POM for Windows to create combination forecasts. The *Time Series Forecasting* Solver also allows you to evaluate your forecasting process with a holdout sample. The forecaster makes a forecast just one period ahead, and learns of given actual demand. Next the solver computes forecasts and forecast errors for the period. The process continues to the next period in the holdout sample with the forecaster committing to a forecast for the next period. To be informed, the forecaster should also be aware of how well the other forecasting methods have been performing, particularly in the recent past. Another way to take advantage of multiple techniques is **focus forecasting**, which selects the best forecast (based on past error measures) from a group of forecasts generated by individual techniques. Every period, all techniques are used to make forecasts for each item. The forecasts are made with a computer because there can be 100,000 SKUs at a company, each needing to be forecast. Using the history file as the starting point for each method, the computer generates forecasts for the current period. The forecasts are compared to actual demand, and the method that produces the forecast with the least error is used to make the forecast for the next period. The method used for each item may change from period to period.

Adding Collaboration to the Process

In step 3 of the forecasting process we try to achieve consensus of the forecast. One way to achieve that consensus in a formal way is to employ **collaborative planning, forecasting, and replenishment (CPFR)**, a process for supply chain integration that allows a supplier and its customers to collaborate on making the forecast by using the Internet. Traditionally, suppliers and buyers in most supply chains prepare independent demand forecasts. With CPFR, firms initiate

combination forecasts

Forecasts that are produced by averaging independent forecasts based on different methods, different sources, or different data.

focus forecasting

A method of forecasting that selects the best forecast from a group of forecasts generated by individual techniques.

collaborative planning, forecasting, and replenishment (CPFR)

A process for supply chain integration that allows a supplier and its customers to collaborate on making the forecast by using the Internet.

Ever wonder how CPFR came into existence? Walmart has long been known for its careful analysis of cash register receipts and for working with suppliers to reduce inventories. To combat the ill effects of forecast errors on inventories, Benchmarking Partners, Inc. was funded in the mid-1990s by Walmart, IBM, SAP, and Manugistics to develop a software package. Walmart initiated the new system with Listerine, a primary product of Warner-Lambert (now produced by Johnson & Johnson). How did it work? Walmart and Warner-Lambert independently calculated the demand they expected for Listerine six months into the future, taking into consideration factors such as past sales trends and sales promotions. If the forecasts differed by more than a predetermined percentage, they exchanged written comments and supporting data. They went through as many cycles as needed to converge to an acceptable forecast. The program was successful; Walmart saw a reduction in stockouts from 15 percent to 2 percent, increased sales, and reduced inventory costs, while Warner-Lambert benefitted from a smoother production plan and lower average costs. The system was later generalized and called collaborative planning, forecasting, and replenishment, or CPFR.

customer-focused operations teams that share with retailers their real-time data and plans, including forecasts, inventories, sales to retailers' shelves, promotions, product plans, and exceptions. CPFR involves four interactive activities:

- **Strategy and Planning:** to establish the ground rules for the collaborative relationship such as business goals, scope of collaboration, and assignment of roles and responsibilities.

- **Demand and Supply Management:** to develop sales forecasts, procedures for order planning, and inventory positions.

- **Execution:** to manage the generation of orders between supplier and customers and the production, shipment, and delivery of products for customer purchase.

- **Analysis:** to monitor the planning process and operations for out of bound conditions and to evaluate achievement of business goals.

Many firms have used CPFR to coordinate forecasts and plans up and down the supply chain. CPFR enables firms to collaborate with their retailers' distribution centers' customers and increase their ability to forecast effectively. The real key to a successful implementation of CPFR is the forging of a cultural alliance that involves peer-to-peer relations and cross-functional teams.

Forecasting as a Nested Process

Forecasting is not a stand-alone activity, but part of a larger process. After all, demand is only half of the equation—the other half is supply. Future plans must be developed to supply the resources needed to meet the forecasted demand. Resources include the workforce, materials, inventories, dollars, and equipment capacity.

LEARNING GOALS IN REVIEW

Learning Goal	Guidelines for Review	MyLab Operations Management Resources
❶ Explain how managers can change demand patterns.	Review the section "Managing Demand". Focus on "Demand Management Options," and the eight ways managers can change demand patterns.	
❷ Describe the two key decisions on making forecasts.	In the section "Key Decisions on Making Forecasts," focus on the considerations for deciding what to forecast and choosing the right forecasting technique.	
❸ Calculate the five basic measures of forecast errors.	Review the section "Forecast Error," to understand CFE, MSE, σ, MAD, and MAPE. Study Figures 2 (a) and (b) for an example. Solved Problem 2 shows an example of MAD and Solved Problem 3 shows MAD and MAPE.	**POM for Windows:** Error Analysis
❹ Compare and contrast the four approaches to judgmental forecasting.	The section "Judgment Methods," explains the differences between salesforce estimates, executive opinion, market research, and the Delphi method.	
❺ Use regression to make forecasts with one or more independent variables.	The "Causal Methods: Linear Regression" section, and Example 2 describe how linear regression, when historical data are available, can express demand as a linear function of one or more independent variables. The computer is an essential tool for linear regression. In addition to Example 2, Solved Problem 1 provides the statistics on how well the regression equation fits the data.	**Active Model:** 1: Linear Regression **OM Explorer Solver:** Regression Analysis **POM for Windows:** Least Squares—Simple and Multiple Regression **POM for Windows:** Regression Projector

Learning Goal	Guidelines for Review	MyLab Operations Management Resources
6 Make forecasts using the five most common statistical approaches for time-series analysis.	The "Time-Series Methods" on explains the naïve method and the five statistical methods of simple moving average, weighted moving average, exponential smoothing, trend projection with regression, and multiplicative seasonal methods that are used. Examples 3 through 6 demonstrate the methods, as do Solved Problems 2 through 4. Also see Experiential Learning 1 for an in-class exercise requiring the use of time-series models to prepare a combination forecast.	**Active Models:** 2: Simple Moving Averages; 3: Exponential Smoothing **OM Explorer Tutors:** 1: Moving Average Method; 2: Weighted Moving Average Method; 3: Exponential Smoothing **OM Explorer Solvers:** Time-Series Forecasting; Trend Projection with Regression; Seasonal Forecasting **POM for Windows:** Time-Series Analysis **Student Data File:** Experiential Exercise 1 Data
7 Describe the big-data approach and the six steps in a typical forecasting process.	See the section "Insights into Effective Demand Forecasting". Study the big-data approach and the six steps involved in the forecasting process. There is much more complexity when you realize the number of SKUs involved and the need to update the history file. Be sure to understand how combination forecasts work into step 2 and how CPFR is integral to step 3.	**Video:** Forecasting and Supply Chain Management at Deckers Outdoor Corporation

Key Equations

Forecast Error

1. Forecast error measures:

$$E_t = D_t - F_t$$

$$\text{CFE} = \Sigma E_t$$

$$\overline{E} = \frac{\text{CFE}}{n}$$

$$\text{MSE} = \frac{\Sigma E_t^2}{n}$$

$$\sigma = \sqrt{\frac{\Sigma (E_t - \overline{E})^2}{n - 1}}$$

$$\text{MAD} = \frac{\Sigma |E_t|}{n}$$

$$\text{MAPE} = \frac{\left(\Sigma |E_t| / D_t \right)(100\%)}{n}$$

Causal Methods: Linear Regression

2. Linear regression:

$$Y = a + bX$$

Time-Series Methods

3. Naïve forecasting:

$$\text{Forecast} = D_t$$

4. Simple moving average:

$$F_{t+1} = \frac{D_t + D_{t-1} + D_{t-2} + \cdots + D_{t-n+1}}{n}$$

5. Weighted moving average:

$$F_{t+1} = \text{Weight}_1(D_t) + \text{Weight}_2(D_{t-1}) + \text{Weight}_3(D_{t-2}) + \cdots + \text{Weight}_n(D_{t-n+1})$$

6. Exponential smoothing:

$$F_{t+1} = \alpha D_t + (1 - \alpha)F_t$$

7. Trend projection using regression:

$$F_t = a + bt$$

8. Tracking signal:

$$\frac{\text{CFE}}{\text{MAD}} \text{ or } \frac{\text{CFE}}{\text{MAD}_t}$$

9. Exponentially smoothed error:

$$\text{MAD}_t = \alpha|E_t| + (1 - \alpha)\text{MAD}_{t-1}$$

Key Terms

additive seasonal method
aggregation
backlog
backorder
big data
causal methods
collaborative planning, forecasting,
    and replenishment (CPFR)
combination forecasts
complementary products
cumulative sum of forecast errors
    (CFE)
Delphi method
demand management

dependent variable
executive opinion
exponential smoothing method
focus forecasting
forecast
forecast error
holdout sample
independent variables
judgment methods
linear regression
market research
mean absolute deviation (MAD)
mean absolute percent error (MAPE)
mean squared error (MSE)

multiplicative seasonal method
naïve forecast
revenue management
salesforce estimates
simple moving average method
standard deviation of the errors (σ)
stockout
technological forecasting
time series
time-series analysis
tracking signal
trend projection with regression
weighted moving average method

Solved Problem 1

Chicken Palace periodically offers carryout five-piece chicken dinners at special prices. Let Y be the number of dinners sold and X be the price. Based on the historical observations and calculations in the following table, determine the regression equation, correlation coefficient, and coefficient of determination. How many dinners can Chicken Palace expect to sell at $3.00 each?

Observation	Price (X)	Dinners Sold (Y)
1	$2.70	760
2	$3.50	510
3	$2.00	980
4	$4.20	250
5	$3.10	320
6	$4.05	480
Total	$19.55	3,300
Average	$3.258	550

SOLUTION

We use the computer (*Regression Analysis* Solver of OM Explorer or *Regression Projector* module of POM for Windows) to calculate the best values of a, b, the correlation coefficient, and the coefficient of determination.

$$a = 1,454.60$$
$$b = -277.63$$
$$r = -0.84$$
$$r^2 = 0.71$$

The regression line is

$$Y = a + bX = 1,454.60 - 277.63X$$

The correlation coefficient ($r = -0.84$) shows a negative correlation between the variables. The coefficient of determination ($r^2 = 0.71$) is not too large, which suggests that other variables (in addition to price) might appreciably affect sales.

If the regression equation is satisfactory to the manager, estimated sales at a price of $3.00 per dinner may be calculated as follows:

$$Y = a + bX = 1,454.60 - 277.63(3.00)$$
$$= 621.71 \text{ or } 622 \text{ dinners}$$

Solved Problem 2

The Polish General's Pizza Parlor is a small restaurant catering to patrons with a taste for European pizza. One of its specialties is Polish Prize pizza. The manager must forecast weekly demand for these special pizzas so that he can order pizza shells weekly. Recently, demand has been as follows:

Week	Pizzas	Week	Pizzas
June 2	50	June 23	56
June 9	65	June 30	55
June 16	52	July 7	60

a. Forecast the demand for pizza for June 23 to July 14 by using the simple moving average method with $n = 3$. Then, repeat the forecast by using the weighted moving average method with $n = 3$ and weights of 0.50, 0.30, and 0.20, with 0.50 applying to the most recent demand.

b. Calculate the MAD for each method.

SOLUTION

a. The simple moving average method and the weighted moving average method give the following results:

Current Week	Simple Moving Average Forecast for Next Week	Weighted Moving Average Forecast for Next Week
June 16	$\dfrac{52 + 65 + 50}{3} = 55.7$ or 56	$[(0.5 \times 52) + (0.3 \times 65) + (0.2 \times 50)] = 55.5$ or 56
June 23	$\dfrac{56 + 52 + 65}{3} = 55.7$ or 58	$[(0.5 \times 56) + (0.3 \times 52) + (0.2 \times 65)] = 56.6$ or 57
June 30	$\dfrac{55 + 56 + 52}{3} = 54.3$ or 54	$[(0.5 \times 55) + (0.3 \times 56) + (0.2 \times 52)] = 54.7$ or 55
July 7	$\dfrac{60 + 55 + 56}{3} = 57.0$ or 57	$[(0.5 \times 60) + (0.3 \times 55) + (0.2 \times 56)] = 57.7$ or 58

Forecasts in each row are for the next week's demand. For example, the simple moving average and weighted moving average forecasts (both are 56 units) are calculated after learning the demand on June 16 and are used for June 23's demand forecast.

b. The mean absolute deviation is calculated as follows:

Week	Actual Demand	SIMPLE MOVING AVERAGE		WEIGHTED MOVING AVERAGE	
		Forecast for This Week	Absolute Errors $\lvert E_t \rvert$	Forecast for This Week	Absolute Errors $\lvert E_t \rvert$
June 23	56	56	$\lvert 56 - 56 \rvert = 0$	56	$\lvert 56 - 56 \rvert = 0$
June 30	55	58	$\lvert 55 - 58 \rvert = 3$	57	$\lvert 55 - 57 \rvert = 2$
July 7	60	54	$\lvert 60 - 54 \rvert = 6$	55	$\lvert 60 - 55 \rvert = 5$
			$\text{MAD} = \dfrac{0 + 3 + 6}{3} = 3.0$		$\text{MAD} = \dfrac{0 + 2 + 5}{3} = 2.3$

For this limited set of data, the weighted moving average method resulted in a slightly lower mean absolute deviation. However, final conclusions can be made only after analyzing much more data.

Solved Problem 3

MyLab Operations Management Video

The monthly demand for units manufactured by the Acme Rocket Company has been as follows:

Month	Units	Month	Units
May	100	September	105
June	80	October	110
July	110	November	125
August	115	December	120

a. Use the exponential smoothing method to forecast the number of units for June to January. The initial forecast for May was 105 units; $\alpha = 0.2$.

b. Calculate the absolute percentage error for each month from June through December and the MAD and MAPE of forecast error as of the end of December.

c. Calculate the tracking signal as of the end of December. What can you say about the performance of your forecasting method?

SOLUTION

a.

Current Month, t	Calculating Forecast for Next Month $F_{t+1} = \alpha D_t + (1 - \alpha)F_t$	Forecast for Month $t + 1$
May	$0.2(100) + 0.8(105) = 104.0$ or 104	June
June	$0.2(80) + 0.8(104.0) = 99.2$ or 99	July
July	$0.2(110) + 0.8(99.2) = 101.4$ or 101	August
August	$0.2(115) + 0.8(101.4) = 104.1$ or 104	September
September	$0.2(105) + 0.8(104.1) = 104.3$ or 104	October
October	$0.2(110) + 0.8(104.3) = 105.4$ or 105	November
November	$0.2(125) + 0.8(105.4) = 109.3$ or 109	December
December	$0.2(120) + 0.8(109.3) = 111.4$ or 111	January

b.

Month, t	Actual Demand, D_t	Forecast, F_t	Error, $E_t = D_t - F_t$	Absolute Error, $\|E_t\|$	Absolute Percentage Error, $(\|E_t\|/D_t)(100\%)$
June	80	104	−24	24	30.0%
July	110	99	11	11	10.0
August	115	101	14	14	12.0
September	105	104	1	1	1.0
October	110	104	6	6	5.5
November	125	105	20	0	16.0
December	120	109	11	11	9.2
Total	765		39	87	83.7%

$$\text{MAD} = \frac{\Sigma |E_t|}{n} = \frac{87}{7} = 12.4 \text{ and MAPE} = \frac{(\Sigma |E_t|/D_t)(100)}{n} = \frac{83.7\%}{7} = 11.96\%$$

c. As of the end of December, the cumulative sum of forecast errors (CFE) is 39. Using the mean absolute deviation calculated in part (b), we calculate the tracking signal:

$$\text{Tracking signal} = \frac{\text{CFE}}{\text{MAD}} = \frac{39}{12.4} = 3.14$$

The probability that a tracking signal value of 3.14 could be generated completely by chance is small. Consequently, we should revise our approach. The long string of forecasts lower than actual demand suggests use of a trend method.

Solved Problem 4

The Northville Post Office experiences a seasonal pattern of daily mail volume every week. The following data for two representative weeks are expressed in thousands of pieces of mail:

Day	Week 1	Week 2
Sunday	5	8
Monday	20	15
Tuesday	30	32
Wednesday	35	30
Thursday	49	45
Friday	70	70
Saturday	15	10
Total	224	210

a. Calculate a seasonal factor for each day of the week.

b. If the postmaster estimates 230,000 pieces of mail to be sorted next week, forecast the volume for each day of the week.

SOLUTION

a. Calculate the average daily mail volume for each week. Then, for each day of the week, divide the mail volume by the week's average to get the seasonal factor. Finally, for each day, add the two seasonal factors and divide by 2 to obtain the average seasonal factor to use in the forecast (see part [b]).

	WEEK 1		WEEK 2		Average Seasonal Factor [(1) + (2)]/2
Day	Mail Volume	Seasonal Factor (1)	Mail Volume	Seasonal Factor (2)	
Sunday	5	5/32 = 0.15625	8	8/30 = 0.26667	0.21146
Monday	20	20/32 = 0.62500	15	15/30 = 0.50000	0.56250
Tuesday	30	30/32 = 0.93750	32	32/30 = 1.06667	1.00209
Wednesday	35	35/32 = 1.09375	30	30/30 = 1.00000	1.04688
Thursday	49	49/32 = 1.53125	45	45/30 = 1.50000	1.51563
Friday	70	70/32 = 2.18750	70	70/30 = 2.33333	2.26042
Saturday	15	15/32 = 0.46875	10	10/30 = 0.33333	0.40104
Total	224		210		
Average	224/7 = 32		210/7 = 30		

b. The average daily mail volume is expected to be 230,000/7 = 32,857 pieces of mail. Using the average seasonal factors calculated in part (a), we obtain the following forecasts:

Day	Calculation		Forecast
Sunday	0.21146(32,857) =		6,948
Monday	0.56250(32,857) =		18,482
Tuesday	1.00209(32,857) =		32,926
Wednesday	1.04688(32,857) =		34,397
Thursday	1.51563(32,857) =		49,799
Friday	2.26042(32,857) =		74,271
Saturday	0.40104(32,857) =		13,177
		Total	230,000

Discussion Questions

1. Figure 9 shows summer air visibility measurements for Denver, Colorado. The acceptable visibility standard is 100, with readings above 100 indicating clean air and good visibility, and readings below 100 indicating temperature inversions caused by forest fires, volcanic eruptions, or collisions with comets.

   a. Is a trend evident in the data? Which time-series techniques might be appropriate for estimating the average of these data?

   b. A medical center for asthma and respiratory diseases located in Denver has great demand for its services when air quality is poor. If you were in charge of developing a short-term (say, 3-day) forecast of visibility, which causal factor(s) would you analyze? In other words, which external factors hold the potential to significantly affect visibility in the *short term*?

   c. Tourism, an important factor in Denver's economy, is affected by the city's image. Air quality, as measured by visibility, affects the city's image. If you were responsible for development of tourism, which causal factor(s) would you analyze to forecast visibility for the *medium term* (say, the next two summers)?

   d. The federal government threatens to withhold several hundred million dollars in Department of Transportation funds unless Denver meets visibility standards within 8 years. How would you proceed to generate a *long-term* judgment forecast of technologies that will be available to improve visibility in the next 10 years?

2. Kay and Michael Passe publish *What's Happening?*—a biweekly newspaper to publicize local events. *What's Happening?* has few subscribers; it typically is sold at checkout stands. Much of the revenue comes from advertisers of garage sales and supermarket specials. In an effort to reduce costs associated with printing too many papers or delivering them to the wrong location, Michael implemented a computerized system to collect sales data. Sales-counter scanners accurately record sales data for each location. Since the system was implemented, total sales volume has steadily declined. Selling advertising space and maintaining shelf space at supermarkets are getting more difficult.

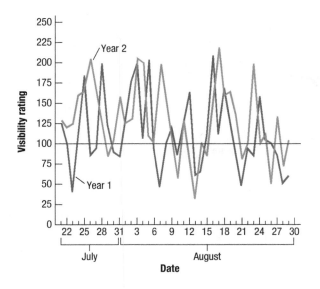

◀ FIGURE 9
Summer Air Visibility Measurements

Reduced revenue makes controlling costs all the more important. For each issue, Michael carefully makes a forecast based on sales data collected at each location. Then, he orders papers to be printed and distributed in quantities matching the forecast. Michael's forecast reflects a downward trend, which *is* present in the sales data. Now only a few papers are left over at only a few locations. Although the sales forecast accurately predicts the actual sales at most locations, *What's Happening?* is spiraling toward oblivion. Kay suspects that Michael is doing something wrong in preparing the forecast but can find no mathematical errors. Tell her what is happening.

Problems

The OM Explorer and POM for Windows software is available to all students. Go to **http://www.pearsonhighered.com/krajewski** to download these computer packages. If you purchased MyLab Operations Management, you also have access to Active Models software and significant help in doing the following problems. Check with your instructor on how best to use these resources. In many cases, the instructor wants you to understand how to do the calculations by hand. At the least, the software provides a check on your calculations. When calculations are particularly complex and the goal is interpreting the results in making decisions, the software entirely replaces the manual calculations.

Causal Methods: Linear Regression

1. Demand for oil changes at Garcia's Garage has been as follows:

Month	Number of Oil Changes
January	41
February	46
March	57
April	52
May	59
June	51
July	60
August	62

a. Use simple linear regression analysis to develop a forecasting model for monthly demand. In this application, the dependent variable, Y, is monthly demand and the independent variable, X, is the month. For January, let $X = 1$; for February, let $X = 2$; and so on.

b. Use the model to forecast demand for September, October, and November. Here, $X = 9$, 10, and 11, respectively.

2. At a hydrocarbon processing factory, process control involves periodic analysis of samples for a certain process quality parameter. The analytic procedure currently used is costly and time consuming. A faster and more economical alternative procedure has been proposed. However, the numbers for the quality parameter given by the alternative procedure are somewhat different from those given by the current procedure, not because of any inherent errors but because of changes in the nature of the chemical analysis.

Management believes that if the numbers from the new procedure can be used to forecast reliably the corresponding numbers from the current procedure, switching to the new procedure would be reasonable and cost effective. The following data were obtained for the quality parameter by analyzing samples using both procedures.

Current (Y)	Proposed (X)	Current (Y)	Proposed (X)
3.0	3.1	3.1	3.1
3.1	3.9	2.7	2.9
3.0	3.4	3.3	3.6
3.6	4.0	3.2	4.1
3.8	3.6	2.1	2.6
2.7	3.6	3.0	3.1
2.7	3.6	2.6	2.8

a. Use linear regression to find a relation to forecast Y, which is the quality parameter from the current procedure, using the values from the proposed procedure, X.

b. Is there a strong relationship between Y and X? Explain.

3. Ohio Swiss Milk Products manufactures and distributes ice cream in Ohio, Kentucky, and West Virginia. The company wants to expand operations by locating another plant in northern Ohio. The size of the new plant will be a function of the expected demand for ice cream within the area served by the plant. A market survey is currently under way to determine that demand.

Ohio Swiss wants to estimate the relationship between the manufacturing cost per gallon and the number of gallons sold in a year to determine the demand for ice cream and, thus, the size of the new plant. The following data have been collected.

a. Develop a regression equation to forecast the cost per gallon as a function of the number of gallons produced.

Plant	Cost per Thousand Gallons (Y)	Thousands ofGallons Sold (X)
1	$ 1,015	416.9
2	973	472.5
3	1,046	250.0
4	1,006	372.1
5	1,058	238.1
6	1,068	258.6
7	967	597.0
8	997	414.0
9	1,044	263.2
10	1,008	372.0
Total	$10,182	3,654.4

b. What are the correlation coefficient and the coefficient of determination? Comment on your regression equation in light of these measures.

c. Suppose that the market survey indicates a demand of 325,000 gallons in the Bucyrus, Ohio area. Estimate the manufacturing cost per gallon for a plant producing 325,000 gallons per year.

4. A manufacturing firm has developed a skills test, the scores from which can be used to predict workers' production rating factors. Data on the test scores of various workers and their subsequent production ratings are shown.

Worker	Test Score	Production Rating	Worker	Test Score	Production Rating
A	53	45	K	54	59
B	36	43	L	73	77
C	88	89	M	65	56
D	84	79	N	29	28
E	86	84	O	52	51
F	64	66	P	22	27
G	45	49	Q	76	76
H	48	48	R	32	34
I	39	43	S	51	60
J	67	76	T	37	32

a. Using POM for Windows' least squares-linear regression module, develop a relationship to forecast production ratings from test scores.

b. If a worker's test score was 80, what would be your forecast of the worker's production rating?

c. Comment on the strength of the relationship between the test scores and production ratings.

5. The materials handling manager of a manufacturing company is trying to forecast the cost of maintenance for the company's fleet of over-the-road tractors. The manager believes that the cost of maintaining the tractors increases with their age. The following data was collected.

Age (years)	Yearly Maintenance Cost ($)	Age (years)	Yearly Maintenance Cost ($)
4.5	619	5.0	1,194
4.5	1,049	0.5	163
4.5	1,033	0.5	182
4.0	495	6.0	764
4.0	723	6.0	1,373
4.0	681	1.0	978
5.0	890	1.0	466
5.0	1,522	1.0	549
5.5	987		

a. Use POM for Windows' least squares-linear regression module to develop a relationship to forecast the yearly maintenance cost based on the age of a tractor.

b. If a section has 20 three-year-old tractors, what is the forecast for the annual maintenance cost?

Time-Series Methods

6. Marianne Kramer, the owner of Handy Man Rentals, rents carpet cleaners to contractors and walk-in customers. She is interested in arriving at a forecast of rentals so that she can order the correct quantities of supplies that go with the cleaners. Data for the last 10 weeks are shown here.

Week	Rentals	Week	Rentals
1	15	6	20
2	16	7	24
3	24	8	27
4	18	9	18
5	23	10	16

a. Prepare a forecast for weeks 6 through 10 by using a 4-week moving average. What is the forecast for week 11?

b. Calculate the mean absolute deviation as of the end of week 10.

7. Sales for the past 12 months at Computer Success are given here.

Month	Sales ($)	Month	Sales ($)
January	3,000	July	6,300
February	3,400	August	7,200
March	3,700	September	6,400
April	4,100	October	4,600
May	4,700	November	4,200
June	5,700	December	3,900

a. Use a 3-month moving average to forecast the sales for the months May through December.

b. Use a 4-month moving average to forecast the sales for the months May through December.

c. Compare the performance of the two methods by using the mean absolute deviation as the performance criterion. Which method would you recommend?

d. Compare the performance of the two methods by using the mean absolute percent error as the performance criterion. Which method would you recommend?

e. Compare the performance of the two methods by using the mean squared error as the performance criterion. Which method would you recommend?

8. Bradley's Copiers sells and repairs photocopy machines. The manager needs weekly forecasts of service calls so that he can schedule service personnel. Use the actual demand in the first period for the forecast for the first week so error measurement begins in the second week. The manager uses exponential smoothing with $\alpha = 0.20$. Forecast the number of calls for week 6, which is the next week.

Week	Actual Service Calls
1	29
2	27
3	41
4	18
5	33

9. Consider the sales data for Computer Success given in Problem 7.

a. Use a 3-month weighted moving average to forecast the sales for the months April through December. Use weights of (4/8), (3/8), and (1/8), giving more weight to more recent data.

b. Use exponential smoothing with $\alpha = 0.6$ to forecast the sales for the months April through December. Assume that the initial forecast for January was $3,200. Start error measurement in April.

c. Compare the performance of the two methods by using the mean absolute deviation as the performance criterion, with error measurement beginning in April. Which method would you recommend?

d. Compare the performance of the two methods by using the mean absolute percent error as the performance criterion, with error measurement beginning in April. Which method would you recommend?

e. Compare the performance of the two methods by using the mean squared error as the performance criterion, with error measurement beginning in April. Which method would you recommend?

10. A convenience store recently started to carry a new brand of soft drink. Management is interested in estimating future sales volume to determine whether it should continue to carry the new brand or replace it with another brand. The table here provides the number of cans sold per week. Use both the trend projection with regression and the exponential smoothing (let $\alpha = 0.4$ with an initial forecast for week 1 of 617) methods to forecast demand for week 13. Compare these methods by using the mean absolute deviation and mean absolute percent error performance criteria. Does your analysis suggest that sales are trending and if so, by how much?

Week	1	2	3	4	5	6	7	8	9	10	11	12
Sales	617	617	648	739	659	623	742	704	724	715	668	740

11. Community Federal Bank in Dothan, Alabama, recently increased its fees to customers who use employees as tellers. Management is interested in whether its new fee policy has increased the number of customers now using its automatic teller machines to the point that more machines are required. The table here provides the number of automatic teller transactions by week. Use trend projection with regression to forecast usage for weeks 13 to 16.

Week	1	2	3	4	5	6	7	8	9	10	11	12
Transactions	512	527	631	434	482	539	577	518	526	636	623	461

12. The number of heart surgeries performed at Heartville General Hospital has increased steadily over the past several years. The hospital's administration is seeking the best method to forecast the demand for such surgeries in year 6. The data for the past 5 years are shown.

Year	Demand
1	45
2	50
3	52
4	56
5	58

The hospital's administration is considering the following forecasting methods. Begin error measurement in year 3 so all methods are compared for the same years.

a. Exponential smoothing, with $\alpha = 0.6$. Let the initial forecast for year 1 be 45, the same as the actual demand.

b. Exponential smoothing, with $\alpha = 0.9$. Let the initial forecast for year 1 be 45, the same as the actual demand.

c. Trend projection with regression.

d. Two-year moving average.

e. Two-year weighted moving average, using weights 0.6 and 0.4, with more recent data given more weight.

f. If MAD is the performance criterion chosen by the administration, which forecasting method should it choose?

g. If MSE is the performance criterion chosen by the administration, which forecasting method should it choose?

h. If MAPE is the performance criterion chosen by the administration, which forecasting method should it choose?

13. The following data are for calculator sales in units at an electronics store over the past 9 weeks.

Week	Sales	Week	Sales
1	46	6	58
2	49	7	62
3	43	8	56
4	50	9	63
5	53		

Use trend projection with regression to forecast sales for weeks 10 to 13. What are the error measures (CFE, MSE, σ, MAD, and MAPE) for this forecasting procedure? How about r^2?

14. The demand for Krispee Crunchies, a favorite breakfast cereal of people born in the 1940s, is experiencing a decline. The company wants to monitor demand for this product closely as it nears the end of its life cycle. The following table shows the actual sales history for January to October. Generate forecasts for November to December, using the trend projection with regression method. Looking at the accuracy of its forecasts over the history file, as well as the other statistics provided, how confident are you in these forecasts for November to December?

Month	Sales	Month	Sales
January	890,000	July	710,000
February	800,000	August	730,000
March	825,000	September	680,000
April	840,000	October	670,000
May	730,000	November	
June	780,000	December	

15. Forrest and Dan make boxes of chocolates for which the demand is uncertain. Forrest says, "That's life." On the other hand, Dan believes that some demand patterns exist that could be useful for planning the purchase of sugar, chocolate, and shrimp. Forrest insists on placing a surprise chocolate-covered shrimp in some boxes so that "You never know what you'll get." Quarterly demand (in boxes of chocolates) for the last 3 years follows:

Quarter	Year 1	Year 2	Year 3
1	3,000	3,300	3,502
2	1,700	2,100	2,448
3	900	1,500	1,768
4	4,400	5,100	5,882
Total	10,000	12,000	13,600

a. Use intuition and judgment to estimate quarterly demand for the fourth year.

b. If the expected sales for chocolates are 14,800 cases for year 4, use the multiplicative seasonal method to prepare a forecast for each quarter of the year. Are any of the quarterly forecasts different from what you thought you would get in part (a)?

16. The manager of Alaina's Garden Center must make the annual purchasing plans for rakes, gloves, and other gardening items. One of the items the company stocks is Fast-Grow, a liquid fertilizer. The sales of this item are seasonal, with peaks in the spring, summer, and fall months. Quarterly demand (in cases) for the past 2 years follows:

Quarter	Year 1	Year 2
1	45	67
2	339	444
3	299	329
4	222	283
Total	905	1,123

If the expected sales for Fast-Grow are 1,850 cases for year 3, use the multiplicative seasonal method to prepare a forecast for each quarter of the year.

17. The manager of a utility company in the Texas panhandle wants to develop quarterly forecasts of power loads for the next year. The power loads are seasonal, and the data on the quarterly loads in megawatts (MW) for the last 4 years are as follows:

Quarter	Year 1	Year 2	Year 3	Year 4
1	103.5	94.7	118.6	109.3
2	126.1	116.0	141.2	131.6
3	144.5	137.1	159.0	149.5
4	166.1	152.5	178.2	169.0

The manager estimates the total demand for the next year at 600 MW. Use the multiplicative seasonal method to develop the forecast for each quarter.

18. Franklin Tooling, Inc., manufactures specialty tooling for firms in the paper-making industry. All of their products are engineer-to-order and so the company never knows exactly what components to purchase for a tool until a customer places an order. However, the company believes that weekly demand for a few components is fairly stable. Component 135.AG is one such item. The last 26 weeks of historical use of component 135.AG is as follows:

Week	Demand	Week	Demand
1	137	14	131
2	136	15	132
3	143	16	124
4	136	17	121
5	141	18	127
6	128	19	118
7	149	20	120
8	136	21	115
9	134	22	106
10	142	23	120
11	125	24	113
12	134	25	121
13	118	26	119

Use OM Explorer's *Time Series Forecasting* Solver to evaluate the following forecasting methods. Start error measurement in the fifth week, so all methods are evaluated over the same time interval. Use the default settings for initial forecasts.

a. Naïve (1-period moving average)
b. Three-period moving average
c. Exponential smoothing, with $\alpha = .28$
d. Trend projection with regression
e. Which forecasting method should management use, if the performance criterion it chooses is:
   - CFE?
   - MSE?
   - MAD?
   - MAPE?

19. Create an Excel spreadsheet on your own that can make combination forecasts for Problem 18. Create a combination forecast using all four techniques from Problem 18. Give each technique an equal weight. Create a second combination forecast by using the three techniques that seem best based on MAD. Give equal weight to each technique. Finally, create a third forecast by equally weighting the two best techniques. Calculate CFE, MAD, MSE, and MAPE for the combination forecast. Are these forecasts better or worse than the forecasting techniques identified in Problem 18?

20. The director of a large public library must schedule employees to reshelf books and periodicals checked out of the library. The number of items checked out will determine the labor requirements. The following data reflect the number of items checked out of the library for the past 3 years.

Month	Year 1	Year 2	Year 3
January	1,847	2,045	1,986
February	2,669	2,321	2,564
March	2,467	2,419	2,635
April	2,432	2,088	2,150
May	2,464	2,667	2,201
June	2,378	2,122	2,663
July	2,217	2,206	2,055
August	2,445	1,869	1,678
September	1,894	2,441	1,845
October	1,922	2,291	2,065
November	2,431	2,364	2,147
December	2,274	2,189	2,451

The director needs a time-series method for forecasting the number of items to be checked out during the next month. Find the best simple moving average forecast you can. Decide what is meant by "best" and justify your decision.

D = **Difficult Problem**

21. Using the data in Problem 20 and the *Time-Series* Solver
D of OM Explorer, find the best exponential smoothing parameter alpha that minimizes MAD. Let the forecast for period 1 be the actual data for period 1, and begin the error analysis in period 2.

22. Using the data in Problem 20, find the trend projection
D with regression model using the *Time-Series Forecasting* Solver of OM Explorer. Compare the performance of this method with the exponential smoothing method from Problem 21. Let the error analysis begin in period 2 (so that both exponential smoothing and trend projection are analyzed over the same time horizon). Which of these two methods would you choose if MAD is the key error measure?

23. Cannister, Inc., specializes in the manufacture of plastic
D containers. The data on the monthly sales of 10-ounce shampoo bottles for the past 5 years are as follows:

Year	1	2	3	4	5
January	742	741	896	951	1,030
February	697	700	793	861	1,032
March	776	774	885	938	1,126
April	898	932	1,055	1,109	1,285
May	1,030	1,099	1,204	1,274	1,468
June	1,107	1,223	1,326	1,422	1,637
July	1,165	1,290	1,303	1,486	1,611
August	1,216	1,349	1,436	1,555	1,608
September	1,208	1,341	1,473	1,604	1,528
October	1,131	1,296	1,453	1,600	1,420
November	971	1,066	1,170	1,403	1,119
December	783	901	1,023	1,209	1,013

a. Using the multiplicative seasonal method, calculate the monthly seasonal indices.

b. Develop a simple linear regression equation to forecast annual sales. For this regression, the dependent variable, Y, is the demand in each year and the independent variable, X, is the index for the year (i.e., $X = 1$ for year 1, $X = 2$ for year 2, and so on until $X = 5$ for year 5).

c. Forecast the annual sales for year 6 by using the regression model you developed in part (b).

d. Prepare the seasonal forecast for each month by using the monthly seasonal indices calculated in part (a).

24. The Midwest Computer Company serves a large number
D of businesses in the Great Lakes region. The company sells supplies and replacements and performs service on all computers sold through seven sales offices. Many items are stocked, so close inventory control is necessary to assure customers of efficient service. Recently, business has been increasing, and management is concerned about stockouts. A forecasting method is needed to estimate requirements several months in advance so that adequate replenishment quantities can be purchased. An example of the sales growth experienced during the last 50 months is the growth in demand for item EP-37, a laser printer cartridge, shown in Table 3.

a. Develop a trend projection with regression solution using OM Explorer. Forecast demand for month 51.

b. A consultant to Midwest's management suggested that new office building leases would be a good leading indicator for company sales. The consultant quoted a recent university study finding that new office building leases precede office equipment and supply sales by 3 months. According to the study findings, leases in month 1 would affect sales in month 4, leases in month 2 would affect sales in month 5, and so on. Use POM for Windows' linear regression module to develop a forecasting model

TABLE 3 | EP-37 SALES AND LEASE DATA

Month	EP-37 Sales	Leases	Month	EP-37 Sales	Leases
1	80	32	26	1,296	281
2	132	29	27	1,199	298
3	143	32	28	1,267	314
4	180	54	29	1,300	323
5	200	53	30	1,370	309
6	168	89	31	1,489	343
7	212	74	32	1,499	357
8	254	93	33	1,669	353
9	397	120	34	1,716	360
10	385	113	35	1,603	370
11	472	147	36	1,812	386
12	397	126	37	1,817	389
13	476	138	38	1,798	399

D = **Difficult Problem**

Month	EP-37 Sales	Leases	Month	EP-37 Sales	Leases
14	699	145	39	1,873	409
15	545	160	40	1,923	410
16	837	196	41	2,028	413
17	743	180	42	2,049	439
18	722	197	43	2,084	454
19	735	203	44	2,083	441
20	838	223	45	2,121	470
21	1,057	247	46	2,072	469
22	930	242	47	2,262	490
23	1,085	234	48	2,371	496
24	1,090	254	49	2,309	509
25	1,218	271	50	2,422	522

for sales, with leases as the independent variable. Forecast sales for month 51.

   c. Which of the two models provides better forecasts? Explain.

25. A certain food item at P&Q Supermarkets has the demand pattern shown in the following 24-period table.

   a. Use the combination forecasting method of the *Time-Series Forecasting* Solver of OM Explorer. Let error analysis begin in month 6, and include (1) a five-period moving average (with a combination weight of 0.33), (2) an exponential smoothing model with $\alpha = 0.20$ (with a combination weight of 0.33), and (3) trend projection (with a combination weight of 0.33). What is the MAD of this model? What is the forecast for month 25?

   b. The need to account for seasonality is apparent if you look at a graph of the trend line. There is a spike in demand in the fifth period of each 5-period cycle. Unfortunately, OM *Explorer's Seasonal Forecasting* Solver does not cover the case where there are five periods in a cycle (or seasons in a year). You must do some manual calculations. Begin by calculating the seasonal factor for each period in each of the first four cycles, and then calculating the average seasonal factor for each period (see Example 6). Now estimate the total demand for cycle 5 using OM Explorer's Trend Projection routine in the *Time-Series* Solver. The dependent variables are the total demands for the first four cycles. Now multiply the average demand estimate for the fifth cycle by the seasonal factor for the fifth period. This is your forecast for month 25. To calculate the errors (including MAD) for the multiplicative seasonal method for all cycles (except for the fifth month in the fifth cycle), calculate MAD manually. You might instead use the Error Analysis Module of POM for Windows.

   c. How do the forecasts by the two methods compare? Which one is likely to give the better forecast, based on MAD?

Period	Demand	Period	Demand
1	33	13	37
2	37	14	43
3	31	15	56
4	39	16	41
5	54	17	36
6	38	18	39
7	42	19	41
8	40	20	58
9	41	21	42
10	54	22	45
11	43	23	41
12	39	24	38

26. The data for the visibility chart in Discussion Question 1 are shown in Table 4. The visibility standard is set at 100. Readings below 100 indicate that air pollution has reduced visibility, and readings above 100 indicate that the air is clearer.

   a. Use several methods to generate a visibility forecast for August 31 of the second year. Which method seems to produce the best forecast?

   b. Use several methods to forecast the visibility index for the summer of the third year. Which method seems to produce the best forecast? Support your choice.

27. Tom Glass forecasts electrical demand for the Flatlands Public Power District (FPPD). The FPPD wants to take its Comstock power plant out of service for maintenance when demand is expected to be low. After shutdown, performing maintenance and getting the plant back on line takes 2 weeks. The utility has enough other generating capacity to satisfy 1,550 megawatts (MW) of demand

D = **Difficult Problem**

TABLE 4 | VISIBILITY DATA

Date	Year 1	Year 2	Date	Year 1	Year 2	Date	Year 1	Year 2
July 22	125	130	Aug 5	105	200	Aug 19	170	160
23	100	120	6	205	110	20	125	165
24	40	125	7	90	100	21	85	135
25	100	160	8	45	200	22	45	80
26	185	165	9	100	160	23	95	100
27	85	205	10	120	100	24	85	200
28	95	165	11	85	55	25	160	100
29	200	125	12	125	130	26	105	110
30	125	85	13	165	75	27	100	50
31	90	105	14	60	30	28	95	135
Aug 1	85	160	15	65	100	29	50	70
2	135	125	16	110	85	30	60	105
3	175	130	17	210	150			
4	200	205	18	110	220			

while Comstock is out of service. Table 5 shows weekly peak demands (in MW) for the past several autumns. When next in year 6 should the Comstock plant be scheduled for maintenance?

28. A manufacturing firm seeks to develop a better forecast **(D)** for an important product, and believes that there is a trend to the data. OM Explorer's *Trend Projection with Regression* Solver has been set up with the 47 demands in the history file. Note the "Load Problem 28 Data" button in the *Trend Projection with Regression* Solver that when clicked will automatically input the demand data. Otherwise, you can enter the demand data directly into the Inputs sheet.

Yr	1	2	3	4
Jan	4507	4589	4084	4535
Feb	4400	4688	4158	4477
Mar	4099	4566	4174	4601

Yr	1	2	3	4
Apr	4064	4485	4225	4648
May	4002	4385	4324	4860
Jun	3963	4377	4220	4998
Jul	4037	4309	4267	5003
Aug	4162	4276	4187	4960
Sep	4312	4280	4239	4943
Oct	4395	4144	4352	5052
Nov	4540	4219	4331	5107
Dec	4471	4052	4371	

a. What is your forecast for December of year 4, making period 1 as the starting period for the regression?

TABLE 5 | WEEKLY PEAK POWER DEMANDS

Year	AUGUST			SEPTEMBER				OCTOBER				NOVEMBER	
	1	2	3	4	5	6	7	8	9	10	11	12	13
1	2,050	1,925	1,825	1,525	1,050	1,300	1,200	1,175	1,350	1,525	1,725	1,575	1,925
2	2,000	2,075	2,225	1,800	1,175	1,050	1,250	1,025	1,300	1,425	1,625	1,950	1,950
3	1,950	1,800	2,150	1,725	1,575	1,275	1,325	1,100	1,500	1,550	1,375	1,825	2,000
4	2,100	2,400	1,975	1,675	1,350	1,525	1,500	1,150	1,350	1,225	1,225	1,475	1,850
5	2,275	2,300	2,150	1,525	1,350	1,475	1,475	1,175	1,375	1,400	1,425	1,550	1,900

b. The actual demand for period 48 was just learned to be 5,100. Add this demand to the Inputs file and change the starting period for the regression to period 2 so that the number of periods in the regression remains unchanged. How much or little does the forecast for period 49 change from the one for period 48? The error measures? Are you surprised?

c. Now change the time when the regression starts to period 25 and repeat the process. What differences do you note now? What forecast will you make for period 49?

VIDEO CASE | Forecasting and Supply Chain Management at Deckers Outdoor Corporation

Deckers Outdoor Corporation's footwear products are among some of the most well-known brands in the world. From UGG sheepskin boots and Teva sport sandals to Simple shoes, Deckers flip-flops, and Tsubo footwear, Deckers is committed to building niche footwear brands into global brands with market leadership positions. Net sales for fiscal year 2007 were close to $449 million. In addition to traditional retail store outlets for Deckers's footwear styles, the company maintains an active and growing "direct to consumer" e-commerce business. Since most retail stores cannot carry every style in every color and size, the company offers the full line for each of its brands directly to consumers through the brands' individual websites. Online sales at its virtual store are handled by its e-commerce group. Customers who want a pair of shoes not available at the retail store can always buy from the virtual store.

Founded in 1973, the company manufactured a single line of sandals in a small factory in southern California. The challenges of managing the raw materials and finished goods inventories were small compared to today's global sourcing and sales challenges for the company's various brands. Today, each brand has its own development team and brand managers who generate, develop, and test-market the seasonal styles that appear on the shelves of retailers such as Nordstrom, Lord & Taylor, REI, the Walking Company, and the company's own UGG brand retail stores in the United States and Japan.

At Deckers, forecasting is the starting point for inventory management, sales and operations planning, resource planning, and scheduling—in short, managing its supply chain. It carries a considerable amount of seasonal stock. Shoes with seasonal demand that are left over at the end of their season must be sold at heavily discounted prices. Its products fall into three categories: (1) carryover items that were sold in prior years, (2) new items that look similar to past models, and (3) completely new designs that are fashionable with no past history.

Twice a year, the brand development teams work on the fall and spring product lines. They come up with new designs about a year in advance of each season. Each brand (UGG, Teva, Simple, Tsubo, and Deckers) contains numerous products. The materials for new designs are selected and tested in prototypes. Approved designs are put into the seasonal lineup. Forecasts must be made at both the product and aggregate levels months before the season begins. "Bottoms-up" forecasts for each product begin by analyzing any available history files of past demand. Judgment forecasts are also important inputs, particularly for the second and third categories of shoes that are not carryovers. For example, Char Nicanor-Kimball is an expert in spotting trends in shoe sales and makes forecasts for the virtual store. For new designs, historical sales on similar items are used to make a best guess on demand for those items. This process is facilitated by a forecasting and inventory system on the company's intranet. At the same time, the sales teams for each brand call on their retail accounts and secure customer orders of approved designs for the coming season. Then, the virtual store forecasts are merged with orders from the retail store orders to get the total seasonal demand forecasted by product. Next, the product forecasts are "rolled up" by category and "top down" forecasts are also made.

Customer orders for Decker footwear are broken down by brand and sent to headquarters in Goletta, California, where the order is entered into the system.

These forecasts then go to top management where some adjustments may be made to account for financial market conditions, consumer credit, weather, demographic factors, and customer confidence. The impact of public relations and advertising must also be considered.

Actually, forecasting continues on throughout the year on a daily and weekly basis to "get a handle" on demand. Comparing actual demand with what was forecasted for different parts of the season also helps the forecasters make better forecasts for the future and better control inventories.

Based on initial demand forecasts, the company must begin sourcing the materials needed to produce the footwear. The company makes most of its products in China and sources many of the raw materials there as well. For UGG products sheepskin sourcing occurs in Australia with top-grade producers, but the rawhide tanning still takes places in China. With potential suppliers identified and assurance from internal engineering that the footwear can be successfully made, the engineering and material data are handed over to the manufacturing department to determine how best to make the footwear in mass quantities. At this point, Deckers places a seasonal "buy" with its suppliers.

The orders for each product are fed into the manufacturing schedules at the Chinese factories. All the products for a given brand are manufactured at the same factory. While Deckers's agents negotiate the raw materials contracts early in the development process, the factories only place the orders for the raw materials when the company sends in the actual orders for the finished goods. No footwear is made by the factories until orders are received.

At the factories, finished goods footwear is inspected and packaged for the month-long ocean voyage from Hong Kong to ports in the United States.

Deckers ships 50 containers a week from its Chinese manufacturing sources, each holding approximately 5,000 pairs of shoes. Ownership of the finished goods transfers from the factories to Deckers in Hong Kong.

When the shipping containers arrive in the United States, the footwear is transferred to Deckers's distribution centers in southern California. Teva products are warehoused in Ventura, California; all other products are handled by the company's state-of-the-art facility in Camarillo, California. Typically, Deckers brings product into the distribution centers 2 to 3 months in advance of expected needs so that the production at the suppliers' factories and the labor activities at the distribution centers are leveled. There are definitive spikes in the demand for footwear, with Teva spiking in quarter 1 and UGG spiking in quarter 4. The leveling approach works to keep costs low in the supply chain. However, it also means that Deckers must maintain sizable inventories. Most shipments from suppliers come in to the distribution centers and are stored in inventory for 1 to 2 months awaiting a customer order. By the time the footwear is stocked in the distribution center, the company knows which retail customers will be getting the various products, based on the orders booked months earlier. Then, according to delivery schedules negotiated with the customers, the company begins filling orders and shipping products to retail locations. The warehouse tracks incoming shipments, goods placed on the shelves for customers, and outgoing orders. The inventory system helps manage the customer order filling process.

Because the booked orders are a relatively large proportion of the total orders from retailers, and the number of unanticipated orders is very small, only small safety stocks are needed to service the retailers. Occasionally, the purchase order from Deckers to one of its suppliers matches the sales order from the customer. In such a case, Deckers uses a "cross-dock" system. When the shipment is received at the distribution center, it is immediately checked in and loaded on another truck for delivery to customers. Cross docking reduces the need to store vast quantities of product for long periods of time and cuts down on warehousing expenses for Deckers. The company has been successful in turning its inventory over about four times a year, which is in line with footwear industry standards.

The online sales traffic is all managed centrally. In fact, for ordering and inventory management purposes, the online side of the business is treated just like another major retail store account. As forecasted seasonal orders are generated by each brand's sales team, a manufacturing order for the online business is placed by the e-commerce sales team at the same time. However, unlike the retail outlets that take delivery of products on a regular schedule, the inventory pledged to the online business is held in the distribution center until a website order is received. Only then is it shipped directly to the consumer who placed the online order. If actual demand exceeds expected demand, Char Nicanor-Kimball checks if more inventory can be secured from other customer orders that have scaled back.

The forecasting and supply chain management challenges now facing Deckers are twofold. First, the company plans to grow the brands that have enjoyed seasonal sales activity into yearround footwear options for consumers by expanding the number of products for those brands. For example, most sales for UGG footwear occur in the fall/winter season. Sales for Teva historically have been in the spring and summer. Product managers are now working to develop styles that will allow the brands to cross over the seasons. Second, the company plans to expand internationally, and will have retail outlets in Europe, China, and other Asian locations in the very near future. Company managers are well aware of the challenges and opportunities such global growth will bring, and are taking steps now to ensure that the entire supply chain is prepared to forecast and handle the demand when the time comes.

QUESTIONS

1. How much does the forecasting process at Deckers correspond with the "typical forecasting process" described at the end of this text?

2. Based on what you see in the video, what kinds of information technology are used to make forecasts, maintain accurate inventory records, and project future inventory levels?

3. What factors make forecasting at Deckers particularly challenging? How can forecasts be made for seasonal, fashionable products for which there is no history file? What are the costs of overforecasting demand for such items? Underforecasting?

4. What are the benefits of leveling aggregate demand by having a portfolio of products that create a 365-day demand?

5. Deckers plans to expand internationally, thereby increasing the volume of shoes it must manage in the supply chain and the pattern of material flows. What implications does this strategy have on forecasting, order quantities, logistics, and relationships with its suppliers and customers?

CASE | Yankee Fork and Hoe Company

The Yankee Fork and Hoe Company is a leading producer of garden tools ranging from wheelbarrows, mortar pans, and hand trucks to shovels, rakes, and trowels. The tools are sold in four different product lines ranging from the top-of-the-line Hercules products, which are rugged tools for the toughest jobs, to the Garden Helper products, which are economy tools for the occasional user. The market for garden tools is extremely competitive because of the simple design of the products and the large number of competing producers. In addition, more people are using power tools, such as lawn edgers, hedge trimmers, and thatchers, reducing demand for their manual counterparts. These factors compel Yankee to maintain low prices while retaining high quality and dependable delivery.

Garden tools represent a mature industry. Unless new manual products can be developed or a sudden resurgence occurs in home gardening, the prospects for large increases in sales are not bright. Keeping ahead of the competition is a constant battle. No one knows this better than Alan Roberts, president of Yankee.

The types of tools sold today are, by and large, the same ones sold 30 years ago. The only way to generate new sales and retain old customers is to provide superior customer service and produce a product with high customer value. This approach puts pressure on the manufacturing system, which has been having difficulties lately. Recently, Roberts has been receiving calls from long-time customers, such as Sears and True Value Hardware Stores, complaining about late shipments. These customers advertise promotions for garden tools and require on-time delivery.

Roberts knows that losing customers like Sears and True Value would be disastrous. He decides to ask consultant Sharon Place to look into the matter and report to him in 1 week. Roberts suggests that she focus on the bow rake as a case in point because it is a high-volume product and has been a major source of customer complaints of late.

Planning Bow Rake Production

A bow rake consists of a head with 12 teeth spaced 1 inch apart, a hardwood handle, a bow that attaches the head to the handle, and a metal ferrule that reinforces the area where the bow inserts into the handle. The bow is a metal strip that is welded to the ends of the rake head and bent in the middle to form a flat tab for insertion into the handle. The rake is about 64 inches long.

Place decides to find out how Yankee plans bow rake production. She goes straight to Phil Stanton, who gives the following account:

> Planning is informal around here. To begin, marketing determines the forecast for bow rakes by month for the next year. Then they pass it along to me. Quite frankly, the forecasts are usually inflated—must be their big egos over there. I have to be careful because we enter into long-term purchasing agreements for steel, and having it just sitting around is expensive. So I usually reduce the forecast by 10 percent or so. I use the modified forecast to generate a monthly final-assembly schedule, which determines what I need to have from the forging and woodworking areas. The system works well if the forecasts are good. But when marketing comes to me and says they are behind on customer orders, as they often do near the end of the year, it wreaks havoc with the schedules. Forging gets hit the hardest. For example, the presses that stamp the rake heads from blanks of steel can handle only 7,000 heads per day, and the bow rolling machine can do only 5,000 per day. Both operations are also required for many other products.

Because the marketing department provides crucial information to Stanton, Place decides to see the marketing manager, Ron Adams. Adams explains how he arrives at the bow rake forecasts.

> Things do not change much from year to year. Sure, sometimes we put on a sales promotion of some kind, but we try to give Phil enough warning before the demand kicks in—usually a month or so. I meet with several managers from the various sales regions to go over shipping data from last year and discuss anticipated promotions, changes in the economy, and shortages we experienced last year. Based on these meetings, I generate a monthly forecast for the next year. Even though we take a lot of time getting the forecast, it never seems to help us avoid customer problems.

The Problem

Place ponders the comments from Stanton and Adams. She understands Stanton's concerns about costs and keeping inventory low and Adams's concern about having enough rakes on hand to make timely shipments. Both are also somewhat concerned about capacity. Yet she decides to check actual customer demand for the bow rake over the past 4 years (in Table 6) before making her final report to Roberts.

QUESTIONS

1. Comment on the forecasting system being used by Yankee. Suggest changes or improvements that you believe are justified.

2. Develop your own forecast for bow rakes for each month of the next year (year 5). Justify your forecast and the method you used.

TABLE 6 | FOUR-YEAR DEMAND HISTORY FOR THE BOW RAKE

Month	DEMAND			
	Year 1	Year 2	Year 3	Year 4
1	55,220	39,875	32,180	62,377
2	57,350	64,128	38,600	66,501
3	15,445	47,653	25,020	31,404
4	27,776	43,050	51,300	36,504
5	21,408	39,359	31,790	16,888
6	17,118	10,317	32,100	18,909
7	18,028	45,194	59,832	35,500
8	19,883	46,530	30,740	51,250
9	15,796	22,105	47,800	34,443
10	53,665	41,350	73,890	68,088
11	83,269	46,024	60,202	68,175
12	72,991	41,856	55,200	61,100

EXPERIENTIAL LEARNING 1 | Forecasting a Vital Energy Statistic

The following time-series data capture the weekly average of East Coast crude oil imports in thousands of barrels per day.

QUARTER 2 YEAR 1		QUARTER 3 YEAR 1		QUARTER 4 YEAR 1		QUARTER 1 YEAR 2	
Week	Data	Week	Data	Week	Data	Week	Data
1	1,160	14	1,116	27	1,073	40	994
2	779	15	1,328	28	857	41	1,307
3	1,134	16	1,183	29	1,197	42	997
4	1,275	17	1,219	30	718	43	1,082
5	1,355	18	1,132	31	817	44	887
6	1,513	19	1,094	32	946	45	1,067
7	1,394	20	1,040	33	725	46	890
8	1,097	21	1,053	34	748	47	865
9	1,206	22	1,232	35	1,031	48	858
10	1,264	23	1,073	36	1,061	49	814
11	1,153	24	1,329	37	1,074	50	871
12	1,424	25	1,096	38	941	51	1,255
13	1,274	26	1,125	39	994	52	980

Your instructor has a "holdout" sample representing the values for week 53 and beyond. Your task is to use the POM for Windows *Time Series Forecasting* module and the history file to project this statistic into the future. If you have MyLab Operations Management, the demand data are available in the *Experiential Exercise 1* Data file. It can be pasted into the Data Table of the *Time Series Forecasting* module. Otherwise, you can enter the demand data directly into the Data Table. Prior to your next class meeting:

a. Use the POM for Windows *Time Series Forecasting* module to locate the best naïve, moving average, weighted moving average, and trend projection with regression models that you think will most accurately forecast demand during the holdout sample. *Begin your error calculations with week 5.*

b. Create an Excel spreadsheet that begins with inputs of the four forecasts from the *Time Series Forecasting* module. Its purpose is to develop a combination forecast that will serve as your team's forecasts for each period. Assign a weight to each forecast model (the sum of all four forecast weights for one period should equal 1.0) and develop a "combination forecast" by multiplying each forecast by its weight. Keep the weights constant for the whole history file as you search for the best set of weights. If you do not like a particular model, give it a weight of 0. Calculate appropriate forecast error measures for your combination forecast in your Excel spreadsheet.

c. Create a management report that shows your period-by-period forecasts and their overall historical CFE and MAPE performance for each model and your combination forecast.

In-Class Exercise—Part 1

a. Input into your Excel spreadsheet the forecasts from the POM for Windows *Time Series Forecasting* module to get the combination forecast for the first period (week 53) in the holdout sample. The combination forecast is considered your team's forecast.

b. Enter the actual data announced by your instructor, and have Excel compute appropriate forecast error measures for your four models and the combination forecast. Decide on any revisions of weights for the combination forecast.

c. Update the POM for Windows *Time Series Forecasting* module with the actual demand for the new period and get the new forecasts.

In-Class Exercise—Part 2

a. Input the forecasts from the POM for Windows *Time Series Forecasting* module into your Excel spreadsheet to get the final combination forecast for the next period (week 54). At this point, you may change this period's weights on each forecasting technique going into the combination forecast. You have no contextual information, but may observe that one model has been performing particularly well in the last few periods. Your team might have different opinions, but you must reach a consensus.

b. Enter the actual data announced by your instructor, with Excel computing appropriate forecast error measures for your four models and the combination forecast.

c. Update the POM for Windows *Time Series Forecasting* module with the actual demand for the new period and get the new forecasts.

In-Class Exercise—Parts 3 and Beyond

Continue in the fashion of Parts 1 and 2 to produce forecasts as directed by your instructor. At the end of the exercise, create a second management report that shows for the holdout sample your period-by-period forecasts, their individual forecast errors, and percent deviations for each model and your combination forecast. Explain your logic regarding any changes made to your combination forecast weights over the holdout period.

Source: This experiential exercise was prepared as an in-class exercise prepared by Dr. John Jensen, University of South Carolina, as a basis for classroom discussion. By permission of John B. Jensen.

Selected References

Forecasting

Armstrong, J. Scott. "Findings from Evidence-based Forecasting: Methods for Reducing Forecast Error." International Journal of Forecasting, vol. 22, no. 3 (2006), pp. 583–598.

Armstrong, J. Scott. (ed.). Principles of Forecasting: A Handbook for Researchers and Practitioners. Norwell, MA: Kluwer Academic Publishers, 2001. Also visit **http://www.forecastingprinciples. com** for valuable information on forecasting, including frequently asked questions, a forecasting methodology tree, and a dictionary.

Attaran, Mohsen, and Sharmin Attaran. "Collaborative Supply Chain Management." Business Process Management Journal, vol. 13, no. 13 (June 2007), pp. 390–404.

Cederlund, Jerold P., Rajiv Kohli, Susan A. Sherer, and Yuliang Yao. "How Motorola Put CPFR into Action." Supply Chain Management Review (October 2007), pp. 28–35.

Daugherty, Patricia J., R. Glenn Richey, Anthony S. Roath, Soonhong Min, Haozhe Chen, Aaron D. Arndt, and Stefan E. Genchev. "Is Collaboration Paying Off for Firms?" Business Horizons (2006), pp. 61–70.

Fildes, Robert, Paul Goodwin, Michael Lawrence, and Konstantinos Nikolopoulos. "Effective Forecasting and Judgmental Adjustments: An Empirical Evaluation and Strategies for Improvement in Supply-Chain Planning." International Journal of Forecasting, vol. 25, no. 1 (2009), pp. 3–23.

Lawrence, Michael, Paul Goodwin, Marcus O'Connor, and Dilek Onkal. "Judgmental Forecasting: A Review of Progress over the Last 25 Years." International Journal of Forecasting (June 2006), pp. 493–518.

Makridakis, S., R. Hogarth, and A. Gaba. "Why Forecasts Fail; What to Do Instead." MIT Sloan Management Review, vol. 51, no. 2 (2010), pp. 83–90.

McCarthy, Teresa, Donna F. Davis, Susan L. Golicic, and John T. Mentzer. "The Evolution of Sales Forecasting Management: A 20-Year Longitudinal Study of Forecasting Practices." Journal of Forecasting, vol. 25 (2006), pp. 303–324.

Min, Hokey, and Wen-Bin Vincent Yu. "Collaborative Planning, Forecasting and Replenishment: Demand Planning in Supply Chain Management." International Journal of Information Technology and Management, vol. 7, no. 1 (2008), pp. 4–20.

Montgomery, David. "Flashpoints for Changing Your Forecasting Process." The Journal of Business Forecasting (Winter 2006–2007), pp. 35–42.

Saffo, Paul. "Six Rules for Effective Forecasting." Harvard Business Review (July–August 2007), pp. 1–30.

Smaros, Johanna. "Forecasting Collaboration in the European Grocery Sector: Observations from a Case Study." Journal of Operations Management, vol. 25, no. 3 (April 2007), pp. 702–716.

Smith, Larry. "West Marine: A CPFR Success Story." Supply Chain Management Review (March 2006), pp. 29–36.

Syntetos, Aris, Konstantinos Nikolopoulos, John Boylan, Robert Fildes, and Paul Goodwin. "The Effects of Integrating Management Judgement into Intermittent Demand Forecasts." International Journal of Production Economics, vol. 118, no. 1 (March, 2009), pp. 72–81.

Wikipedia. "Collaborative Planning, Forecasting, and Replenishment." **http:en.wikipedia.org/wiki/Collaborative Planning Forecasting and Replenishment** (April, 2011).

Glossary

additive seasonal method A method in which seasonal forecasts are generated by adding or subtracting a constant to the estimate of average demand per season.

aggregation The act of clustering several similar services or products so that forecasts and plans can be made for whole families.

backlog An accumulation of customer orders that a manufacturer has promised for delivery at some future date.

backorder A customer order that cannot be filled when promised or demanded but is filled later.

big data Data sets that are so large or complex that traditional data processing applications are inadequate to deal with them.

causal methods A quantitative forecasting method that uses historical data on independent variables, such as promotional campaigns, economic conditions, and competitors' actions, to predict demand.

collaborative planning, forecasting, and replenishment (CPFR) A process for supply chain integration that allows a supplier and its customers to collaborate on making the forecast by using the Internet.

combination forecasts Forecasts that are produced by averaging independent forecasts based on different methods, different sources, or different data.

complementary products Services or products that have similar resource requirements but different demand cycles.

cumulative sum of forecast errors (CFE) A measurement of the total forecast error that assesses the bias in a forecast.

Delphi method A process of gaining consensus from a group of experts while maintaining their anonymity.

demand management The process of changing demand patterns using one or more demand options.

dependent variable The variable that one wants to forecast.

executive opinion A forecasting method in which the opinions, experience, and technical knowledge of one or more managers are summarized to arrive at a single forecast.

exponential smoothing method A weighted moving average method that calculates the average of a time series by implicitly giving recent demands more weight than earlier demands.

focus forecasting A method of forecasting that selects the best forecast from a group of forecasts generated by individual techniques.

forecast A prediction of future events used for planning purposes.

forecast error The difference found by subtracting the forecast from actual demand for a given period.

holdout sample Actual demands from the more recent time periods in the time series that are set aside to test different models developed from the earlier time periods.

independent variables Variables that are assumed to affect the dependent variable and thereby "cause" the results observed in the past.

judgment methods A forecasting method that translates the opinions of managers, expert opinions, consumer surveys, and salesforce estimates into quantitative estimates.

linear regression A causal method in which one variable (the dependent variable) is related to one or more independent variables by a linear equation.

market research A systematic approach to determine external consumer interest in a service or product by creating and testing hypotheses through data-gathering surveys.

mean absolute deviation (MAD) A measurement of the dispersion of forecast errors.

mean absolute percent error (MAPE) A measurement that relates the forecast error to the level of demand and is useful for putting forecast performance in the proper perspective.

mean squared error (MSE) A measurement of the dispersion of forecast errors.

multiplicative seasonal method A method whereby seasonal factors are multiplied by an estimate of average demand to arrive at a seasonal forecast.

naïve forecast A time-series method whereby the forecast for the next period equals the demand for the current period, or Forecast $= D_t$.

revenue management Varying price at the right time for different customer segments to maximize revenues yielded by existing supply capacity.

salesforce estimates The forecasts that are compiled from estimates of future demands made periodically by members of a company's salesforce.

simple moving average method A time-series method used to estimate the average of a demand time series by averaging the demand for the n most recent time periods.

standard deviation of the errors (σ) A measurement of the dispersion of forecast errors.

stockout An order that cannot be satisfied, resulting in a loss of the sale.

technological forecasting An application of executive opinion to keep abreast of the latest advances in technology.

time series The repeated observations of demand for a service or product in their order of occurrence.

time-series analysis A statistical approach that relies heavily on historical demand data to project the future size of demand and recognizes trends and seasonal patterns.

tracking signal A measure that indicates whether a method of forecasting is accurately predicting actual changes in demand.

trend projection with regression A forecasting model that is a hybrid between a time-series technique and the causal method.

weighted moving average method A time-series method in which each historical demand in the average can have its own weight; the sum of the weights equals 1.0.

PROJECT MANAGEMENT

BURJ KHALIFA

robertharding/Alamy Stock Photo

The Burj Khalifa in Dubai, UAE, completed in 2010, is the tallest
man-made structure in the world.

What has concrete equivalent to the weight of 100,000 elephants;
aluminum equivalent to the weight of that used in five A380 aircraft;
15 million gallons of water sustainably collected a year; the longest
single running elevator, which travels at 33 feet per second and reaches
140 floors and required 22 million labor hours to build? The answer is the

From Chapter 7 of *Operations Management: Processes and Supply Chains*, Twelfth Edition. Lee J. Krajewski,
Manoj K. Malhotra, Larry P. Ritzman. Copyright © 2019 by Pearson Education, Inc. All rights reserved.

Burj Khalifa, presently the tallest building in the world at 2,722 feet. Located in the heart of downtown Dubai, United Arab Emirates (UAE), it incorporates a 304-room Armani hotel in the first 15 floors and has the world's highest nightclub, restaurant, swimming pool, and observation deck. At the peak of construction, the project employed more than 12,000 employees from 100 countries. Even with this short description, it is clear that constructing the Burj Khalifa was a complex affair. Let's take a peek at how that project was designed and executed.

Every project has a life cycle that consists of four major phases: (1) definition and organization, (2) planning, (3) execution, and (4) closeout. In the case of the Burj Khalifa, that cycle took 6 years.

Definition and Organization

The decision to build the Burj Khalifa was made by the Dubai government to make Dubai a hub for finance, trade, and tourism in the Middle East. From the get-go, the structure had to be the tallest building in the world. It was to contain residential apartments, offices, a hotel, restaurants, and observation decks, and be the centerpiece of a large-scale, mixed-use development that included homes, hotels, parks, shopping malls, and an artificial lake. Emaar Properties, the developer of the project, wanted the development to be strikingly modern while maintaining the culture of its surroundings. The design of the tower itself incorporates cultural and historical elements particular to the region such as a spiral minaret, which grows slender as it rises. The start date for excavation was set for January 2004, with the finish date 48 months later. At the start of the project, the budget was $876 million for a tower 2,388 feet tall.

Planning

Planning for the Burj Khalifa not only entailed assembling a schedule of activities properly sequenced for technical reasons; it also involved planning for a number of engineering challenges because of the uniqueness of the project. The planning, too, involved design-test-redesign cycles for many key structural elements to enhance their effectiveness and safety in light of the environment the Burj Khalifa finds itself in. Here are two examples of the engineering challenges.

Wind The winds in the UAE average 8 mph but can have gusts as high as 80 mph. You can imagine the forces against a building a half-mile tall. After many wind tunnel tests, the engineers developed a Y-shaped design that not only afforded aesthetic advantages and breathtaking views from all rooms, but also provided a buttress against wind from any direction. The structural system enables the building to support itself laterally and keeps it from twisting. Even so, at its tallest point, the building sways 4.9 feet.

Concrete Given the high temperatures in the UAE and the weight of the building, many tests of the various concrete mixes were required. These tests included durability, compressive strength, creep and shrinkage, water penetration, and pump simulations, which had to certify that the concrete could be pumped up to 2,000 feet—a world record. The project required 431,000 cubic yards of concrete and 61,000 tons of steel rebar.

Execution

The execution phase of any project is the time frame over which most of the project's resources will be expended and progress toward the target completion date will be measured. Maintaining the project schedule of individual tasks was paramount toward completing the Burj Khalifa project on time. To that end, a 3-day cycle was established. Tasks were sequenced in a repetitive way, and the latest technologies employed, so that one story was raised every 3 days. However, as in any project, things happen to disrupt the schedule. For example, the most common reason for schedule delays and cost overruns in any project is scope creep. Emaar Properties decided in 2008 to change the final height of the building, making it 334 feet taller than the original plan. Further, it said that the luxury finishes for the apartments and offices that were decided in 2004, when the tower was originally conceived, would be replaced by upgraded finishes to make them more aesthetically attractive and functionally superior. These changes, in conjunction with a 4-month delay because of economic conditions in Dubai, increased costs and added to the duration of the project. All told, the project's cost was $624 million over budget and took 9 months longer than planned.

Closeout

The closeout phase of a project involves writing final reports and assessing the performance of the management team regarding three critical goals of any project: to complete the project on time or better (time), to stay within budget (cost), and to meet the specifications to the satisfaction of the customer (quality). Regarding the Burj Khalifa, we have seen that both the budget and the target completion date were exceeded, largely due to economic conditions and scope creep. The quality of the tower can be judged by the materials and technology used in its construction, its functionality, and its achievement of the strategic objectives of its owners. The materials and technology used in the construction of the tower were the best available at the time. Mixed reinforced concrete, tested many times, and the latest technologies for pumping the concrete are just two examples of the quality of construction. The project's functionality objectives had been met, with the launching of the Armani hotel, offices, apartments, restaurants, observation decks, and nightclub. As for the strategic objectives, the tower certainly is a world phenomenon. It holds many awards, such as the building with the highest occupied floor, highest outdoor observation deck, highest restaurant, highest nightclub, longest travel distance for elevators, and highest vertical pumping of concrete for a building, among many other achievements. It draws international tourists to Dubai just to see the structure and enjoy its amenities. However, the record for being the world's tallest building may be short-lived. The Jeddah Tower, in Saudi Arabia, is scheduled for completion in 2019 at a height of 3,281 feet. And the beat goes on.

Sources: Jennifer Dombrowski, "10 Fun Facts About the Burj Khali-fa, **http://luxeadddddventuretraveler.com** (accessed September 29, 2106); Ahmad Abdelrazaq, S. E., Kyung Jun Kim, and Jae Ho Kim, "Brief on the Construction Planning of the Burj Dubai Project, Dubai, UAE, *CTBUH 8th World Congress 2008*; **https://en.wikipedia.org/wiki/Burj_Khalifa** (accessed September 29, 2016); **http://www.turnerconstruction.com/experience/project/28/burj-khalifa**; **https://www.ukessays.com/esays/economics/analysis-of-the-burj-khalifa-tower-project-economics-essay.php** (March 23, 2015).

LEARNING GOALS *After reading this text, you should be able to:*

1 Explain the major activities associated with defining and organizing a project.

2 Describe the procedure for constructing a project network.

3 Develop the schedule of a project.

4 Analyze cost–time trade-offs in a project network.

5 Assess the risk of missing a project deadline.

6 Identify the options available to monitor and control projects.

project

An interrelated set of activities with a definite starting and ending point, which results in a unique outcome for a specific allocation of resources.

project management

A systemized, phased approach to defining, organizing, planning, monitoring, and controlling projects.

program

An interdependent set of projects that have a common strategic purpose.

Companies such as Turner Construction and Samsung Engineering & Construction, project manager and primary construction contractor, respectively, for the Burj Khalifa project, are experts at managing large projects. They master the ability to schedule activities and monitor progress within strict time, cost, and performance guidelines. A **project** can be defined as an interrelated set of activities with a definite starting and ending point, which results in a unique outcome for a specific allocation of resources.

Projects are common in everyday life as well as in business. Planning weddings, remodeling bathrooms, writing term papers, and organizing surprise parties are examples of small projects in everyday life. Conducting company audits, planning mergers, creating advertising campaigns, reengineering processes, developing new services or products, and establishing a strategic alliance are examples of large projects in business.

Recall from the opening vignette, the three main goals of any project are (1) to complete the project on time or earlier, (2) to stay within budget, and (3) to meet the specifications to the satisfaction of the customer; these three goals are often referred to as the *iron triangle*. When we must undertake projects with some uncertainty involved, it helps to have flexibility with respect to resource availability, deadlines, and budgets. Consequently, projects can be complex and challenging to manage. **Project management**—a systemized, phased approach to defining, organizing, planning, monitoring, and controlling projects—is one way to overcome that challenge.

Projects often cut across organizational lines because they require the skills of multiple professions and organizations. Furthermore, each project is unique, even if it is routine, requiring new combinations of skills and resources in the project process. For example, projects for adding a new branch office, installing new computers in a department, or developing a sales promotion may be initiated several times a year. Each project may have been done many times before; however, differences arise with each replication. Uncertainties, such as the advent of new technologies or the activities of competitors, can change the character of projects and require responsive countermeasures. Finally, projects are temporary because personnel, materials, and facilities are organized to complete them within a specified time frame and then are disbanded.

Projects, and the application of project management, facilitate the implementation of operations strategy and enable the fruition of all the changes and improvements to the processes discussed. However, the power of this approach goes beyond the focus on any one project. Operations strategy initiatives often require the coordination of many interdependent projects. Such a collection of projects is called a **program**, which is an interdependent set of projects with a common strategic purpose. As new project proposals come forward, management must assess their fit to the current operations strategy and ongoing initiatives and have a means to prioritize them, because funds for projects are often limited. Projects also can be used to implement changes to processes and supply chains. For example, projects involving the implementation of major information technologies may affect all of a firm's core processes and supporting processes as well as some of their suppliers' and customers' processes. As such, projects are a useful tool for improving processes and supply chains.

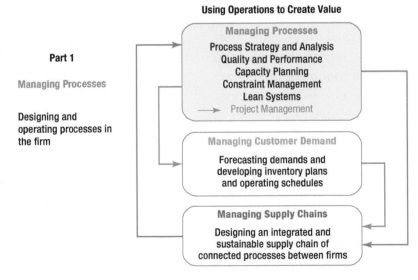

Part 1

Managing Processes

Designing and operating processes in the firm

Using Operations to Create Value

Managing Processes
Process Strategy and Analysis
Quality and Performance
Capacity Planning
Constraint Management
Lean Systems
→ Project Management

Managing Customer Demand
Forecasting demands and developing inventory plans and operating schedules

Managing Supply Chains
Designing an integrated and sustainable supply chain of connected processes between firms

Defining and Organizing Projects

A clear understanding of a project's organization and how personnel are going to work together to complete the project are keys to success. In this section, we will address (1) defining the scope and objectives, (2) selecting the project manager and team, and (3) recognizing the organizational structure.

Defining the Scope and Objectives of a Project

A thorough statement of a project's scope, time frame, and allocated resources is essential to managing the project. This statement is often referred to as the *project objective statement*. The scope provides a succinct statement of project objectives and captures the essence of the desired project outcomes in the form of major deliverables, which are concrete outcomes of the project. Changes to the scope of a project inevitably increase costs and delay completion. Collectively, changes to scope are called *scope creep* and, in sufficient quantity, are primary causes of failed projects. The time frame for a project should be as specific as possible, as in "the project should be completed by January 1, 2020." Finally, although specifying an allocation of resources to a project may be difficult during the early stages of planning, it is important for managing the project. The allocation should be expressed as a dollar figure or as full-time equivalents of personnel time. A specific statement of allocated resources makes it possible to make adjustments to the scope of the project as it proceeds.

Selecting the Project Manager and Team

Once the project is selected, a project manager must be chosen. The qualities of a good project manager should be well aligned with the roles a project manager must play.

- *Facilitator.* The project manager often must resolve conflicts between individuals or departments to ensure that the project has the appropriate resources for the job to be completed. Successful project managers have good leadership skills and a *systems view*, which encompasses the interaction of the project, its resources, and its deliverables with the firm as a whole.
- *Communicator.* Project progress and requests for additional resources must be clearly communicated to senior management and other stakeholders in a project. The project manager must also frequently communicate with the project team to get the best performance.
- *Decision Maker.* Good project managers will be sensitive to the way the team performs best and be ready to make tough decisions, if necessary. The project manager must organize the team meetings, specify how the team will make decisions, and determine the nature and timing of reports to senior management.

Selecting the project team is just as important as the selection of the project manager. Several characteristics should be considered.

- *Technical Competence.* Team members should have the technical competence required for the tasks to which they will be assigned.
- *Sensitivity.* All team members should be sensitive to interpersonal conflicts that may arise. Senior team members should be politically sensitive to help mitigate problems with upper-level management.
- *Dedication.* Team members should feel comfortable solving project problems that may spill over into areas outside their immediate expertise. They should also be dedicated to getting the project done, as opposed to maintaining a comfortable work schedule.

Recognizing Organizational Structure

The relationship of the project manager to the project team is determined by the firm's organizational structure. Each of the three types of organizational structure described here has its own implications for project management.

- *Functional.* The project is housed in a specific department or functional area, presumably the one with the most interest in the project. Assistance from personnel in other functional areas must be negotiated by the project manager. In such cases, the project manager has less control over project timing than if the entire scope of the project fell within the purview of the department.
- *Pure Project.* The team members work exclusively for the project manager on a particular project. This structure simplifies the lines of authority and is particularly effective for large projects that consist of enough work for each team member to work full time. For small projects, it could result in significant duplication of resources across functional areas.

- *Matrix.* The matrix structure is a compromise between the functional and pure project structures. The project managers of the firm's projects all report to a program manager who coordinates resource and technological needs across the functional boundaries. The matrix structure allows each functional area to maintain control over who works on a project and the technology that is used. However, team members, in effect, have two bosses: the project manager and the department manager. Resolving these line-of-authority conflicts requires a strong project manager.

Constructing Project Networks

After the project is defined and organized, the team must formulate the specific work to be accomplished and the relationships between the activities in the project. Constructing a project network involves two steps: (1) defining the work breakdown structure, and (2) diagramming the network.

Defining the Work Breakdown Structure

work breakdown structure (WBS)

A statement of all work that has to be completed.

activity

The smallest unit of work effort consuming both time and resources that the project manager can schedule and control.

The **work breakdown structure (WBS)** is a statement of all work that has to be completed. Perhaps the single most important contributor to delay is the omission of work that is germane to the successful completion of the project. The project manager must work closely with the team to identify all activities. An **activity** is the smallest unit of work effort consuming both time and resources that the project manager can schedule and control. Typically, in the process of accumulating activities, the team generates a hierarchy to the work breakdown. Major work components are broken down to smaller tasks that ultimately are broken down to activities that are assigned to individuals. Figure 1 shows a WBS for a major project involving the relocation of a hospital. In the interest of better serving the surrounding community, the board of St. John's Hospital has decided to move to a new location. The project involves constructing a new hospital and making it operational. The work components at level 1 in the WBS can be broken down into smaller units of work in level 2 that could be further divided at level 3, until the project manager gets to activities at a level of detail that can be scheduled and controlled. For example, "Organizing and Site Preparation" has been divided into six activities at level 2 in Figure 1. We have kept our example simple so that the concept of the WBS can be easily understood. If our activities in the example are divided into even smaller units of work, it is easy to see that the total WBS for a project of this size may include many more than 100 activities. Regardless of the project, care must be taken to include all important activities in the WBS to avoid project delays. Often overlooked are the activities required to plan the project, get management approval at various stages, run pilot tests of new services or products, and prepare final reports.

This view of the construction site for the Papworth Hospital in Cambridge, UK shows the extent of the activities that must take place simultaneously. Projects such as this have complex work breakdown structures and network diagrams.

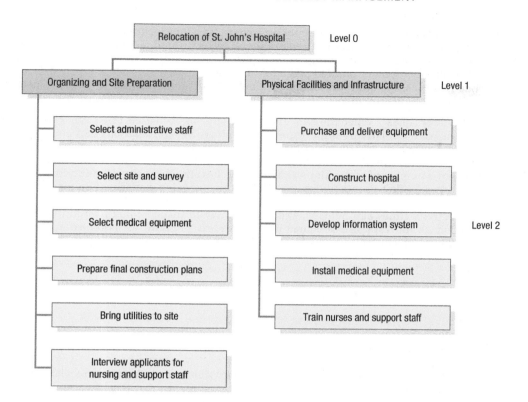

◄ **FIGURE 1**
Work Breakdown Structure for
the St. John's Hospital Project

Each activity in the WBS must have an "owner" who is responsible for doing the work. *Activity ownership* avoids confusion in the execution of activities and assigns responsibility for timely completion. The team should have a defined procedure for assigning activities to team members, which can be democratic (consensus of the team) or autocratic (assigned by the project manager).

Diagramming the Network

Network planning methods can help managers monitor and control projects. These methods treat a project as a set of interrelated activities that can be visually displayed in a **network diagram**, which consists of nodes (circles) and arcs (arrows) that depict the relationships between activities. Two network planning methods were developed in the 1950s. The **program evaluation and review technique (PERT)** was created for the U.S. Navy's Polaris missile project, which involved 3,000 separate contractors and suppliers. The **critical path method (CPM)** was developed as a means of scheduling maintenance shutdowns at chemical-processing plants. Although early versions of PERT and CPM differed in their treatment of activity time estimates, today the differences are minor. For purposes of our discussion, we refer to them collectively as PERT/CPM. These methods offer several benefits to project managers, including the following:

1. Considering projects as networks forces project teams to identify and organize the data required and to identify the interrelationships between activities. This process also provides a forum for managers of different functional areas to discuss the nature of the various activities and their resource requirements.

2. Networks enable project managers to estimate the completion time of projects, an advantage that can be useful in planning other events and in conducting contractual negotiations with customers and suppliers.

3. Reports based on project networks highlight the activities that are crucial to completing projects on schedule. They also highlight the activities that may be delayed without affecting completion dates, thereby freeing up resources for other, more critical activities.

4. Network methods enable project managers to analyze the time and cost implications of resource trade-offs.

Diagramming the project network involves establishing precedence relationships and estimating activity times.

Establishing Precedence Relationships
A **precedence relationship** determines a sequence for undertaking activities; it specifies that one activity cannot start until a preceding activity has been

network diagram

A visual display, designed to depict the relationships between activities, that consists of nodes (circles) and arcs (arrows).

program evaluation and review technique (PERT)

A network planning method created for the U.S. Navy's Polaris missile project in the 1950s, which involved 3,000 separate contractors and suppliers.

critical path method (CPM)

A network planning method developed in the 1950s as a means of scheduling maintenance shutdowns at chemical-processing plants.

precedence relationship

A relationship that determines a sequence for undertaking activities; it specifies that one activity cannot start until a preceding activity has been completed.

completed. For example, brochures announcing a conference for executives must first be designed by the program committee (activity A) before they can be printed (activity B). In other words, activity A must *precede* activity B. For large projects, establishing precedence relationships is essential because incorrect or omitted precedence relationships will result in costly delays. The precedence relationships are represented by a network diagram, similar to what we used for analyzing line balancing problems.

Estimating Activity Times   When the same type of activity has been done many times before, time estimates will have a relatively high degree of certainty. Several methods can be used to get time estimates in such an environment. First, statistical methods can be used if the project team has access to data on actual activity times experienced in the past. Second, if activity times improve with the number of replications, the times can be estimated using learning curve models. Finally, the times for first-time activities are often estimated using managerial opinions based on similar prior experiences. If the estimates involve a high degree of uncertainty, probability distributions for activity times can be used. We discuss how to incorporate uncertainty in project networks when we address risk assessment later in this text. For now, we assume that the activity times are known with certainty.

MyLab Operations Management

EXAMPLE 1	Diagramming the St. John's Hospital Project

Judy Kramer, the project manager for the St. John's Hospital project, divided the project into two major modules. She assigned John Stewart the overall responsibility for the Organizing and Site Preparation module and Sarah Walker the responsibility for the Physical Facilities and Infrastructure module. Using the WBS shown in Figure 1, the project team developed the precedence relationships, activity time estimates, and activity responsibilities shown in the following table.

Activity	Immediate Predecessors	Activity Times (wks)	Responsibility
ST. JOHN'S HOSPITAL PROJECT			Kramer
START		0	
ORGANIZING and SITE PREPARATION			Stewart
A. Select administrative staff	Start	12	Johnson
B. Select site and survey	Start	9	Taylor
C. Select medical equipment	A	10	Adams
D. Prepare final construction plans	B	10	Taylor
E. Bring utilities to site	B	24	Burton
F. Interview applicants for nursing and support staff	A	10	Johnson
PHYSICAL FACILITIES and INFRASTRUCTURE			Walker
G. Purchase and deliver equipment	C	35	Sampson
H. Construct hospital	D	40	Casey
I. Develop information system	A	15	Murphy
J. Install medical equipment	E, G, H	4	Pike
K. Train nurses and support staff	F, I, J	6	Ashton
FINISH	K	0	

For purposes of our example, we will assume a work week consists of five work days. Draw the network diagram for the hospital project.

SOLUTION

The network diagram, activities, and activity times for the hospital project are shown in Figure 2. The diagram depicts activities as circles, with arrows indicating the sequence in which they are to be performed. Activities A and B emanate from a *start* node because they have no immediate predecessors. The arrows connecting activity A to activities C, F, and I indicate that all three require completion of activity A before they can begin. Similarly, activity B must be completed before activities D and E can begin, and so on. Activity K connects to a *finish* node because no activities follow it. The start and finish nodes do not actually represent activities; they merely provide beginning and ending points for the network.

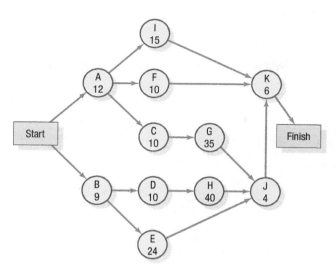

▲ **FIGURE 2**
Network Showing Activity Times for the St. John's Hospital Project

Developing the Project Schedule

A key advantage of network planning methods is the creation of a schedule of project activities that will help managers achieve the objectives of the project. Given a project network, managers can (1) estimate the completion time of a project by finding the critical path, (2) identify the start and finish times for each activity for a project schedule, and (3) calculate the amount of slack time for each activity.

Critical Path

A crucial aspect of project management is estimating the time of completion of a project. If each activity in relocating the hospital were done in sequence, with work proceeding on only one activity at a time, the time of completion would equal the sum of the times for all the activities, or 175 weeks. However, Figure 2 indicates that some activities can be carried on simultaneously, given adequate resources. We call each sequence of activities between the project's start and finish a **path**. The network describing the hospital relocation project has five paths: (1) A–I–K, (2) A–F–K, (3) A–C–G–J–K, (4) B–D–H–J–K, and (5) B–E–J–K. The **critical path** is the sequence of activities between a project's start and finish that takes the longest time to complete. Thus, the activities along the critical path determine the completion time of the project; that is, if one of the activities on the critical path is delayed, the entire project will be delayed. The estimated times for the paths in the hospital project network are:

path

The sequence of activities between a project's start and finish.

critical path

The sequence of activities between a project's start and finish that takes the longest time to complete.

Path	Estimated Time (weeks)
A–I–K	33
A–F–K	28
A–C–G–J–K	67
B–D–H–J–K	69
B–E–J–K	43

The activity string B–D–H–J–K is estimated to take 69 weeks to complete. As the longest, it constitutes the critical path. Because the critical path defines the completion time of the project, Judy Kramer and the project team should focus on these activities and any other path that is close in length to the critical path.

earliest finish time (EF)

An activity's earliest start time plus its estimated duration, t, or $EF = ES + t$.

earliest start time (ES)

The earliest finish time of the immediately preceding activity.

Project Schedule

The typical objective is to finish the project as early as possible as determined by the critical path. The project schedule is specified by the start and finish times for each activity. For any activity, managers can use the earliest start and finish times, the latest start and finish times (and still finish the project on time), or times in between these extremes if the activity is not on the critical path.

- **Earliest Start and Earliest Finish Times** The earliest start and earliest finish times are obtained as follows:

    1. The **earliest finish time (EF)** of an activity equals its earliest start time plus its estimated duration, t, or $EF = ES + t$.

        The **earliest start time (ES)** for an activity is the earliest finish time of the immediately preceding activity. For activities with more than one preceding activity, ES is the latest of the earliest finish times of the preceding activities.

        To calculate the duration of the entire project, we determine the EF for the last activity on the critical path.

An in-production Boeing 787 Dreamliner aircraft for Qatar Airways sits under construction at the Boeing production facilities and factory at Paine Field in Everett, Washington, February 17, 2012.

latest finish time (LF)

The latest start time of the activity that immediately follows.

latest start time (LS)

The latest finish time minus its estimated duration, t, or $LS = LF - t$.

- **Latest Start and Latest Finish Times** To obtain the latest start and latest finish times, we must work backward from the finish node. We start by setting the latest finish time of the project equal to the earliest finish time of the last activity on the critical path.

    1. The **latest finish time (LF)** for an activity is the latest start time of the activity that immediately follows. For activities with more than one activity that immediately follow, LF is the earliest of the latest start times of those activities.

    2. The **latest start time (LS)** for an activity equals its latest finish time minus its estimated duration, t, or $LS = LF - t$.

EXAMPLE 2	Calculating Start and Finish Times for the Activities

Calculate the ES, EF, LS, and LF times for each activity in the hospital project. Which activity should Kramer start immediately? Figure 2 contains the activity times.

SOLUTION

To compute the early start and early finish times, we begin at the start node at time 0. Because activities A and B have no predecessors, the earliest start times for these activities are also zero. The earliest finish times for these activities are

$$EF_A = 0 + 12 = 12 \text{ and } EF_B = 0 + 9 = 9$$

Because the earliest start time for activities I, F, and C is the earliest finish time of activity A,

$$ES_I = 12, ES_F = 12, \text{ and } ES_C = 12$$

Similarly,

$$ES_D = 9 \text{ and } ES_E = 9$$

After placing these ES values on the network diagram (Figure 3), we determine the EF times for activities I, F, C, D, and E:

$$EF_I = 12 + 15 = 27, EF_F = 12 + 10 = 22, EF_C = 12 + 10 = 22,$$
$$EF_D = 9 + 10 = 19, \text{ and } EF_E = 9 + 24 = 33$$

The earliest start time for activity G is the latest EF time of all immediately preceding activities. Thus,

$$ES_G = EF_C = 22, ES_H = EF_D = 19$$
$$EF_G = ES_G + t = 22 + 35 = 57, EF_H = ES_H + t = 19 + 40 = 59$$

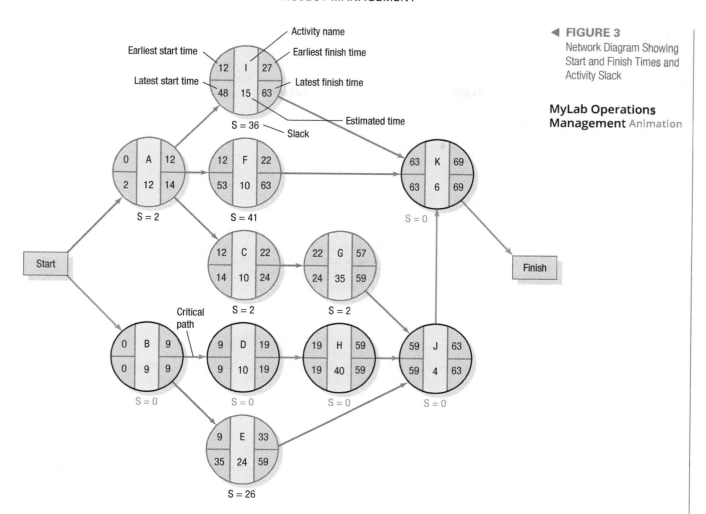

◀ FIGURE 3
Network Diagram Showing
Start and Finish Times and
Activity Slack

**MyLab Operations
Management** Animation

The project team can now determine the earliest time any activity can be started. Because activity J has several predecessors, the earliest time that activity J can begin is the latest of the EF times of any of its preceding activities: EF_G, EF_H, or EF_E. Thus, $EF_J = 59 + 4 = 63$. Similarly, $ES_K = 63$ and $EF_K = 63 + 6 = 69$. Because activity K is the last activity on the critical path, the earliest the project can be completed is week 69. The earliest start and finish times for all activities are shown in Figure 3.

To compute the latest start and latest finish times, we begin by setting the latest finish activity time of activity K at week 69, which is its earliest finish time as determined in Figure 3. Thus, the latest start time for activity K is

$$LS_K = LF_K - t = 69 - 6 = 63$$

If activity K is to start no later than week 63, all its predecessors must finish no later than that time. Consequently,

$$LF_I = 63, LF_F = 63, \text{ and } LF_J = 63$$

The latest start times for these activities are shown in Figure 3 as

$$LS_I = 63 - 15 = 48, LS_F = 63 - 10 = 53, \text{ and } LS_J = 63 - 4 = 59$$

After obtaining LS_J, we can calculate the latest start times for the immediate predecessors of activity J:

$$LS_G = 59 - 35 = 24, LS_H = 59 - 40 = 19, \text{ and } LS_E = 59 - 24 = 35$$

Similarly, we can now calculate the latest start times for activities C and D:

$$LS_C = 24 - 10 = 14 \text{ and } LS_D = 19 - 10 = 9$$

Activity A has more than one immediately following activity: I, F, and C. The earliest of the latest start times is 14 for activity C. Thus,

$$LS_A = 14 - 12 = 2$$

Similarly, activity B has two immediate followers: D and E. Because the earliest of the latest start times of these activities is 9,

$$LS_B = 9 - 9 = 0$$

The earliest or latest start times can be used for developing a project schedule. For example, Kramer should start activity B immediately because the latest start time is zero; otherwise, the project will not be completed by week 69. When the LS is greater than the ES for an activity, that activity could be scheduled for any date between ES and LS. Such is the case for activity E, which could be scheduled to start anytime between week 9 and week 35, depending on the availability of resources. The earliest start and earliest finish times and the latest start and latest finish times for all activities are shown in Figure 3.

activity slack

The maximum length of time that an activity can be delayed without delaying the entire project, calculated as S = LS − ES or S = LF − EF.

MyLab Operations Management

Active Model 1 in MyLab Operations Management provides additional insight on Gantt charts and their uses for the St. John's Hospital project.

Gantt chart

A project schedule, usually created by the project manager using computer software, that superimposes project activities, with their precedence relationships and estimated duration times, on a time line.

▼ **FIGURE 4**
MS Project Gantt Chart for the St. John's Hospital Project Schedule

Activity Slack

The maximum length of time that an activity can be delayed without delaying the entire project is called **activity slack**. Consequently, *activities on the critical path have zero slack.* Information on slack can be useful because it highlights activities that need close attention. In this regard, activity slack is the amount of schedule slippage that can be tolerated for an activity before the entire project will be delayed. Slack at an activity is reduced when the estimated time duration of an activity is exceeded or when the scheduled start time for the activity must be delayed because of resource considerations. Activity slack can be calculated in one of two ways for any activity:

$$S = LS - ES \text{ or } S = LF - EF$$

Computers calculate activity slack and prepare periodic reports for large projects, enabling managers to monitor progress. Using these reports, managers can sometimes manipulate slack to overcome scheduling problems. When resources can be used on several different activities in a project, they can be taken from activities with slack and given to activities that are behind schedule until the slack is used up. The slack for each activity in the hospital project is shown in Figure 3.

Gantt Chart The project manager, often with the assistance of computer software, creates the project schedule by superimposing project activities, with their precedence relationships and estimated duration times, on a time line. The resulting diagram is called a **Gantt chart**. Figure 4 shows a Gantt chart for the hospital project created with Microsoft Project,

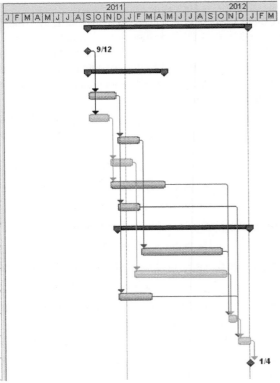

	Task Name	Duration	Start	Finish	Predecessors
1	⊟ St John's Hospital Project	69 wks	Mon 9/12/11	Fri 1/4/13	
2	Start	0 wks	Mon 9/12/11	Mon 9/12/11	
3	⊟ Organizing and Site Prep	33 wks	Mon 9/12/11	Fri 4/27/12	
4	A. Select Staff	12 wks	Mon 9/12/11	Fri 12/2/11	2
5	B. Select Site	9 wks	Mon 9/12/11	Fri 11/11/11	2
6	C. Select Equipment	10 wks	Mon 12/5/11	Fri 2/10/12	4
7	D. Construction Plans	10 wks	Mon 11/14/11	Fri 1/20/12	5
8	E. Utilities	24 wks	Mon 11/14/11	Fri 4/27/12	5
9	F. Interviews	10 wks	Mon 12/5/11	Fri 2/10/12	4
10	⊟ Facilities and Infrastructure	57 wks	Mon 12/5/11	Fri 1/4/13	
11	G. Purchase Equipment	35 wks	Mon 2/13/12	Fri 10/12/12	6
12	H. Construct Hospital	40 wks	Mon 1/23/12	Fri 10/26/12	7
13	I. Information System	15 wks	Mon 12/5/11	Fri 3/16/12	4
14	J. Install Equipment	4 wks	Mon 10/29/12	Fri 11/23/12	8,11,12
15	K. Train Staff	6 wks	Mon 11/26/12	Fri 1/4/13	9,13,14
16	Finish	0 wks	Fri 1/4/13	Fri 1/4/13	15

a popular software package for project management. The critical path is shown in red. The chart clearly shows which activities can be undertaken simultaneously and when they should be started. Figure 4 also shows the earliest start schedule for the project. Microsoft Project can also be used to show the latest start schedule or to change the definition of the work week to declare Saturday and Sunday as work days, for example. Gantt charts are popular because they are intuitive and easy to construct.

Analyzing Cost–Time Trade-Offs

Keeping costs at acceptable levels is almost always as important as meeting schedule dates. In this section, we discuss the use of PERT/CPM methods to obtain minimum-cost schedules.

The reality of project management is that there are always cost–time trade-offs. For example, a project can often be completed earlier than scheduled by hiring more workers or running extra shifts. Such actions could be advantageous if savings or additional revenues accrue from completing the project early. *Total project costs* are the sum of direct costs, indirect costs, and penalty costs. These costs are dependent either on activity times or on project completion time. *Direct costs* include labor, materials, and any other costs directly related to project activities. *Indirect costs* include administration, depreciation, financial, and other variable overhead costs that can be avoided by reducing total project time: The shorter the duration of the project, the lower the indirect costs will be. Finally, a project may incur *penalty costs* if it extends beyond some specific date, whereas *an incentive* may be provided for early completion. Managers can shorten individual activity times by using additional direct resources, such as overtime, personnel, or equipment. Thus, a project manager may consider *crashing*, or expediting, some activities to reduce overall project completion time and total project costs.

People work at the construction site of the electric railway in Dire Dawa, Ethiopia. The first overseas electric railway built to Chinese standards started having its tracks laid in Dire Dawa, Ethiopia, on May 8, 2014. The railway, which will stretch 740 kilometers linking Ethiopian capital Addis Ababa with Djibouti's capital Djibouti, was inaugurated in October, 2016, with a total investment of 4 billion U.S. dollars.

Xinhua / Alamy Stock Photo

Cost to Crash

To assess the benefit of crashing certain activities—from either a cost or a schedule perspective—the project manager needs to know the following times and costs:

1. The **normal time (NT)** is the time necessary to complete an activity under normal conditions.

2. The **normal cost (NC)** is the activity cost associated with the normal time.

3. The **crash time (CT)** is the shortest possible time to complete an activity.

4. The **crash cost (CC)** is the activity cost associated with the crash time.

Our cost analysis is based on the assumption that direct costs increase linearly as activity time is reduced from its normal time. This assumption implies that for every week the activity time is reduced, direct costs increase by a proportional amount. For example, suppose that the normal time for activity C in the hospital project is 10 weeks and is associated with a direct cost of $4,000. Also, suppose that we can crash its time to only 5 weeks at a total cost of $7,000; the net time reduction is 5 weeks at a net cost increase of $3,000. We assume that crashing activity C costs $3,000/5 = $600 per week—an assumption of linear marginal costs that is illustrated in Figure 5. Thus, if activity C were expedited by 2 weeks (i.e., its time reduced from 10 weeks to 8 weeks), the estimated direct costs would be $4,000 + 2($600) = $5,200. For any activity, the cost to crash an activity by 1 week is

$$\text{Cost to crash per period} = \frac{CC - NC}{NT - CT}$$

normal time (NT)

In the context of project management, the time necessary to complete an activity under normal conditions.

normal cost (NC)

The activity cost associated with the normal time.

crash time (CT)

The shortest possible time to complete an activity.

crash cost (CC)

The activity cost associated with the crash time.

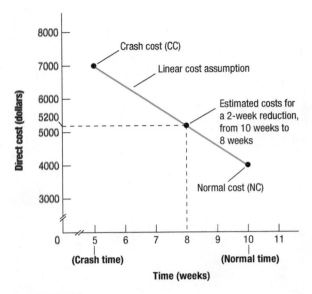

▲ FIGURE 5
Cost–Time Relationships in
Cost Analysis

Table 1 contains direct cost and time data, as well as the costs of crashing per week for the activities in the hospital project.

Minimizing Costs

The objective of cost analysis is to determine the project schedule that minimizes total project costs. Suppose that project indirect costs are $8,000 per week. Suppose also that, after week 65, the Regional Hospital Board imposes on St. John's a penalty cost of $20,000 per week if the hospital is not fully operational. With a critical path completion time of 69 weeks, the hospital faces potentially large penalty costs unless the schedule is changed. For every week that the project is shortened—to week 65—the hospital saves 1 week of penalty *and* indirect costs, or $28,000. For reductions beyond week 65, the savings are only the weekly indirect costs of $8,000.

The minimum possible project duration can be found by using the crash times of each activity for scheduling purposes. However, the cost of that schedule could be prohibitive. Project managers are most interested in minimizing the costs of their projects so that budgets are not exceeded. In determining the **minimum-cost schedule**, we start with the normal time schedule and crash activities along the critical path, whose length equals the length of the project. We want to determine

TABLE 1 | DIRECT COST AND TIME DATA FOR THE ST. JOHN'S HOSPITAL PROJECT

Activity	Normal Time (NT) (wks)	Normal Cost (NC) ($)	Crash Time (CT) (wks)	Crash Cost (CC) ($)	Maximum Time Reduction (wks)	Cost of Crashing per Week ($)
A	12	$12,000	11	13,000	1	1,000
B	9	50,000	7	64,000	2	7,000
C	10	4,000	5	7,000	5	600
D	10	16,000	8	20,000	2	2,000
E	24	120,000	14	200,000	10	8,000
F	10	10,000	6	16,000	4	1,500
G	35	500,000	25	530,000	10	3,000
H	40	1,200,000	35	1,260,000	5	12,000
I	15	40,000	10	52,500	5	2,500
J	4	10,000	1	13,000	3	1,000
K	6	30,000	5	34,000	1	4,000
	Totals	$1,992,00		$2,209,50		

minimum-cost schedule

A schedule determined by starting with the normal time schedule and crashing activities along the critical path, in such a way that the costs of crashing do not exceed the savings in indirect and penalty costs.

how much we can add in crash costs without exceeding the savings in indirect and penalty costs. The procedure involves the following steps:

Step 1. Determine the project's critical path(s).

Step 2. Find the activity or activities on the critical path(s) with the lowest cost of crashing per week.

Step 3. Reduce the time for this activity until (a) it cannot be further reduced, (b) another path becomes critical, or (c) the increase in direct costs exceeds the indirect and penalty cost savings that result from shortening the project. If more than one path is critical, the time for an activity on each path may have to be reduced simultaneously.

Step 4. Repeat this procedure until the increase in direct costs is larger than the savings generated by shortening the project.

EXAMPLE 3 — Find a Minimum-Cost Schedule

Determine the minimum-cost schedule for the St. John's Hospital project. Use the information provided in Table 1 and Figure 3.

MyLab Operations Management

Active Model 2 in MyLab Operations Management provides additional insight on cost analysis for the St. John's Hospital project.

SOLUTION

The projected completion time of the project is 69 weeks. The project costs for that schedule are $1,992,000 in direct costs, $69(\$8,000) = \$552,000$ in indirect costs, and $(69 - 65)(\$20,000) = \$80,000$ in penalty costs, for total project costs of $2,624,000. The five paths in the network have the following normal times:

A–I–K:	33 weeks
A–F–K:	28 weeks
A–C–G–J–K:	67 weeks
B–D–H–J–K:	69 weeks
B–E–J–K:	43 weeks

It will simplify our analysis if we can eliminate some paths from further consideration. If all activities on A–C–G–J–K were crashed, the path duration would be 47 weeks. Crashing all activities on B–D–H–J–K results in a project duration of 56 weeks. Because the *normal* times of A–I–K, A–F–K, and B–E–J–K are less than the minimum times of the other two paths, we can disregard those three paths; they will never become critical regardless of the crashing we may do.

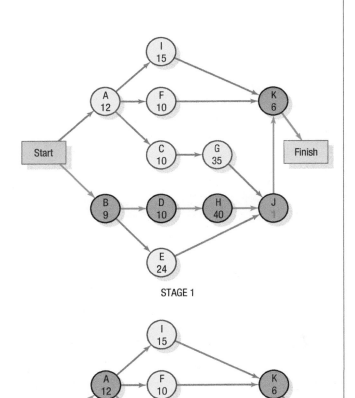

STAGE 1

Step 1. The critical path is B–D–H–J–K.

Step 2. The cheapest activity to crash per week is J at $1,000, which is much less than the savings in indirect and penalty costs of $28,000 per week.

Step 3. Crash activity J by its limit of 3 weeks because the critical path remains unchanged. The new expected path times are

A–C–G–J–K: 64 weeks and B–D–H–J–K: 66 weeks

The net savings are $3(\$28,000) - 3(\$1,000) = \$81,000$. The total project costs are now $\$2,624,000 - \$81,000 = \$2,543,000$.

STAGE 1

STAGE 2

Step 1. The critical path is still B–D–H–J–K.

Step 2. The cheapest activity to crash per week is now D at $2,000.

Step 3. Crash D by 2 weeks. The first week of reduction in activity D saves $28,000 because it eliminates 1 week of penalty costs, as well as indirect costs. Crashing D by a second week saves only $8,000 in indirect costs because, after week 65, no more penalty costs are incurred. These savings still exceed the cost of crashing D for a second week. Updated path times are

A–C–G–J–K: 64 weeks and B–D–H–J–K: 64 weeks

STAGE 2

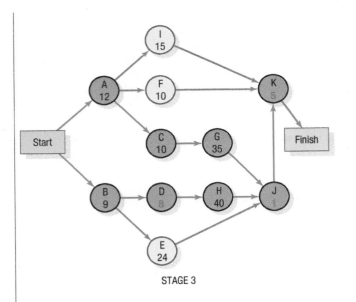

STAGE 3

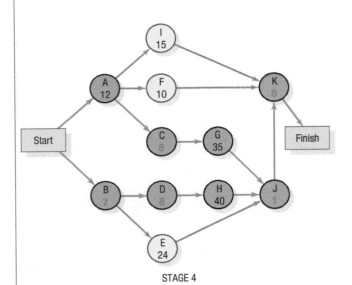

STAGE 4

The net savings are $28,000 + $8,000 − 2($2,000) = $32,000. Total project costs are now $2,543,000 − $32,000 = $2,511,000.

STAGE 3

Step 1. After crashing D, we now have two critical paths. *Both* critical paths must now be shortened to realize any savings in indirect project costs. If one is shortened and the other is not, the length of the project remains unchanged.

Step 2. Our alternatives are to crash one of the following combinations of activities—(A, B), (A, H), (C, B), (C, H), (G, B), (G, H)—or to crash activity K, which is on both critical paths (J has already been crashed). We consider only those alternatives for which the cost of crashing is less than the potential savings of $8,000 per week. The only viable alternatives are (C, B) at a cost of $7,600 per week and K at $4,000 per week. We choose activity K to crash.

Step 3. We crash activity K to the greatest extent possible—a reduction of 1 week—because it is on both critical paths. Updated path times are

A−C−G−J−K: 63 weeks and B−D−H−J−K: 63 weeks

The net savings are $8,000 − $4,000 = $4,000. Total project costs are $2,511,000 − $4,000 = $2,507,000.

STAGE 4

Step 1. The critical paths are B−D−H−J−K and A−C−G−J−K.

Step 2. The only viable alternative at this stage is to crash activities B and C simultaneously at a cost of $7,600 per week. This amount is still less than the savings of $8,000 per week.

Step 3. Crash activities B and C by 2 weeks, the limit for activity B. Updated path times are

A−C−G−J−K: 61 weeks and B−D−H−J−K: 61 weeks

Net savings are 2($8,000) − 2($7,600) = $800. Total project costs are $2,507,000 − $800 = $2,506,200.
The following table summarizes the analysis.

Stage	Crash Activity	Time Reduction (wks)	Resulting Critical Path(s)	Project Duration (wks)	Project Direct Costs, Last Trial ($000)	Crash Cost Added ($000)	Total Indirect Costs ($000)	Total Penalty Costs ($000)	Total Project Costs ($000)
0	—	—	B–D–H–J–K	69	1,992.0	—	552.0	80.0	2,624.0
1	J	3	B–D–H–J–K	66	1,992.0	3.0	528.0	20.0	2,543.0
2	D	2	B–D–H–J–K	64	1,995.0	4.0	512.0	0.0	2,511.0
			A–C–G–J–K						
3	K	1	B–D–H–J–K	63	1,999.0	4.0	504.0	0.0	2,507.0
			A–C–G–J–K						
4	B, C	2	B–D–H–J–K	61	2,003.0	15.2	488.0	0.0	2,506.2
			A–C–G–J–K						

DECISION POINT
Because the crash costs exceed weekly indirect costs, any other combination of activities will result in a net increase in total project costs. The minimum-cost schedule is 61 weeks, with a total cost of $2,506,200. To obtain this schedule, the project team must crash activities B, D, J, and K to their limits and activity C to 8 weeks. The other activities remain at their normal times. This schedule costs $117,800 less than the normal-time schedule.

Assessing and Analyzing Risks

Risk is a measure of the probability and consequence of not reaching a defined project goal. Risk involves the notion of uncertainty as it relates to project timing and costs. Often, project teams must deal with uncertainty caused by labor shortages, weather, supply delays, or the outcomes of critical tests. In this section, we discuss risk management plans and the tools managers can use to analyze the risks, such as simulation and statistical analysis, which enable managers to estimate the probability of completing a project on time and the potential for near-critical paths to affect the project completion time.

Risk-Management Plans

A major responsibility of the project manager at the start of a project is to develop a **risk-management plan**, which identifies the key risks to a project's success and prescribes ways to circumvent them. A good risk-management plan will quantify the risks, predict their impact on the project, and provide contingency plans. Project risk can be assessed by examining four categories:

risk-management plan

A plan that identifies the key risks to a project's success and pre-scribes ways to circumvent them.

- **Strategic Fit** The project may not be a good strategic fit in that it may not be clearly linked to the strategic goals of the firm.

- **Service/Product Attributes** If the project involves the development of a new service or product, there may be market, technological, or legal risks. There is a chance that competitors may offer a superior product or a technological discovery may render the service or product obsolete before it even hits the market. There may also be a legal risk of potential lawsuits or liability that could force a design change after product development has begun.

- **Project Team Capability** The project team may not have the capability to complete the project successfully because of the size and complexity of the project or the technology involved.

- **Operations** There may be an operations risk because of poor information accuracy, lack of communication, missing precedence relationships, or bad estimates for activity times.

These risks should be identified and the significant ones should have contingency plans in case something goes wrong. The riskier a project is, the more likely the project will experience difficulties, as Managerial Practice 1 shows.

Simulation PERT/CPM networks can be used to quantify risks associated with project timing. Often, the uncertainty associated with an activity can be reflected in the activity's time duration. For example, an activity in a new product development project might be developing the enabling technology to manufacture it, an activity that may take from 8 months to 1 year. To incorporate uncertainty into the network model, probability distributions of activity times can be calculated using two approaches: (1) computer simulation and (2) statistical analysis. With simulation, the time for each activity is randomly chosen from its probability distribution. The critical path of the network is determined, and the completion date of the project computed. The procedure is repeated many times, which results in a probability distribution for the completion date. We will have more to say about simulation when we discuss near critical paths later in this text.

MyLab Operations Management

MANAGERIAL PRACTICE **1**   San Francisco—Oakland Bay Bridge

San Francisco, California, has many noteworthy attractions: gardens, museums, Golden Gate Park, seafood and barking seals at Fisherman's Wharf, and the San Francisco Giants baseball team. The team was preparing to play in game 3 of the 1989 World Series against the Oakland Athletics when a 7.1 magnitude earthquake struck the Bay Area, minutes before the start of the game, resulting in the loss of many lives and billions of dollars in damage. Included in the damage was a 50-foot section of the upper deck of the Bay Bridge, which was closed until November 18, 1989, while the section was replaced. However, the Bay Bridge replacement project, which was needed to protect against future earthquakes, was not completed until September 12, 2013, at a cost of $6.4 billion, one of the most costly projects in the history of California. Are you wondering how that can happen? The answer lies at the heart of engaging in what we refer to as a risky project.

Aerial Archives/Alamy Stock Photo

The eastern span replacement of the San Francisco—Oakland Bay Bridge was built between 2002 and 2013. It is the largest public works project in California history. The construction project was complex; the span is engineered to withstand the largest earthquake expected over a 1,500-year period, and it is expected to last at least 150 years with proper maintenance. Projects such as this pose many risks for project managers.

The two major indicators of project performance are time and cost. Let's explore these two factors for the Bay Bridge replacement project.

Time Shortly after the initial repair of the bridge, engineers determined that the eastern span of the bridge had to be made more earthquake resistant. Several design proposals were submitted. One proposal was to retrofit the existing bridge by replacing or supplementing the existing supports, doing little to change the appearance of the existing structure. However, the design was called into question for lack of robustness in an earthquake. The second type of design would replace the entire eastern span of the bridge. Debate arose as two designs emerged, one lacking esthetics but meeting the structural requirements and having a lower price tag, called the *freeway on stilts*, and the other the result of a contest having a more innovative and dramatic appearance but costing more. It was referred to as the *signature span*. Meanwhile, in 1997, there was political bickering about whether the bridge should be built to the north or the south of the existing bridge. One of the complaints was that with the existing placement and design the bridge would cast a shadow over prime development sites on Yerba Buena Island, which is within the province of San Francisco. Consequently, San Francisco restricted soil engineers' access to the proposed site for 2 years while a bridge design compromise was worked out. Finally the revised signature span proposal was accepted, and on January 29, 2002, construction began with an estimated completion date in 2007. However, in 2004, the governor of California announced that insufficient funds were available for the signature span design and that the "freeway on stilts" should be constructed instead. After 6 months of delay, in 2005, additional funding was found and the original signature span design was reapproved. Once the project was in full swing, additional unforeseen hurdles such as technical challenges, permitting, weather, and design revisions caused long delays that added years to the original project deadlines. Consequently, because the project was extremely complex and involved an esthetically pleasing but seldom built design, securing accurate time estimates for the activities was nearly impossible.

Cost As project delays mounted, costs increased. In 1997, the cost for the signature span design was estimated to be $1.5 billion. By 2002, when approval for the start of the project was obtained, the cost for steel rose dramatically, primarily because of a building boom in China. The entire project required 100,000 tons of structural steel; the total project cost was reestimated to be about $6.2 billion. Contractors were now considering uncertainties in construction costs due to the innovative design as well

as the increase in steel costs in their cost estimates. Further, the delay in 2004 over the funding of the signature span design added an estimated $83 million to the cost of the project. Additional problems, including defective rods anchoring the roadway to earthquake safety structures, broken bolts connecting portions of the bridge deck to concrete columns, and water leaks due to a problem with the caulking between the steel guardrails and the roadway, added cost as well. All told, the project was estimated to cost $6.4 billion.

Projects of this size and complexity are inherently risky; contingency plans should cover the most likely disruptions. Schedule and budget problems are not unusual; however, the job of project managers is to manage the risks and minimize the deviations.

Sources: **http://en.wikipedia.org/wiki/Eastern_span_replacement_of_the_San_Francisco_Oakland** Bay Bridge (2013); Rick Weinberg, "26: World Series halted by Bay Area earthquake," **http://sports.espn.go.com/espn25** (2013); Jason Dearen, "After 24 years, $6.4 Billion S.F. Bay Bridge Project Draws to Close," **http://cnsnews.com/news/article** (2013); Jaxon Van Derbeken, "Bay Bridge's new problem: leaks," **http://www.sfgate.com/bayarea/article** (2014).

Statistical Analysis

The statistical analysis approach requires that activity times be stated in terms of three reasonable time estimates:

1. The **optimistic time (a)** is the shortest time in which an activity can be completed, if all goes exceptionally well.

2. The **most likely time (m)** is the probable time required to perform an activity.

3. The **pessimistic time (b)** is the longest estimated time required to perform an activity.

With three time estimates—the optimistic, the most likely, and the pessimistic—the project manager has enough information to estimate the probability that an activity will be completed on schedule. To do so, the project manager must first calculate the mean and variance of a probability distribution for each activity. In PERT/CPM, each activity time is treated as though it were a random variable derived from a beta probability distribution. This distribution can have various shapes, allowing the most likely time estimate (m) to fall anywhere between the pessimistic (b) and optimistic (a) time estimates. The most likely time estimate is the *mode* of the beta distribution, or the time with the highest probability of occurrence. This condition is not possible with the normal distribution, which is symmetrical, because the normal distribution requires the mode to be equidistant from the end points of the distribution. Figure 6 shows the difference between the two distributions.

optimistic time (a)

The shortest time in which an activity can be completed, if all goes exceptionally well.

most likely time (m)

The probable time required to perform an activity.

pessimistic time (b)

The longest estimated time required to perform an activity.

▼ **FIGURE 6**

Differences Between Beta and Normal Distributions for Project Risk Analysis

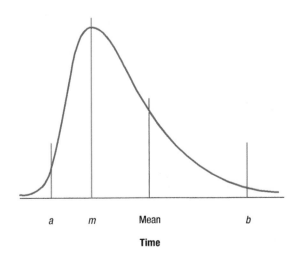

(a) **Beta distribution:** The most likely time (m) has the highest probability and can be placed anywhere between the optimistic (a) and pessimistic (b) times.

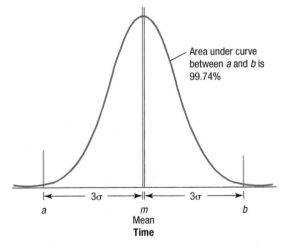

(b) **Normal distribution:** The mean and most likely times must be the same. If a and b are chosen to be 6σ apart, there is a 99.74% chance that the actual activity time will fall between them.

Two key assumptions are required. First, we assume that a, m, and b can be estimated accurately. The estimates might best be considered values that define a reasonable time range for the activity duration negotiated between the project manager and the team members responsible for the activities. Second, we assume that the standard deviation, σ, of the activity time is one-sixth the range $b - a$. Thus, the chance that actual activity times will fall between a and b is high. Why does this assumption make sense? If the activity time followed the normal distribution, six standard deviations would span approximately 99.74 percent of the distribution.

Even with these assumptions, derivation of the mean and variance of each activity's probability distribution is complex. These derivations show that the mean of the beta distribution can be estimated by using the following weighted average of the three time estimates:

$$t_e = \frac{a + 4m + b}{6}$$

Note that the most likely time has four times the weight of the pessimistic and optimistic estimates. The variance of the beta distribution for each activity is

$$\sigma^2 = \left(\frac{b - a}{6}\right)^2$$

The variance, which is the standard deviation squared, increases as the difference between b and a increases. This result implies that the less certain a person is in estimating the actual time for an activity, the greater will be the variance.

EXAMPLE 4	**Calculating Means and Variances**

Suppose that the project team has arrived at the following time estimates for activity B (Select Site and Survey) of the St. John's Hospital project:

$$a = 7 \text{ weeks}, m = 8 \text{ weeks, and } b = 15 \text{ weeks}$$

a. Calculate the expected time and variance for activity B.

b. Calculate the expected time and variance for the other activities in the project.

SOLUTION

a. The expected time for activity B is

$$t_e = \frac{7 + 4(8) + 15}{6} = \frac{54}{6} = 9 \text{ weeks}$$

Note that the expected time (9 weeks) does not equal the most likely time (8 weeks) for this activity. These times will be the same only when the most likely time is equidistant from the optimistic and pessimistic times. We calculate the variance for activity B as

$$\sigma^2 = \left(\frac{15 - 7}{6}\right)^2 = \left(\frac{8}{6}\right)^2 = 1.78$$

b. The following table shows expected activity times and variances for the activities listed in the project description.

	TIME ESTIMATES (WKS)			ACTIVITY STATISTICS	
Activity	Optimistic (*a*)	Most Likely (*m*)	Pessimistic (*b*)	Expected Time (*t_e*)	Variance (*σ^2*)
A	11	12	13	12	0.11
B	7	8	15	9	1.78
C	5	10	15	10	2.78

Activity	TIME ESTIMATES (WKS)			ACTIVITY STATISTICS	
	Optimistic (a)	Most Likely (m)	Pessimistic (b)	Expected Time (t_e)	Variance (σ²)
D	8	9	16	10	1.78
E	14	25	30	24	7.11
F	6	9	18	10	4.00
G	25	36	41	35	7.11
H	35	40	45	40	2.78
I	10	13	28	15	9.00
J	1	2	15	4	5.44
K	5	6	7	6	0.11

DECISION POINT

The project team should notice that the greatest uncertainty lies in the time estimate for activity I, followed by the estimates for activities E and G. These activities should be analyzed for the source of the uncertainties, and actions should be taken to reduce the variance in the time estimates.

Analyzing Probabilities

Because time estimates for activities involve uncertainty, project managers are interested in determining the probability of meeting project completion deadlines. To develop the probability distribution for project completion time, we assume that the duration time of one activity does not depend on that of any other activity. This assumption enables us to estimate the mean and variance of the probability distribution of the time duration of the entire project by summing the duration times and variances of the activities along the critical path. However, if one work crew is assigned two activities that can be done at the same time, the activity times will be interdependent and the assumption is not valid. In addition, if other paths in the network have small amounts of slack, one of them might become the critical path before the project is completed; we should calculate a probability distribution for those paths as well.

Because of the assumption that the activity duration times are independent random variables, we can make use of the central limit theorem, which states that the sum of a group of independent, identically distributed random variables approaches a normal distribution as the number of random variables increases. The mean of the normal distribution is the sum of the expected activity times on the path. In the case of the critical path, it is the earliest expected finish time for the project:

$$T_E = \sum \text{(Expected activity times on the critical path)} = \text{Mean of normal distribution}$$

Similarly, because of the assumption of activity time independence, we use the sum of the variances of the activities along the path as the variance of the time distribution for that path. That is, for the critical path,

$$\sigma_P^2 = \sum \text{(Variances of activities on the critical path)}$$

To analyze probabilities of completing a project by a certain date using the normal distribution, we focus on the *critical path* and use the z-transformation formula:

$$z = \frac{T - T_E}{\sigma_P}$$

where

$$T = \text{due date for the project}$$

Given the value of z, we use the Normal Distribution appendix to find the probability that the project will be completed by time T, or sooner. An implicit assumption in this approach is that no other path will become critical during the time span of the project. Example 5, part (a), demonstrates this calculation for the St. John's Hospital project.

The procedure for assessing the probability of completing any activity in a project by a specific date is similar to the one just discussed. However, instead of the critical path, we would use the longest time path of activities from the start node to the activity node in question.

Near-Critical Paths

A project's duration is a function of its critical path. However, paths that are close to the same duration as the critical path may ultimately become the critical path over the life of the project. In practice, at the start of the project, managers typically do not know the activity times with certainty and may never know which path was the critical path until the actual activity times are known at the end of the project. Nonetheless, this uncertainty does not reduce the usefulness of identifying the probability of one path or another causing a project to exceed its target completion time; it helps to identify the activities that need close management attention. To assess the chances of near-critical paths delaying the project completion, we can focus on the longest paths in the project network keeping in mind that both duration and variance along the path must be considered. Shorter paths with high variances could have just as much a chance to delay the project as longer paths with smaller variances. We can then estimate the probability that a given path will exceed the project target completion time. We demonstrate that approach using statistical analysis in Example 5, part (b).

Alternatively, simulation can be used to estimate the probabilities. The advantage of simulation is that you are not restricted to the use of the beta distribution for activity times. Also, activity or path dependencies, such as decision points that could involve different groups of activities to be undertaken, can be incorporated in a simulation model much more easily than with the statistical analysis approach. Fortunately, regardless of the approach used, it is rarely necessary to evaluate every path in the network. In large networks, many paths will have both short durations and low variances, making them unlikely to affect the project duration.

| EXAMPLE 5 | Calculating the Probability of Completing a Project by a Given Date |

MyLab Operations Management

Active Model 3 in MyLab Operations Management provides additional insight on probability analysis for the St. John's Hospital project.

Calculate the probability that St. John's Hospital will become operational in 72 weeks, using (a) the critical path and (b) near-critical path A–C–G–J–K.

SOLUTION

a. The critical path B–D–H–J–K has a length of 69 weeks. From the table in Example 4, we obtain the variance of path B–D–H–J–K: $\sigma_P^2 = 1.78 + 1.78 + 2.78 + 5.44 + 0.11 = 11.89$. Next, we calculate the z-value:

$$z = \frac{72 - 69}{\sqrt{11.89}} = \frac{3}{3.45} = 0.87$$

Using the Normal Distribution appendix, we go down the lefthand column until we arrive at the value 0.8 and then across until we arrive at the 0.07 column, which shows a tabular value of 0.8078. Consequently, we find that the probability is about 0.81 that the length of path B–D–H–J–K will be no greater than 72 weeks. Because this path is the critical path, there is a 19 percent probability that the project will take longer than 72 weeks. This probability is shown graphically in Figure 7.

b. From the table in Example 4, we determine that the sum of the expected activity times on path A–C–G–J–K is 67 weeks and that $\sigma_P^2 = 0.11 + 2.78 + 7.11 + 5.44 + 0.11 = 15.55$. The z-value is

$$z = \frac{72 - 67}{\sqrt{15.55}} = \frac{5}{3.94} = 1.27$$

The probability is about 0.90 that the length of path A–C–G–J–K will be no greater than 72 weeks.

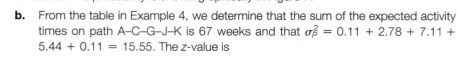

Length of critical path / Normal distribution: Mean = 69 weeks; σ_p = 3.45 weeks

Probability of meeting the schedule is 0.8078 / Probability of exceeding 72 weeks is 0.1922

69 72

Project duration (weeks)

▲ FIGURE 7
Probability of Completing the St. John's Hospital Project on Schedule

DECISION POINT

The project team should be aware of the 10 percent chance that path A–C–G–J–K will exceed the target completion date of week 72. Although the probability is not high for that path, activities A, C, and G bear watching during the first 57 weeks of the project to make sure no more than 2 weeks of slippage occurs in their schedules. This attention is especially important for activity G, which has a high time variance.

Monitoring and Controlling Projects

Once project planning is over, the challenge becomes keeping the project on schedule within the budget of allocated resources. In this section, we discuss how to monitor project status and resource usage. In addition, we identify the features of project management software useful for monitoring and controlling projects.

Monitoring Project Status

A good tracking system will help the project team accomplish its project goals. Effective tracking systems collect information on three topics: (1) open issues, (2) risks, and (3) schedule status.

Open Issues and Risks   One of the duties of the project manager is to make sure that issues that have been raised during the project actually get resolved in a timely fashion. The tracking system should remind the project manager of due dates for open issues and who was responsible for seeing that they are resolved. Likewise, it should provide the status of each risk to project delays specified in the risk management plan so that the team can review them at each meeting. To be effective, the tracking system requires team members to update information periodically regarding their respective responsibilities.

Schedule Status   Even the best laid project plans can go awry. A tracking system that provides periodic monitoring of slack time in the project schedule can help the project manager control activities along the critical path. Periodic updating of the status of ongoing activities in the project allows the tracking system to recalculate activity slacks and indicate those activities that are behind schedule or are in danger of using up all of their slack. Managers can then focus on those activities and reallocate resources as needed.

Monitoring and controlling shipbuilding projects is critical to keeping these complex projects on schedule. Here a propeller is attached to an ocean-going vessel.

Monitoring Project Resources

Experience has shown that the resources allocated to a project are consumed at an uneven rate that is a function of the timing of the schedules for the project's activities. Projects have a *life cycle* that consists of four major phases: (1) definition and organization, (2) planning, (3) execution, and (4) closeout. Figure 8 shows that each of the four phases requires different resource commitments.

We have already discussed the activities associated with the project definition and organization and project planning phases. The phase that takes the most resources is the *execution phase*, during which managers focus on activities pertaining to deliverables. The project schedule becomes very important because it shows when each resource devoted to a given activity will be required. Monitoring the progress of activities throughout the project is important to avoid potential overloading of resources. Problems arise when a specific resource, such as a construction crew or staff specialist, is required on several activities with overlapping schedules. Project managers have several options to alleviate resource problems, including the following:

▼ FIGURE 8
Project Life Cycle

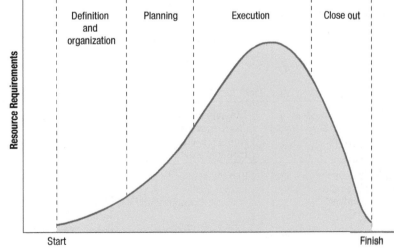

- *Resource Leveling.* The attempt to reduce the peaks and valleys in resource needs by shifting the schedules of conflicting activities within their earliest and latest start dates. Software packages such as MS Project have algorithms that move activities to avoid violating resource constraints.

- *Resource Allocation.* The assignment of resources to the most important activities. Most popular project management software packages have a few priority rules that can be used to decide which activity a critical resource should be scheduled to perform when conflicts arise. For example, for all the activities requiring a given resource, assign the resource to the one with the earliest start time. An activity slack report identifies potential candidates for resource shifting—shift resources from high slack activities to those behind schedule.

- *Resource Acquisition.* The addition of more of an overloaded resource to maintain the schedule of an activity. Obviously, this tactic is constrained by the project budget.

Controlling Projects

Project managers have the responsibilities of accounting for the effective use of the firm's resources as well as managing the activities to achieve the time and quality goals of the project. The firm's assets include the physical assets, human resources, and financial resources. Physical assets are controlled by the timely maintenance of machines and equipment so that their failure does not delay the project. Inventories must be received, stored for future use, and replenished. Project managers are also responsible for human resource development. Projects provide a rich environment to develop future leaders; project managers can take advantage of the situation by assigning team members important activities to aid in their managerial development. Last, but not least, project managers must control the expenditures of the firm's financial resources. Most project management software packages contain accounting reports, budget reports, capital investment controls, and cash flow reports. Deviations from the project plan, often referred to as variances, must be periodically reported and analyzed for their causes.

Monitoring and controlling projects are ongoing activities throughout the execution phase of the project life cycle. The project **closeout**, however, is an activity that many project managers forget to include in their consideration of resource usage. The purpose of this final phase in the project life cycle is to write final reports and complete remaining deliverables. A key ingredient of the report should be a thorough analysis of the achievement of the iron triangle goals: on time, within budget, and meet the specifications of the project to the satisfaction of the customer. An important aspect of this phase, however, is compiling the team's recommendations for improving the project process of which they were a part. Many team members will be assigned to other projects where they can apply what they learned.

closeout

An activity that includes writing final reports, completing remaining deliverables, and compiling the team's recommendations for improving the project process.

LEARNING GOALS IN REVIEW

Learning Goal	Guidelines for Review	MyLab Operations Management Resources
1 Explain the major activities associated with defining and organizing a project.	Read the opener to the text, which shows the four major phases of the project to build the Burj Khalifa tower, the introduction to the text, and the section "Defining and Organizing Projects".	**Video:** Project Management at the Phoenician
2 Describe the procedure for constructing a project network.	Focus on the section "Constructing Project Networks," paying close attention to Example 1.	**SmartDraw**—Free trial
3 Develop the schedule of a project.	Review the section "Developing the Project Schedule". The schedule is determined when activity slacks and the critical path are computed. Focus on Example 2 and Figure 3.	**Active Model Exercise:** 1: Gantt Chart **OME Solver:** Single Time Estimates **POM for Windows:** Single Time Estimates **MS Project**—Free trial
4 Analyze cost–time trade-offs in a project network.	The section "Analyzing Cost–Time Trade-offs," and Example 3 demonstrate how the relevant costs must be considered to minimize costs. Figure 5 explains a key assumption in the analysis. Solved Problem 1 contains a detailed solution.	**Active Model Exercise:** 2: Cost Analysis **POM for Windows:** Crashing
5 Assess the risk of missing a project deadline.	See the section "Assessing and Analyzing Risks," which explains the risks faced by project managers and how to compute the probabilities. Be sure to understand Examples 4 and 5 and Solved Problem 2.	**Active Model Exercise:** 3: Probability Analysis **OME Solver:** Three Time Estimates **POM for Windows:** Triple Time Estimates; Mean/Standard Deviation Given **Simquick Simulation Exercise:** Software Development Company
6 Identify the options available to monitor and control projects.	See the section "Monitoring and Controlling Projects".	**OME Solver:** Project Budgeting **POM for Windows:** Cost Budgeting

Key Equations

Developing the Project Schedule

1. Start and finish times:

t = estimated time duration of the activity

ES = latest of the EF times of all activities immediately preceding activity

EF = ES + t

LF = earliest of the LS times of all activities immediately following activity

LS = LF − t

2. Activity slack:

$$S = LS - ES \text{ or } S = LF - EF$$

Analyzing Cost–Time Trade-offs

3. Project costs:

$$\text{Crash cost per period} = \frac{\text{Crash cost} - \text{Normal cost}}{\text{Normal time} - \text{Crash time}}$$

$$= \frac{CC - NC}{NT - CT}$$

Assessing and Analyzing Risks

4. Activity time statistics:

t_e = mean of an activity's beta distribution

$$t_e = \frac{a + 4m + b}{6}$$

σ^2 = variance of the activity time

$$\sigma^2 = \left(\frac{b - a}{6}\right)^2$$

5. z-transformation formula:

$$z = \frac{T - T_E}{\sigma_P}$$

where

T = due date for the project

$T_E = \sum$ (expected activity times on the critical path)

$\quad$ = mean of normal distribution of critical path time

σ_P = standard deviation of critical path time distribution

Key Terms

activity
activity slack
closeout
crash cost (CC)
crash time (CT)
critical path
critical path method (CPM)
earliest finish time (EF)
earliest start time (ES)
Gantt chart

latest finish time (LF)
latest start time (LS)
minimum-cost schedule
most likely time (m)
network diagram
normal cost (NC)
normal time (NT)
optimistic time (a)
path
pessimistic time (b)

precedence relationship
program
program evaluation and review
$\quad$ technique (PERT)
project
project management
risk-management plan
work breakdown structure (WBS)

Solved Problem 1

MyLab Operations Management Video

Your company has just received an order from a good customer for a specially designed electric motor. The contract states that, starting on the 13th day from now, your firm will experience a penalty of $100 per day until the job is completed. Indirect project costs amount to $200 per day. The data on direct costs and activity precedence relationships are given in Table 2.

TABLE 2 | ELECTRIC MOTOR PROJECT DATA

Activity	Normal Time (days)	Normal Cost ($)	Crash Time (days)	Crash Cost ($)	Immediate Predecessor(s)
A	4	1,000	3	1,300	None
B	7	1,400	4	2,000	None
C	5	2,000	4	2,700	None
D	6	1,200	5	1,400	A
E	3	900	2	1,100	B
F	11	2,500	6	3,750	C
G	4	800	3	1,450	D, E
H	3	300	1	500	F, G

a. Draw the project network diagram.
b. What completion date would you recommend?

SOLUTION

a. The network diagram, including normal activity times, for this procedure is shown in Figure 9. Keep the following points in mind while constructing a network diagram.

  1. Always have start and finish nodes.
  2. Try to avoid crossing paths to keep the diagram simple.
  3. Use only one arrow to directly connect any two nodes.
  4. Put the activities with no predecessors at the left and point the arrows from left to right.
  5. Be prepared to revise the diagram several times before you come up with a correct and uncluttered diagram.

b. With these activity durations, the project will be completed in 19 days and incur a $700 penalty. Determining a good completion date requires the use of the minimum-cost schedule procedure. Using the data provided in Table 2, you can determine the maximum crash-time reduction and crash cost per day for each activity. For example, for activity A:

$$\text{Maximum crash time} = \text{Normal time} - \text{Crash time}$$
$$= 4 \text{ days} - 3 \text{ days} = 1 \text{ day}$$

$$\text{Crash cost per day} = \frac{\text{Crash cost} - \text{Normal cost}}{\text{Normal time} - \text{Crash time}}$$
$$= \frac{CC - NC}{NT - CT}$$
$$= \frac{\$1,300 - \$1,000}{4 \text{ days} - 3 \text{ days}} = \$300$$

FIGURE 9 ▶
Network Diagram for the Electric Motor Project

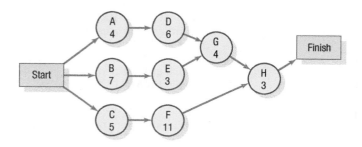

Activity	Crash Cost per Day ($)	Maximum Time Reduction (days)
A	300	1
B	200	3
C	700	1
D	200	1
E	200	1
F	250	5
G	650	1
H	100	2

Table 3 summarizes the analysis and the resultant project duration and total cost. The critical path is C–F–H at 19 days, which is the longest path in the network. The cheapest of these activities to crash is H, which costs only an extra $100 per day to crash. Doing so saves $200 + $100 = $300 per day in indirect and penalty costs. If you crash this activity for 2 days (the maximum), the lengths of the paths are now

A–D–G–H: 15 days, B–E–G–H: 15 days, and C–F–H: 17 days

The critical path is still C–F–H. The next cheapest critical activity to crash is F at $250 per day. You can crash F only 2 days because at that point you will have three critical paths. Further reductions in project duration will require simultaneous crashing of more than one activity (D, E, and F). The cost to do so, $650, exceeds the savings, $300. Consequently, you should stop. Note that every activity is critical. The project costs are minimized when the completion date is day 15. However, some goodwill costs may be associated with disappointing a customer who wants delivery in 12 days.

TABLE 3 | PROJECT COST ANALYSIS

Stage	Crash Activity	Time Reduction (days)	Resulting Critical Path(s)	Project Duration (days)	Project Direct Costs, Last Trial ($)	Crash Cost Added ($)	Total Indirect Costs ($)	Total Penalty Costs ($)	Total Project Costs ($)
0	—	—	C–F–H	19	10,100	—	3,800	700	14,600
1	H	2	C–F–H	17	10,100	200	3,400	500	14,200
2	F	2	A–D–G–H	15	10,300	500	3,000	300	14,100
			B–E–G–H						
			C–F–H						

Solved Problem 2

An advertising project manager developed the network diagram shown in Figure 10 for a new advertising campaign. In addition, the manager gathered the time information for each activity, as shown in the accompanying table.

Activity	TIME ESTIMATES (WKS)			Immediate Predecessor(s)
	Optimistic	Most Likely	Pessimistic	
A	1	4	7	—
B	2	6	7	—
C	3	3	6	B
D	6	13	14	A
E	3	6	12	A, C
F	6	8	16	B
G	1	5	6	E, F

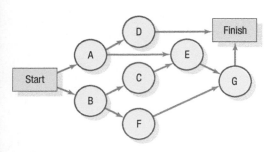

▲ FIGURE 10
Network Diagram for the
Advertising Project

a. Calculate the expected time and variance for each activity.
b. Calculate the activity slacks and determine the critical path, using the expected activity times.
c. What is the probability of completing the project within 23 weeks?

SOLUTION

a. The expected time and variance for each activity are calculated as follows:

$$t_e = \frac{a + 4m + b}{6}$$

Activity	Expected Time (wks)	Variance (σ^2)
A	4.0	1.00
B	5.5	0.69
C	3.5	0.25
D	12.0	1.78
E	6.5	2.25
F	9.0	2.78
G	4.5	0.69

b. We need to calculate the earliest start, latest start, earliest finish, and latest finish times for each activity. Starting with activities A and B, we proceed from the beginning of the network and move to the end, calculating the earliest start and finish times:

Activity	Earliest Start (wks)	Earliest Finish (wks)
A	0	0 + 4.0 = 4.0
B	0	0 + 5.5 = 5.5
C	5.5	5.5 + 3.5 = 9.0
D	4.0	4.0 + 12.0 = 16.0
E	9.0	9.0 + 6.5 = 15.5
F	5.5	5.5 + 9.0 = 14.5
G	15.5	15.5 + 4.5 = 20.0

Based on expected times, the earliest finish for the project is week 20, when activity G has been completed. Using that as a target date, we can work backward through the network, calculating the latest start and finish times (shown graphically in Figure 11):

Activity	Latest Start (wks)	Latest Finish (wks)
G	15.5	20.0
F	6.5	15.5
E	9.0	15.5
D	8.0	20.0
C	5.5	9.0
B	0.0	5.5
A	4.0	8.0

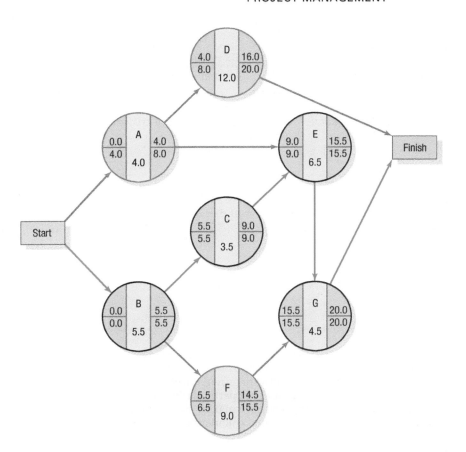

We now calculate the activity slacks and determine which activities are on the critical path:

Activity	START (WKS)		FINISH (WKS)		Slack	Critical Activity
	Earliest	Latest	Earliest	Latest		
A	0.0	4.0	4.0	8.0	4.0	No
B	0.0	0.0	5.5	5.5	0.0	Yes
C	5.5	5.5	9.0	9.0	0.0	Yes
D	4.0	8.0	16.0	20.0	4.0	No
E	9.0	9.0	15.5	15.5	0.0	Yes
F	5.5	6.5	14.5	15.5	1.0	No
G	15.5	15.5	20.0	20.0	0.0	Yes

The paths, and their total expected times and variances, are

Path	Total Expected Time (wks)	Total Variance (σ_P^2)
A–D	4 + 12 = 16	1.00 + 1.78 = 2.78
A–E–G	4 + 6.5 + 4.5 = 15	1.00 + 2.25 + 0.69 = 3.94
B–C–E–G	5.5 + 3.5 + 6.5 + 4.5 = 20	0.69 + 0.25 + 2.25 + 0.69 = 3.88
B–F–G	5.5 + 9 + 4.5 = 19	0.69 + 2.78 + 0.69 = 4.16

The critical path is B–C–E–G, with a total expected time of 20 weeks. However, path B–F–G is 19 weeks and has a large variance.

c. We first calculate the z-value:

$$z = \frac{T - T_E}{\sigma_P} = \frac{23 - 20}{\sqrt{3.88}} = 1.52$$

Using the Normal Distribution appendix, we find that the probability of completing the project in 23 weeks or fewer is 0.9357. Because the length of path B–F–G is close to that of the critical path and has a large variance, it might well become the critical path during the project.

Discussion Questions

1. One of your colleagues comments that software is the ultimate key to project management success. How would you respond?

2. Explain how to determine the slack for each activity in a project. Why is it important for managers to know where the slack is in their projects?

3. Define risk as it applies to projects. What are the major sources of risk in a project?

Problems

The OM Explorer and POM for Windows software is available to all students. Go to **http://www.pearsonhighered.com/krajewski** to download these computer packages. If you purchased MyLab Operations Management, you also have access to Active Models software and significant help in doing the following problems. Check with your instructor on how best to use these resources. In many cases, the instructor wants you to understand how to do the calculations by hand. At the least, the software provides a check on your calculations. When calculations are particularly complex and the goal is interpreting the results in making decisions, the software replaces entirely the manual calculations.

Developing the Project Schedule

1. Consider the following data for a project to install a new server at the Northland Pines High School.

Activity	Activity Time (days)	Immediate Predecessor(s)
A	2	—
B	4	A
C	5	A
D	2	B
E	1	B
F	8	B, C
G	3	D, E
H	5	F
I	4	F
J	7	G, H, I

   a. Draw the network diagram.

   b. Calculate the critical path for this project.

   c. How much slack is in each of the activities G, H, and I?

2. The following information is known about a project to upgrade a point-of-sale system at Kids and Tots Apparel.

Activity	Activity Time (days)	Immediate Predecessor(s)
A	7	—
B	2	A

Activity	Activity Time (days)	Immediate Predecessor(s)
C	4	A
D	4	B, C
E	4	D
F	3	E
G	5	E

   a. Draw the network diagram for this project.

   b. Determine the critical path and project duration.

   c. Calculate the slack for each activity.

3. A project for improving a billing process has the following precedence relationships and activity times.

Activity	Activity Time (wks)	Immediate Predecessor(s)
A	3	—
B	11	—
C	7	A
D	13	B, C
E	10	B
F	6	D
G	5	E
H	8	F, G

a. Draw the network diagram.

b. Calculate the slack for each activity. Which activities are on the critical path?

4. The following information is available about a project to organize an event to honor the mayor of West Allis at the Nathan Hale High School.

Activity	Activity Time (days)	Immediate Predecessor(s)
A	3	—
B	4	—
C	5	—
D	4	—
E	7	A
F	2	B, C, D
G	4	E, F
H	6	F
I	4	G
J	3	G
K	3	H

a. Draw the network diagram.

b. Find the critical path.

5. The following information has been gathered for a project to install a new machine lathe at Diamond Manufacturing, Inc.

Activity	Activity Time (wks)	Immediate Predecessor(s)
A	4	—
B	7	A
C	9	B
D	3	B
E	14	D
F	10	C, D
G	11	F, E

a. Draw the network diagram.

b. Calculate the slack for each activity and determine the critical path. How long will the project take?

6. Consider the following information for a project to add a drive-through window at Crestview Bank.

Activity	Activity Time (wks)	Immediate Predecessor(s)
A	5	—
B	2	—
C	6	—
D	2	A, B
E	7	B
F	3	D, C
G	9	E, C
H	11	F, G

a. Draw the network diagram for this project.

b. Specify the critical path.

c. Calculate the slack for activities A and D.

7. Consider the following data for a project to reorganize the office space at Platinum Financial Advisors.

Activity	Expected Time t_e (wks)	Immediate Predecessor(s)
A	5	—
B	3	—
C	2	A
D	5	B
E	4	C, D
F	7	D

a. Draw the network diagram for this project.

b. Identify the critical path and estimate the project's duration.

c. Calculate the slack for each activity.

8. Paul Silver, owner of Sculptures International, just initiated a new art project. The following data are available for the project.

Activity	Activity Time (days)	Immediate Predecessor(s)
A	4	—
B	1	—
C	3	A
D	2	B
E	3	C, D

a. Draw the network diagram for the project.

b. Determine the project's critical path and duration.

c. What is the slack for each activity?

9. Reliable Garage is completing production of the J2000 kit car. The following data are available for the project.

Activity	Activity Time (days)	Immediate Predecessor(s)
A	2	—
B	6	A
C	4	B
D	5	C
E	7	C
F	5	C
G	5	F
H	3	D, E, G

a. Draw the network diagram for the project.

b. Determine the project's critical path and duration.

c. What is the slack for each activity?

10. The following information concerns a project to raise money for the Kids Against Crime Foundation.

Activity	Activity Time (days)	Immediate Predecessor(s)
A	10	—
B	11	—
C	9	A, B
D	5	A, B
E	8	A, B
F	13	C, E
G	5	C, D
H	10	G
I	6	F, G
J	9	E, H
K	11	I, J

a. Draw the network diagram for this project.

b. Determine the critical path and project completion time.

11. Consider a project to produce custom door moldings for
Ⓓ GMC Acadia crossover vehicles, described in Table 4.

Analyzing Cost–Time Trade-offs

12. Table 5 contains information about an environmental cleanup project in the township of Hiles. Shorten the project 3 weeks by finding the minimum-cost schedule. Assume that project indirect costs and penalty costs are negligible. Identify activities to crash while minimizing the additional crash costs.

TABLE 5 | ENVIRONMENTAL PROJECT DATA

Activity	Normal Time (wks)	Crash Time (wks)	Cost to Crash ($/wk)	Immediate Predecessor(s)
A	7	6	200	None
B	12	9	250	None
C	7	6	250	A
D	6	5	300	A
E	1	1	—	B
F	1	1	—	C, D
G	3	1	200	D, E
H	3	2	350	F
I	2	2	—	G

13. The Advanced Tech Company has a project to design an integrated information database for a major bank. Data for the project are given in Table 6. Indirect project costs amount to $300 per day. The company will incur a $150 per day penalty for each day the project lasts beyond day 14.

a. If you start the project immediately, when will it be finished?

b. You are interested in completing your project as soon as possible. You have only one option. Suppose you could assign Employee A, currently assigned to activity G, to help Employee B, currently assigned to activity F. Each week that Employee A helps Employee B will result in activity G increasing its time by 1 week and activity F reducing its time by 1 week. How many weeks should Employee A work on activity F?

TABLE 4 | PROJECT DATA FOR GMC ACADIA

Activity	Activity Time (wks)	Immediate Predecessor(s)
START	0	—
A	3	START
B	4	START
C	4	B
D	4	A
E	5	A, B
F	6	D, E
G	2	C, E
FINISH	0	F, G

a. What is the project's duration if only normal times are used?

b. What is the minimum-cost schedule?

c. What is the critical path for the minimum-cost schedule?

TABLE 6 | DATABASE DESIGN PROJECT DATA

Activity	Normal Time (days)	Normal Cost ($)	Crash Time (days)	Crash Cost ($)	Immediate Predecessor(s)
A	6	1,000	5	1,200	—
B	4	800	2	2,000	—
C	3	600	2	900	A, B
D	2	1,500	1	2,000	B
E	6	900	4	1,200	C, D
F	2	1,300	1	1,400	E
G	4	900	4	900	E
H	4	500	2	900	G

14. You are the manager of a project to improve a billing process at your firm. Table 7 contains the data you will need to conduct a cost analysis of the project. Indirect costs are $1,600 per week, and penalty costs are $1,200 per week after week 12.

a. What is the minimum-cost schedule for this project?

b. What is the difference in total project costs between the earliest completion time of the project using "normal" times and the minimum-cost schedule you derived in part (a)?

Ⓓ = **Difficult Problem**

TABLE 7 | DATA FOR THE BILLING PROCESS PROJECT

Activity	Immediate Predecessor(s)	Normal Time (wks)	Crash Time (wks)	Normal Cost ($)	Crash Cost ($)
A	—	4	1	5,000	8,000
B	—	5	3	8,000	10,000
C	A	1	1	4,000	4,000
D	B	6	3	6,000	12,000
E	B, C	7	6	4,000	7,000
F	D	7	6	4,000	7,000

15. Table 8 contains data for the installation of new equipment in a manufacturing process at Excello Corporation. Your company is responsible for the installation project. Indirect costs are $15,000 per week, and a penalty cost of $9,000 per week will be incurred by your company for every week the project is delayed beyond week 9.

a. What is the shortest time duration for this project regardless of cost?

b. What is the minimum total cost associated with completing the project in 9 weeks?

c. What is the total time of the minimum-cost schedule?

TABLE 8 | DATA FOR THE EQUIPMENT INSTALLATION PROJECT

Activity	Immediate Predecessor(s)	Normal Time (wks)	Crash Time (wks)	Normal Cost ($)	Crash Cost ($)
A	—	2	1	7,000	10,000
B	—	2	2	3,000	3,000
C	A	3	1	12,000	40,000
D	B	3	2	12,000	28,000
E	C	1	1	8,000	8,000
F	D, E	5	3	5,000	15,000
G	E	3	2	9,000	18,000

16. The diagram in Figure 12 was developed for the project launch of Kitty Condo, a new product in the luxury cat cage market. Suppose that you, as project manager, are interested in finding ways to speed up the project at minimal additional cost. Determine the schedule for completing the project in 25 days at minimum cost. Penalty and project-overhead costs are negligible. Time and cost data for each activity are shown in Table 9.

TABLE 9 | PROJECT ACTIVITY AND COST DATA

Activity	NORMAL Time (days)	NORMAL Cost ($)	CRASH Time (days)	CRASH Cost ($)
A	12	1,300	11	1,900
B	13	1,050	9	1,500
C	18	3,000	16	4,500
D	9	2,000	5	3,000
E	12	650	10	1,100
F	8	700	7	1,050
G	8	1,550	6	1,950
H	2	600	1	800
I	4	2,200	2	4,000

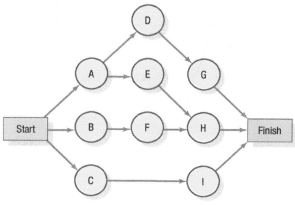

▲ FIGURE 12
Network Diagram for Kitty Condo

17. You are in charge of a project at the local community center. The center needs to remodel one of the rooms in time for the start of a new program. Delays in the project mean that the center must rent other space at a nearby church at additional cost. Time and cost data for your project are contained in Table 10. Your interest is in minimizing the cost of the project to the community center.

    a. Using the *normal times* for each activity, what is the earliest date you can complete the project?

    b. Suppose the variable overhead costs are $50 per day for your project. Also, suppose that the center must pay $40 per day for a temporary room on day 15 or beyond. Find the minimum-cost project schedule.

TABLE 10 | DATA FOR THE COMMUNITY CENTER PROJECT

Activity	Normal Time (days)	Normal Cost ($)	Crash Time (days)	Crash Cost ($)	Immediate Predecessor(s)
START	0	0	0	0	—
A	10	50	8	150	START
B	4	40	2	200	START
C	7	70	6	160	B
D	2	20	1	50	A, C
E	3	30	3	30	A, C
F	8	80	5	290	B
G	5	50	4	180	D
H	6	60	3	180	E, F
FINISH	0	0	0	0	G, H

18. The information in Table 11 is available for a large fundraising project.

    a. Determine the critical path and the expected completion time of the project.

    b. Plot the total project cost, starting from day 1 to the expected completion date of the project, assuming the earliest start times for each activity. Compare that result to a similar plot for the latest start times. What implication does the time differential have for cash flows and project scheduling?

TABLE 11 | FUNDRAISING PROJECT DATA

Activity	Activity Time (days)	Activity Cost ($)	Immediate Predecessor(s)
A	3	100	—
B	4	150	—
C	2	125	A
D	5	175	B
E	3	150	B
F	4	200	C, D
G	6	75	C
H	2	50	C, D, E
I	1	100	E
J	4	75	D, E
K	3	150	F, G
L	3	150	G, H, I
M	2	100	I, J
N	4	175	K, M
O	1	200	H, M
P	5	150	N, L, O

19. You are the project manager of the software installation project in Table 12. You would like to find the minimum-cost schedule for your project. There is a $1,000-per-week penalty for each week the project is delayed beyond week 25. In addition, your project team determined that indirect project costs are $2,500 per week.

    a. What would be your target completion week?

    b. How much would you save in total project costs with your schedule?

TABLE 12 | DATA FOR SOFTWARE INSTALLATION PROJECT

Activity	Immediate Predecessors	Normal Time (wks)	Normal Cost ($)	Crash Time (wks)	Crash Cost ($)
A	—	5	2,000	3	4,000
B	—	8	5,000	7	8,000
C	A	10	10,000	8	12,000
D	A, B	4	3,000	3	7,000
E	B	3	4,000	2	5,000
F	D	9	8,000	6	14,000
G	E, F	2	2,000	2	2,000
H	G	8	6,000	5	9,000
I	C, F	9	7,000	7	15,000

Assessing and Analyzing Risks

20. Jordanne King, the project manager for Webjets International, Inc., compiled a table showing time estimates for each of the activities of a project to upgrade the company's Web page, including optimistic, most likely, and pessimistic.

  a. Calculate the expected time, t_e, for each activity.

  b. Calculate the variance, σ^2, for each activity.

Activity	Optimistic (days)	Most Likely (days)	Pessimistic (days)
A	3	8	19
B	12	15	18
C	2	6	16
D	4	9	20
E	1	4	7

21. Recently, you were assigned to manage a project to remodel the seminar room for your company. You have constructed a network diagram depicting the various activities in the project (Figure 13). In addition, you have asked your team to estimate the amount of time that they would expect each of the activities to take. Their responses are shown in the following table.

Activity	TIME ESTIMATES (DAYS)		
	Optimistic	Most Likely	Pessimistic
A	5	8	11
B	4	8	11
C	5	6	7
D	2	4	6
E	4	7	10

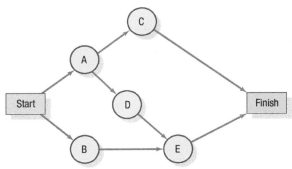

▲ **FIGURE 13**
Network Diagram for Problem 21

  a. What is the expected completion time of the project?

  b. What is the probability of completing the project in 21 days?

  c. What is the probability of completing the project in 17 days?

22. In Solved Problem 2, estimate the probability that the noncritical path B–F–G will take more than 20 weeks. *Hint:* Subtract from 1.0 the probability that B–F–G will take 20 weeks or less.

23. The director of continuing education at Bluebird University just approved the planning for a sales training seminar. Her administrative assistant identified the various activities that must be done and their relationships to each other, as shown in Table 13.

TABLE 13 ACTIVITIES FOR THE SALES TRAINING SEMINAR

Activity	Description	Immediate Predecessor(s)
A	Design brochure and course announcement	—
B	Identify prospective teachers	—
C	Prepare detailed outline of course	—
D	Send brochure and student applications	A
E	Send teacher applications	B
F	Select teacher for course	C, E
G	Accept students	D
H	Select text for course	F
I	Order and receive texts	G, H
J	Prepare room for class	G

Because of the uncertainty in planning the new course, the assistant also has supplied the following time estimates for each activity.

Activity	TIME ESTIMATES (DAYS)		
	Optimistic	Most Likely	Pessimistic
A	5	7	8
B	6	8	12
C	3	4	5
D	11	17	25
E	8	10	12
F	3	4	5
G	4	8	9
H	5	7	9
I	8	11	17
J	4	4	4

The director wants to conduct the seminar 47 working days from now. What is the probability that everything will be ready in time?

24. Gabrielle Kramer, owner of Pet Paradise, is opening a new store in Columbus, Ohio. Her major concern is the hiring of a manager and several associates who are animal lovers. She also has to coordinate the renovation of a building that was previously owned by a chic clothing store. Kramer has gathered the data shown in Table 14.

a. How long is the project expected to take?

b. Suppose that Kramer has a personal goal of completing the project in 14 weeks. What is the probability that it will happen this quickly?

TABLE 14 | DATA FOR THE PET PARADISE PROJECT

			TIME (WKS)		
Activity	Description	Immediate Predecessor(s)	a	m	b
A	Interview for new manager	—	1	3	6
B	Renovate building	—	6	9	12
C	Place ad for associates and interview applicants	—	6	8	16
D	Have new manager prospects visit	A	2	3	4
E	Purchase equipment for new store and install	B	1	3	11
F	Check employee applicant references and make final selection	C	5	5	5
G	Check references for new manager and make final selection	D	1	1	1
H	Hold orientation meetings and do payroll paperwork	E, F, G	3	3	3

25. **Ⓓ** The project manager of Good Public Relations gathered the data shown in Table 15 for a new advertising campaign.

a. How long is the project likely to take?

b. What is the probability that the project will take more than 38 weeks?

c. Consider the path A–E–G–H–J. What is the probability that this path will exceed 38 weeks?

TABLE 15 | ACTIVITY DATA FOR ADVERTISING PROJECT

	TIME ESTIMATES (WKS)			
Activity	Optimistic	Most Likely	Pessimistic	Immediate Predecessor(s)
A	8	10	12	START
B	5	8	17	START
C	7	8	9	START
D	1	2	3	B
E	8	10	12	A, C
F	5	6	7	D, E
G	1	3	5	D, E
H	2	5	8	F, G
I	2	4	6	G
J	4	5	8	H
K	2	2	2	H

26. **Ⓓ** Consider the office renovation project data in Table 16. A "zero" time estimate means that the activity could take a very small amount of time and should be treated as a numeric zero in the analysis.

a. Based on the critical path, find the probability of completing the office renovation project by 39 days.

b. Find the date by which you would be 90 percent sure of completing the project.

Ⓓ = Difficult Problem

TABLE 16 | DATA FOR THE OFFICE RENOVATION PROJECT

Activity	TIME ESTIMATES (DAYS)			Immediate Predecessor(s)
	Optimistic	Most Likely	Pessimistic	
START	0	0	0	—
A	6	10	14	START
B	0	1	2	A
C	16	20	30	A
D	3	5	7	B
E	2	3	4	D
F	7	10	13	C
G	1	2	3	D
H	0	2	4	G
I	2	2	2	C, G
J	2	3	4	I
K	0	1	2	H
L	1	2	3	J, K
FINISH	0	0	0	E, F, L

Active Model Exercise

Active Model 1, Gantt Chart, appears in MyLab Operations Management. It allows you to evaluate the sensitivity of the project time to changes in activity times and activity predecessors. In this exercise we use the data from Example 2 to develop a Gantt chart.

QUESTIONS

1. Activity B and activity K are critical activities. Describe the difference that occurs on the graph when you increase activity B versus when you increase activity K.

2. Activity F is not critical. Use the scroll bar to determine how many weeks you can increase activity F until it becomes critical.

3. Activity A is not critical. How many weeks can you increase activity A until it becomes critical? What happens when activity A becomes critical?

4. What happens when you increase activity A by 1 week after it becomes critical?

5. Suppose that building codes may change and, as a result, activity C would have to be completed before activity D could be started. How would this affect the project?

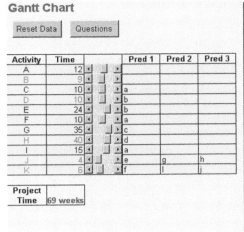

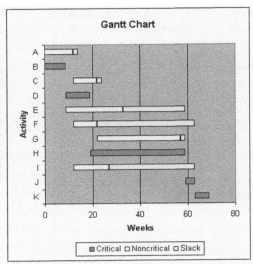

VIDEO CASE | Project Management at Choice Hotels International

Choice Hotels International is the company behind well-known hotel brands that range from budget-friendly EconoLodge and Rodeway Inns to Quality, Comfort Inns and its luxury brands, Ascend and Cambria. Over 6,400 properties are part of the franchisor's offerings in both domestically and abroad. This translates to over 500,000 rooms around the globe.

To help hotel guests find and book those rooms, Choice Hotels maintains a robust central reservation system, or CRS, that must connect travel agents, online reservation websites such as Trivago and Kayak, and mobile app users to the company's daily available inventory. On the back end, the system also must connect to each property's front check-in desk system and the organization's revenue management systems. For Choice, the CRS is the heart of their hotel operations and it could not operate without it.

The company first developed its CRS back in the 1980s using the latest project management techniques and information technology (IT) available. But the company's growth, coupled with dramatic changes in information technology and the cost of maintaining inflexible systems built for last century business that couldn't scale with growth, have compelled the organization in 2014 to embark on a multi-million dollar, multi-year project, called choiceEDGE, to replace this mission-critical system by 2017. To replace such a vital system, Todd Davis, Choice's Chief Information Officer (CIO), knew they couldn't just remove the old software and hardware systems and then plug in brand-new ones. The risk was too high. Nor could they rely on a linear systems development approach that would require the company to deliver a finished solution that would be outdated at the end of several years of work. The world of business and technology were changing too rapidly to wait. The company has seen hospitality industry competitors spend hundreds of millions doing just that, with failed outcomes.

Instead, senior management at Choice Hotels committed to a new IT project management approach, called "Agile," that allowed development to occur iteratively around "projects within projects" so as each requirement outlined in its work breakdown structure (WBS) was completed, it could be deployed without disruption to the entire enterprise. This approach both minimized risk of business disruption and allowed new features to be seamlessly rolled out without the need for major workforce training initiatives. It also allowed franchisees to start seeing the benefit of the new "heart" just months after helping to define the desired business outcomes instead of waiting years.

To get started, Choice defined its project scope and objectives with input from its various stakeholders: thousands of franchisees, dozens of external business partners, millions of customers, and thousands of employees. Brian Kirkland, Vice President of Engineering, was chosen to head up the project team of nearly 120 systems architects, "scrum masters" (daily project managers), software developers, and quality assurance professionals at Choice's Scottsdale, Arizona location. From the start, Kirkland wanted the team to use all the tools available to manage the project. For example, early on in the project, Denise Tower, Director of IT Project Management and Delivery, used a WBS and Gantt charts to identify the critical path. Kirkland and his team quickly realized that the system's underlying distribution engine (the platform upon which all the functionality rested) was in the critical path. Any problems or delays would cause downstream delays and cost the company software programmer idle time. So resources were shifted to getting this core system functionality in place and off the critical path. Resources were then redirected back toward completion of the business outcomes that relied on the distribution engine, which were delivered weekly throughout the project's entire development process. Daily monitoring meetings,

Cambria Hotels and Suites, such as this one on Times Square in New York, is a luxury product of Choice Hotels. With over 6,400 properties across all of its brands, and more than 500,000 rooms to fill, Choice must have a flexible and reliable reservation system to remain competitive.

called "daily stand-ups," were held each morning to keep the focus on the work at hand, and assured issues got priority attention for resolution to avoid those parts of the project ending up in the critical path and causing downstream delays.

Today, choiceEDGE is capable of quickly scaling to meet the business demands it faces in the competitive hospitality industry. The system processes over 250 million transactions a day that include simple shopping queries for room rates and availability, pricing and inventory updates, or actual room bookings. Amazon Web Services is used for cloud storage. And as the demand for mobile access to its systems continues to grow, the company's IT department is equipped to rapidly respond.

QUESTIONS:

1. Assess the four categories of a risk-management plan for the choiceEDGE project. Given the information in the case, how risky is this project for Choice Hotels?

2. Go online to research "Agile" information systems development and the role of "scrum masters" in helping organizations manage successful IT projects. Why are leading organizations now turning to this approach for developing their systems projects?

3. Assume you are Denise Tower and have responsibility for the overall management of the choiceEDGE IT project. Describe what you might need to do to monitor and control the project to assure scope, budget, and schedule are managed.

CASE   The Pert Mustang

Roberts Auto Sales and Service (RASAS) consists of three car dealerships that sell and service several makes of American and Japanese cars, two auto parts stores, a large body shop and car painting business, and an auto salvage yard. Vicky Roberts, owner of RASAS, went into the car business when she inherited a Ford dealership from her father. She was able to capitalize on her knowledge and experience to build her business into the diversified and successful mini-empire it is today. Her motto, "Sell 'em today, repair 'em tomorrow!" reflects a strategy that she refers to in private as "Get 'em coming and going."

Roberts has always retained a soft spot in her heart for high-performance Mustangs and just acquired a 1965 Shelby Mustang GT 350 that needs a lot of restoration. She also notes the public's growing interest in the restoration of vintage automobiles. Roberts is thinking of expanding into the vintage car restoration business and needs help in assessing the feasibility of such a move. She wants to restore her 1965 Shelby Mustang to mint condition, or as close to mint condition as possible. If she decides to go into the car restoring business, she can use the Mustang as an exhibit in sales and advertising and take it to auto shows to attract business for the new shop.

Roberts believes that many people want the thrill of restoring an old car themselves, but they do not have the time to run down all the old parts. Still, others just want to own a vintage auto because it is different and many of them have plenty of money to pay someone to restore an auto for them.

Roberts wants the new business to appeal to both types of people. For the first group, she envisions serving as a parts broker for NOS ("new old stock"), new parts that were manufactured many years ago and are still packaged in their original cartons. It can be a time-consuming process to find the right part. RASAS could also machine new parts to replicate those that are hard to find or that no longer exist.

In addition, RASAS could assemble a library of parts and body manuals for old cars to serve as an information resource for do-it-yourself restorers. The do-it-yourselfers could come to RASAS for help in compiling parts lists, and RASAS could acquire the parts for them. For others, RASAS would take charge of the entire restoration.

Roberts asked the director of service operations to take a good look at her Mustang and determine what needs to be done to restore it to the condition it was in when it came from the factory more than 40 years ago. She wants to restore this car in time to exhibit it at the Detroit Auto Show. If the car gets a lot of press, it will be a real public relations coup for RASAS—especially if Roberts decides to enter this new venture. Even if she does not, the car will be a showpiece for the rest of the business.

Roberts asked the director of service operations to prepare a report about what is involved in restoring the car and whether it can be done in time for the Detroit show in 45 working days using PERT/CPM. The parts manager, the body shop manager, and the chief mechanic have provided the following estimates of times and activities that need to be done, as well as cost estimates.

a. Order all needed material and parts (upholstery, windshield, carburetor, and oil pump). Time: 2 days. Cost (telephone calls and labor): $100.

b. Receive upholstery material for seat covers. Cannot be done until order is placed. Time: 30 days. Cost: $2,100.

c. Receive windshield. Cannot be done until order is placed. Time: 10 days. Cost: $800.

d. Receive carburetor and oil pump. Cannot be done until order is placed. Time: 7 days. Cost: $1,750.

e. Remove chrome from body. Can be done immediately. Time: 1 day. Cost: $200.

f. Remove body (doors, hood, trunk, and fenders) from frame. Cannot be done until chrome is removed. Time: 1 day. Cost: $300.

g. Have fenders repaired by body shop. Cannot be done until body is removed from frame. Time: 4 days. Cost: $1,000.

h. Repair doors, trunk, and hood. Cannot be done until body is removed from frame. Time: 6 days. Cost: $1,500.

i. Pull engine from chassis. Do after body is removed from frame. Time: 1 day. Cost: $200.

j. Remove rust from frame. Do after the engine has been pulled from the chassis. Time: 3 days. Cost $900.

k. Regrind engine valves. Do after the engine has been pulled from the chassis. Time: 5 days. Cost: $1,000.

l. Replace carburetor and oil pump. Do after engine has been pulled from chassis and after carburetor and oil pump have been received. Time: 1 day. Cost: $200.

m. Rechrome the chrome parts. Chrome must have been removed from the body first. Time: 3 days. Cost: $210.

n. Reinstall engine. Do after valves are reground and carburetor and oil pump have been installed. Time: 1 day. Cost: $200.

o. Put doors, hood, and trunk back on frame. The doors, hood, and trunk must have been repaired first. The frame must have had its rust removed first. Time: 1 day. Cost: $240.

p. Rebuild transmission and replace brakes. Do so after the engine has been reinstalled and the doors, hood, and trunk are back on the frame. Time: 4 days. Cost: $2,000.

q. Replace windshield. Windshield must have been received. Time: 1 day. Cost: $100.

r. Put fenders back on. The fenders must have been repaired first, the transmission rebuilt, and the brakes replaced. Time: 1 day. Cost: $100.

s. Paint car. Cannot be done until the fenders are back on and windshield replaced. Time: 4 days. Cost: $1,700.

t. Reupholster interior of car. Must have received upholstery material first. Car must have been painted first. Time: 7 days. Cost: $2,400.

u. Put chrome parts back on. Car must have been painted and chrome parts rechromed first. Time: 1 day. Cost: $100.

v. Pull car to the Detroit Auto Show. Must have completed reupholstery of interior and have put the chrome parts back on. Time: 2 days. Cost: $1,000.

Roberts wants to limit expenditures on this project to what could be recovered by selling the restored car. She has already spent $50,000 to acquire the car. In addition, she wants a brief report on some of the aspects of the proposed business, such as how it fits in with RASAS's other businesses and what RASAS's operations task should be with regard to cost, quality, customer service, and flexibility.

In the restoration business there are various categories of restoration. A basic restoration gets the car looking great and running, but a mint-condition restoration puts the car back in original condition—as it was "when it rolled off the line." When restored cars are resold, a car in mint condition commands a much higher price than one that is just a basic restoration. As cars are restored, they can also be customized. That is, something is put on the car that could not have been on the original. Roberts wants a mint-condition restoration for her Mustang without customization. (The proposed new business would accept any kind of restoration a customer wanted.)

The total budget cannot exceed $70,000 including the $50,000 Roberts has already spent. In addition, Roberts cannot spend more than $3,600 in any week given her present financial position. Even though much of the work will be done by Roberts's own employees, labor and materials costs must be considered. All relevant costs have been included in the cost estimates.

QUESTIONS

1. Using the information provided, prepare the report that Vicky Roberts requested, assuming that the project will begin immediately. Assume 45 working days are available to complete the project, including transporting the car to Detroit before the auto show begins. Your report should briefly discuss the aspects of the proposed new business, such as the competitive priorities that Roberts asked about.

2. Construct a table containing the project activities using the letter assigned to each activity, the time estimates, and the precedence relationships from which you will assemble the network diagram.

3. Draw a network diagram of the project similar to Figure 3. Determine the activities on the critical path and the estimated slack for each activity.

4. Prepare a project budget showing the cost of each activity and the total for the project. Can the project be completed within the budget? Will the project require more than $3,600 in any week? To answer this question, assume that activities B, C, and D must be paid for when the item is received (the earliest finish time for the activity). Assume that the costs of all other activities that span more than 1 week can be prorated. Each week contains 5 work days. If problems exist, how might Roberts overcome them?

Source: This case was prepared by and is used by permission of Dr. Sue P. Siferd, Professor Emerita, Arizona State University (Updated September, 2007).

Selected References

Project Management

Goldratt, E. M. Critical Chain. Great Barrington, MA: North River, 1997.

"A Guide to Project Management Body of Knowledge." Available from the Project Management Institute at **www.pmi.org**, 2013.

Hartvigsen, David. SimQuick: Process Simulation with Excel, 2nd ed. Upper Saddle River, NJ: Prentice Hall, 2004.

Kerzner, Harold. Advanced Project Management: Best Practices on Implementation, 2nd ed. New York: John Wiley & Sons, 2004.

Kerzner, Harold. Project Management: A Systems Approach to Planning, Scheduling, and Controlling, 11th ed. New York: John Wiley & Sons, 2013.

Lewis, J. P. Mastering Project Management, 2nd ed. New York: McGraw-Hill, 2007.

Mantel Jr., Samuel J., Jack R. Meredith, Scott M. Shafer, and Margaret M. Sutton. Project Management in Practice, 4th ed. New York: John Wiley & Sons, 2010.

Meredith, Jack R., and Samuel J. Mantel, Project Management: A Managerial Approach, 8th ed. New York: John Wiley & Sons, 2011.

Muir, Nancy C. Microsoft Project 2010 for Dummies. New York: John Wiley & Sons, 2010.

Nicholas, John M., and Herman Stein. Project Management for Engineering, Business, and Technology, 4th ed. London, U.K.: Routledge, 2012.

Srinivasan, Mandyam, Darren Jones, and Alex Miller. "CORPS Capabilities." APICS Magazine (March 2005), pp. 46–50.

Glossary

activity The smallest unit of work effort consuming both time and resources that the project manager can schedule and control.

activity slack The maximum length of time that an activity can be delayed without delaying the entire project, calculated as $S = LS - ES$ or $S = LF - EF$.

closeout An activity that includes writing final reports, completing remaining deliverables, and compiling the team's recommendations for improving the project process.

crash cost (CC) The activity cost associated with the crash time.

crash time (CT) The shortest possible time to complete an activity.

critical path The sequence of activities between a project's start and finish that takes the longest time to complete.

critical path method (CPM) A network planning method developed in the 1950s as a means of scheduling maintenance shutdowns at chemical-processing plants.

earliest finish time (EF) An activity's earliest start time plus its estimated duration, t, or $EF = ES + t$.

earliest start time (ES) The earliest finish time of the immediately preceding activity.

Gantt chart A project schedule, usually created by the project manager using computer software, that superimposes project activities, with their precedence relationships and estimated duration times, on a time line.

latest finish time (LF) The latest start time of the activity that immediately follows.

latest start time (LS) The latest finish time minus its estimated duration, t, or $LS = LF - t$.

minimum-cost schedule A schedule determined by starting with the normal time schedule and crashing activities along the critical path, in such a way that the costs of crashing do not exceed the savings in indirect and penalty costs.

most likely time (m) The probable time required to perform an activity.

network diagram A visual display, designed to depict the relationships between activities, that consists of nodes (circles) and arcs (arrows).

normal cost (NC) The activity cost associated with the normal time.

normal time (NT) In the context of project management, the time necessary to complete an activity under normal conditions.

optimistic time (a) The shortest time in which an activity can be completed, if all goes exceptionally well.

path The sequence of activities between a project's start and finish.

pessimistic time (b) The longest estimated time required to perform an activity.

precedence relationship A relationship that determines a sequence for undertaking activities; it specifies that one activity cannot start until a preceding activity has been completed.

program An interdependent set of projects that have a common strategic purpose.

program evaluation and review technique (PERT) A network planning method created for the U.S. Navy's Polaris missile project in the 1950s, which involved 3,000 separate contractors and suppliers.

project An interrelated set of activities with a definite starting and ending point, which results in a unique outcome for a specific allocation of resources.

project management A systemized, phased approach to defining, organizing, planning, monitoring, and controlling projects.

risk-management plan A plan that identifies the key risks to a project's success and prescribes ways to circumvent them.

work breakdown structure (WBS) A statement of all work that has to be completed.

INVENTORY MANAGEMENT

Ford's Smart Inventory Management System (SIMS)

Ford dealership car sales lot.

As you pass a large car dealership and see the hundreds of new cars neatly arranged in the lot, have you ever wondered how it was decided to stock those particular units in the dealership's inventory? According to Bryan Goodman, a research scientist at Ford, it really matters what is on the lot at the moment a customer arrives. Having the wrong models, colors, or options could

From Chapter 9 of *Operations Management: Processes and Supply Chains*, Twelfth Edition. Lee J. Krajewski, Manoj K. Malhotra, Larry P. Ritzman. Copyright © 2019 by Pearson Education, Inc. All rights reserved.

have a big effect on sales. The answer, however, is not larger inventories. One problem is figuring out what the customers want, and the number of possibilities can be mind boggling. On a given vehicle, customers may have multiple choices on features such as exterior color, trim, interior seating, entertainment, navigation, and the like. The number of combinations on some models could be in the millions. Another problem with large inventories is that inventory holding costs can be prohibitive; it costs about $10 per vehicle per day.

Ford's answer was to employ a *big-data approach*. A team of 200 big-data and analytics experts from a range of disciplines focused on three areas: ascertaining what customers want, managing vehicle complexity, and delivering the right cars with the right features to individual dealers. To do that, Ford integrates and analyzes several data streams, including data on what has already been built and sold at a dealership, what has been sold in the context of what was in inventory at the time of the sale, sales patterns of other Ford dealerships in the area, plus what customers are searching for and configuring on company websites. These data are then combined with economic data to predict vehicle sales relative to housing starts, employment rates, and the like. The system, called the Smart Inventory Management System, or SIMS, requires the support of supercomputers with 1.5 terabytes of RAM to analyze all of that data on a timely basis. Relevant data are sent to dealers on a weekly basis, and it is up to them whether to follow the order recommendations. Dealers are in the best position to fine-tune orders because they can better evaluate additional information on the ground using their experience and intuition. Nonetheless, there is a 98 percent match between what SIMS recommends and what is actually ordered. Each week, 50,000 vehicle orders are placed in North America alone.

The new system was rolled out in 2009 and has become a major success. Its recommendations saved dealers $90 per vehicle. By reducing the time a vehicle spends on the lots, dealers have enjoyed quicker inventory turnover. However, the value of SIMS goes beyond new car inventories. By tailoring the bulk of the company's production to customers' preferences, assembly plant schedules and parts forecasts have been significantly improved. It is estimated that SIMS is worth more than $100 million a year to Ford.

Sources: Julia King, "How Analytics Helped Ford Turn Its Fortunes," http:/www.computerworld.com (December 2, 2013); Kathleen Burke, "Ford Data Crunchers Help Dealers Fine-Tune Inventory," **http://www.autonews.com** (August 18, 2014); Chanelle Bessette, "Ford's $100 Million Data Machine," **http:/fortune.com** (June 2, 2014).

LEARNING GOALS *After reading this text, you should be able to:*

1 Identify the advantages, disadvantages, and costs of holding inventory.

2 Define the different types of inventory and the roles they play in supply chains.

3 Explain the tactics for reducing inventories in supply chains.

4 Use ABC analysis to determine the items deserving most attention and tightest inventory control.

5 Calculate the economic order quantity and apply it to various situations.

6 Determine the order quantity and reorder point for a continuous review inventory control system.

7 Determine the review interval and target inventory level for a periodic review inventory control system.

Inventory management, the planning and controlling of inventories to meet the competitive priorities of the organization, is an important concern for managers in all types of businesses. We have seen how forecasting can help us determine the sizing and timing of customer demands for goods or services. **Inventory management** is the first of the tools we discuss in Part 2 of this text that is focused on how to satisfy that demand. Effective inventory management is essential for realizing the full potential of any supply chain. The challenge is not to pare inventories to the bone to reduce costs or to have plenty around to satisfy all demands, but to have the right amount to achieve the competitive priorities of the business most efficiently. This type of efficiency can only happen if the right amount of inventory is flowing through the supply chain—through suppliers, the firm, warehouses or distribution centers, and customers. Much of inventory management involves **lot sizing**, which is the determination of how frequently and in what quantity to order inventory. We make ample reference to the term **lot size**, which is the quantity of an inventory item that management either buys from a supplier or manufactures using internal processes. In this text, we focus on the decision-making aspects of inventory management.

Inventories are important to all types of organizations, their employees, and their supply chains. Inventories profoundly affect everyday operations because they must be counted, paid for, used in operations, used to satisfy customers, and managed. Inventories require an investment of funds, as does the purchase of a new machine. Monies invested in inventory are not available for investment in other things; thus, they represent a drain on the cash flows of an organization. Nonetheless, companies realize that the availability of products is a key selling point in many markets and downright critical in many more.

So, is inventory a boon or a bane? Certainly, too much inventory on hand reduces profitability, and too little inventory on hand creates shortages in the supply chain and ultimately damages customer confidence. Inventory management, therefore, involves trade-offs. Let us discover how companies can effectively manage inventories across the organization.

inventory management
The planning and controlling of inventories to meet the competitive priorities of the organization.

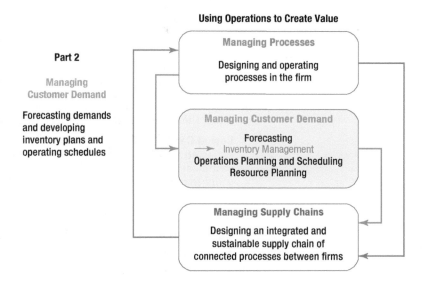

Using Operations to Create Value

Managing Processes
Designing and operating processes in the firm

Part 2

Managing Customer Demand

Forecasting demands and developing inventory plans and operating schedules

Managing Customer Demand
Forecasting
→ Inventory Management
Operations Planning and Scheduling
Resource Planning

Managing Supply Chains
Designing an integrated and sustainable supply chain of connected processes between firms

lot sizing
The determination of how frequently and in what quantity to order inventory.

lot size
The quantity of an inventory item that management either buys from a supplier or manufactures using internal processes.

Inventory Trade-offs

The value of inventory management becomes apparent when the complexity of the supply chain is recognized. The performance of numerous suppliers determines the inward flow of materials and services to a firm. The performance of the firm determines the outward flow of services or products to the next stage of the supply chain. The flow of materials, however, determines inventory levels. **Inventory** is a stock of materials used to satisfy customer demand or to support the production of services or goods. Figure 1 shows how inventories are created at one node in a supply chain through the analogy of a water tank. The flow of water into the tank raises the water level. The inward flow of water represents input materials, such as steel, component parts, office supplies, or a finished product. The water level represents the amount of inventory held at a plant, service facility, warehouse, or retail outlet. The flow of water from the tank lowers the water level in the tank. The outward flow of water represents the demand for materials in inventory, such as customer orders for a Huffy bicycle or service requirements for supplies such as soap, food, or furnishings. The rate of the outward flow also reflects the ability of the firm to match the demand for services or products. Another possible outward flow is that of scrap, which also lowers the level of usable inventory. Together, the difference between input flow rate and the output flow rate determines the level of inventory. Inventories rise when more material flows into the tank than flows out; they fall when more material flows out than flows in. Figure 1 also shows clearly why firms utilize Six Sigma and total quality management (TQM) to reduce defective materials: The larger the scrap flows, the larger the input flow of materials required for a given level of output.

A fundamental question in supply chain management is how much inventory to have. The answer to this question involves a trade-off between the advantages and disadvantages of holding inventory. Depending on the situation, the pressures for having small inventories may or may not exceed the pressures for having large inventories.

inventory
A stock of materials used to satisfy customer demand or to support the production of services or goods.

▼ **FIGURE 1**
Creation of Inventory

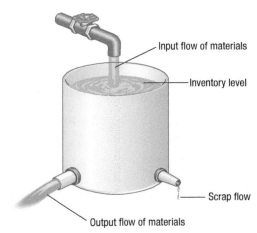

Input flow of materials

Inventory level

Scrap flow

Output flow of materials

Pressures for Small Inventories

An inventory manager's job is to balance the advantages and disadvantages of both small and large inventories and find a happy medium between the two levels. The primary reason for keeping inventories small is that inventory represents a temporary monetary investment. As such, the firm incurs an opportunity cost, which we call the cost of capital, arising from the money tied up in inventory that could be used for other purposes. The **inventory holding cost** (or *carrying cost*) is the sum of the cost of capital plus the variable costs of keeping items on hand, such as storage and handling costs and taxes, insurance, and shrinkage costs. When these components change with inventory levels, so does the holding cost.

Companies usually state an item's holding cost per period of time as a percent of its value. The annual cost to maintain one unit in inventory typically ranges from 15 to 35 percent of its value. Suppose that a firm's holding cost is 20 percent. If the average value of total inventory is 20 percent of sales, the average annual cost to hold inventory is 4 percent [0.20(0.20)] of total sales. This cost is sizable in terms of gross profit margins, which often are less than 10 percent. Thus, the components of holding cost create pressures for small inventories.

Cost of Capital   The cost of capital is the opportunity cost of investing in an asset relative to the expected return on assets of similar risk. Inventory is an asset; consequently, we should use a cost measure that adequately reflects the firm's approach to financing assets. Most firms use the *weighted average cost of capital (WACC)*, which is the average of the required return on a firm's stock equity and the interest rate on its debt, weighted by the proportion of equity and debt in its portfolio. The cost of capital usually is the largest component of holding cost, as high as 15 percent of inventory value, depending on the particular capitalization portfolio of the firm. Firms typically update the WACC on an annual basis because it is used to make many financial decisions.

Storage and Handling Costs   Inventory takes up space and must be moved into and out of storage. Storage and handling costs may be incurred when a firm rents space on either a long- or short-term basis. An inventory holding cost is incurred when a firm could use storage space productively in some other way.

Taxes, Insurance, and Shrinkage   More taxes are paid if end-of-year inventories are high, and the cost of insuring the inventories increases, too. Shrinkage takes three forms. The first, *pilferage*, or theft of inventory by customers or employees, is a significant percentage of sales for some businesses. The second form of shrinkage, called *obsolescence*, occurs when inventory cannot be used or sold at full value, owing to model changes, engineering modifications, or unexpectedly low demand. Obsolescence is a big expense in the retail clothing industry. Drastic discounts on seasonal clothing frequently must be offered on many of these products at the end of a season. Finally, *deterioration* through physical spoilage or damage due to rough or excessive material handling results in lost value. Food and beverages, for example, lose value and might even have to be discarded when their shelf life is reached. When the rate of deterioration is high, building large inventories may be unwise.

Pressures for Large Inventories

Given the costs of holding inventory, why not eliminate it altogether? Let us look briefly at the pressures related to maintaining large inventories.

Customer Service   Creating inventory can speed delivery and improve the firm's on-time delivery of goods. High inventory levels reduce the potential for stockouts and backorders, which are key concerns of wholesalers and retailers. A *stockout* is an order that cannot be satisfied, resulting in loss of the sale. A *backorder* is a customer order that cannot be filled when promised or demanded but is filled later. Customers do not like waiting for backorders to be filled. Many of them will take their business elsewhere. Sometimes, customers are given discounts for the inconvenience of waiting.

Ordering Cost   Each time a firm places a new order, it incurs an **ordering cost**, or the cost of preparing a purchase order for a supplier or a production order for manufacturing. For the same item, the ordering cost is the same, regardless of the order size. The purchasing agent must take the time to decide how much to order and, perhaps, select a supplier and negotiate terms. Time also is spent on paperwork, follow-up, and receiving the item(s). In the case of a production order for a manufactured item, a blueprint and routing instructions often must accompany the order. However, the Internet streamlines the order process and reduces the costs of placing orders.

Setup Cost   The cost involved in changing over a machine or workspace to produce a different item is the **setup cost**. It includes labor and time to make the changeover, cleaning, and sometimes new tools or equipment. Scrap or rework costs are also higher at the start of the production run. Setup cost also is independent of order size, which creates pressure to make or order a large supply of the items and hold them in inventory rather than order smaller batches.

---

inventory holding cost

The sum of the cost of capital and the variable costs of keeping items on hand, such as storage and handling, taxes, insurance, and shrinkage.

ordering cost

The cost of preparing a purchase order for a supplier or a production order for manufacturing.

setup cost

The cost involved in changing over a machine or workspace to produce a different item.

Labor and Equipment Utilization By creating more inventory, management can increase workforce productivity and facility utilization in three ways. First, placing larger, less frequent production orders reduces the number of unproductive setups, which add no value to a service or product. Second, holding inventory reduces the chance of the costly rescheduling of production orders because the components needed to make the product are not in inventory. Third, building inventories improves resource utilization by stabilizing the output rate when demand is cyclical or seasonal. The firm uses inventory built during slack periods to handle extra demand in peak seasons. This approach minimizes the need for extra shifts, hiring, layoffs, overtime, and additional equipment.

Transportation Cost Sometimes, outbound transportation cost can be reduced by increasing inventory levels. Having inventory on hand allows more full-carload shipments to be made and minimizes the need to expedite shipments by more expensive modes of transportation. Inbound transportation costs can also be reduced by creating more inventory. Sometimes, several items are ordered from the same supplier. Placing these orders at the same time will increase inventories because some items will be ordered before they are actually needed; nonetheless, it may lead to rate discounts, thereby decreasing the costs of transportation and raw materials.

Payments to Suppliers A firm often can reduce total payments to suppliers if it can tolerate higher inventory levels. Suppose that a firm learns that a key supplier is about to increase its prices. In this case, it might be cheaper for the firm to order a larger quantity than usual—in effect delaying the price increase—even though inventory will increase temporarily. A firm can also take advantage of quantity discounts this way. A **quantity discount**, whereby the price per unit drops when the order is sufficiently large, is an incentive to order larger quantities.

quantity discount

A drop in the price per unit when an order is sufficiently large.

MANAGERIAL PRACTICE 1 — Inventory Management at Netflix

Netflix is a $4 billion company specializing in delivering movies and TV programs directly to the homes of customers via streaming or DVD for a subscription fee. It employs more than 2,000 employees worldwide, has more than 65 million streaming customers in over 50 countries, and has 5.3 million DVD customers in the United States, which is the only DVD market for Netflix. The inventory, of course, comes in the form of DVDs (also blue-ray discs). Netflix holds a DVD inventory valued at $2 billion; that amounts to about 89 million discs distributed across 33 warehouses located across the country. That inventory must be carefully managed: New releases of movies must be purchased in adequate quantities while older movies cannot simply be discarded because many customers like to see the "classics." The *composition* of the inventory of discs supports one of Netflix's competitive priorities—variety. However, if it were not for the fact that Netflix designed a process to minimize the lead time in processing customer requests for a disc, the inventory of discs needed to support variety would balloon to enormous proportions.

Another of Netflix's competitive priorities is delivery speed, as evidenced by its goal of delivering a disc by "the next business day." That is, once a customer has returned a disc in his possession, the next disc in his queue will be delivered in a day. This goal was necessary to compete against the bricks-and-mortar video stores where customers could get a movie the same day they wanted it. The *size* of the inventory helps support delivery speed. The inventory of discs consists of two parts: those discs in the possession of customers, and those in stock waiting for a request. Netflix had two options for processing a customer's request for a new disc once his disc is returned to the warehouse: (1) send the next disc in the customer's queue from the stockpiled inventory of discs, or (2) process the returned discs quickly and satisfy the customer's request for the next disc in his queue from those being returned that day. Each warehouse can handle tens of thousands of orders per day, so a good number of requests could be

Automation increases delivery speed. Here, DVDs are stuffed into mailing envelopes that will be printed with shipping addresses.

Ricardo Ramirez Buxeda/Orlando Sentinel/MCT via Getty Images satisfied with in-transit returns. Netflix opted for the second option, thereby reducing the need for a larger stockpile of discs. The process at a typical warehouse begins when unmarked trucks arrive at the post office at around 3 a.m. to pick up cartons of returned discs. The trucks deliver the discs to the Netflix warehouse. Upon arrival, a machine sucks up a returned Netflix mailer into the system at a rate of 3,400 per hour and proceeds to slice open the envelop, identify and clean the disc inside, check to see if the disc works, and then reinsert it into the original sleeve. The discs are scanned into the inventory using barcodes. As soon as a disc is scanned, the last renter receives an email confirming the return and is told what disc that renter will receive next. If anyone has ordered that disc, it is sorted by ZIP code and prepared for shipment. Other discs return to inventory. Finally, outgoing discs are stuffed into new mailing envelopes and sent through a label machine that scans their barcodes and prints shipping addresses. Warehouse trucks are loaded with cartons of discs and return to the post office. The entire process is highly automated. For example, at the Fremont hub, it used to take about 100 employees to do all of the work. Today, it only takes 25 employees, largely assisting the machines.

While it is clear that streaming will eventually overtake the business of shipping DVDs directly to the homes of customers, what lessons can we take away from Netflix's DVD process? First, properly managed inventories can support the competitive priorities of variety and delivery speed. Second, process design can help to reduce the need for excessive inventory investment. These are lessons that can be applied to most any business.

Sources: Emily Steel, "Netflix Refines Its DVD Business, Even as Streaming Unit Booms," https://www.nttimes.com/2015/07/27/business/while-its-streaming-service-booms-netflix-streamlines-old-business.html (July, 26, 2015) Christopher Borrelli, "How Netflix Gets Your Movies to Your Mailbox So Fast," *Chicago Tribune* (August 4, 2009); Tracy V. Wilson and Stephanie Crawford, "How Netflix Works," How Stuff Works, **http://electronics.howstufworks.com**; Rick Newman, "How Netflix (and Blockbuster) Killed Blockbuster," *US News*, **http://moneyusnews.com** (September 23, 2010).

raw materials (RM)

The inventories needed for the production of services or goods.

work-in-process (WIP)

Items, such as components or assemblies, needed to produce a final product in manufacturing or service operations.

finished goods (FG)

The items in manufacturing plants, warehouses, and retail outlets that are sold to the firm's customers.

independent demand items

Items for which demand is influenced by market conditions and is not related to the inventory decisions for any other item held in stock or produced.

Types of Inventory

Inventories can be classified in several ways. In this section we discuss accounting inventories and operational inventories.

Accounting Inventories

Inventory exists in three aggregate categories that are useful for accounting purposes. **Raw materials (RM)** are the inventories needed for the production of services or goods. They are considered to be inputs to the transformation processes of the firm. **Work-in-process (WIP)** consists of items, such as components or assemblies, needed to produce a final product in manufacturing. WIP is also present in some service operations, such as repair shops, restaurants, check-processing centers, and package delivery services. **Finished goods (FG)** in manufacturing plants, warehouses, and retail outlets are the items sold to the firm's customers. The finished goods of one firm may actually be the raw materials for another.

Figure 2 shows how inventory can be held in different forms and at various stocking points. In this example, raw materials—the finished goods of the supplier—are held both by the supplier and the manufacturer. Raw materials at the plant pass through one or more processes, which transform them into various levels of WIP inventory. Final processing of this inventory yields finished goods inventory. Finished goods can be held at the plant, the distribution center (which may be a warehouse owned by the manufacturer or the retailer), and retail locations.

An important distinction regarding the three categories of inventories is the nature of the demand they experience. For example, take finished goods, which are **independent demand items**—that is, items for which demand is influenced by market conditions and is not related to the inventory decisions for any other item held in stock or produced. Retailers, such as JCPenney and Dillards, deal with finished goods. Examples of independent demand items include:

- Wholesale and retail merchandise
- Service support inventory, such as stamps and mailing labels for post offices, office supplies for law firms, and laboratory supplies for research universities

Raw materials, work-in-progress, and finished goods inventories can all be stocked in the same facility. Modern warehouses allow for efficient inventory access.

Marcin Balcerzak/Shutterstock

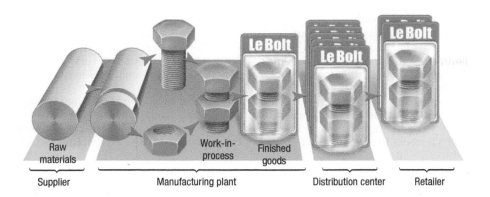

- Product and replacement-part distribution inventories
- Maintenance, repair, and operating (MRO) supplies—that is, items that do not become part of the final service or product, such as employee uniforms, fuel, paint, and machine repair parts

Managing an independent demand inventory can be tricky because demand is influenced by external factors. For example, the owner of a bookstore may not be sure how many copies of the latest bestseller novel customers will purchase during the coming month. As a result, the manager may decide to stock extra copies as a safeguard. Independent demand, such as the demand for various book titles, must be *forecasted*. There is, however, a whole different type of demand for certain items that must be considered. **Dependent demand items**, consisting of raw materials and WIP inventories, are those items whose required quantity varies with the production plans for other items held in the firm's inventory. These items are required as components or inputs to a service or product. Dependent demand should be calculated, not forecasted, and exhibits a pattern very different from that of independent demand.

dependent demand items

Items whose required quantity varies with the production plans for other items held in the firm's inventory.

Operational Inventories

Inventories can also be classified by how they are created. In this context, inventory takes four forms: (1) cycle, (2) safety stock, (3) anticipation, and (4) pipeline. They cannot be identified physically; that is, an inventory manager cannot look at a pile of widgets and identify which ones are cycle inventory and which ones are safety stock inventory. However, conceptually, each of the four types comes into being in an entirely different way. Once you understand these differences, you can prescribe different ways to reduce inventory.

Cycle Inventory The portion of total inventory that varies directly with lot size is called **cycle inventory**. Two principles apply:

1. The lot size, Q, varies directly with the elapsed time (or cycle) between orders. If a lot is ordered every 5 weeks, the average lot size must equal 5 weeks' demand.

2. The longer the time between orders for a given item, the greater the cycle inventory must be.

At the beginning of the interval, the cycle inventory is at its maximum, or Q. At the end of the interval, just before a new lot arrives, cycle inventory drops to its minimum, or 0. The average cycle inventory is the average of these two extremes:

$$\text{Average cycle inventory} = \frac{Q + 0}{2} = \frac{Q}{2}$$

This formula is exact only when the demand rate is constant and uniform. However, it does provide a reasonably good estimate even when demand rates are not constant. Factors other than the demand rate (e.g., scrap losses) also may cause estimating errors when this simple formula is used.

cycle inventory

The portion of total inventory that varies directly with lot size.

safety stock inventory

Surplus inventory that a company holds to protect against uncertainties in demand, lead time, and supply changes.

Safety Stock Inventory To avoid customer service problems and the hidden costs of unavailable components, companies hold safety stock. **Safety stock inventory** is surplus inventory that protects against uncertainties in demand, lead time, and supply changes. Safety stocks are desirable when suppliers fail to deliver either the desired quantity on the specified date or items of acceptable quality, or when manufactured items require significant amounts of scrap or rework. Safety stock inventory ensures that operations are not disrupted when such problems occur, allowing subsequent operations to continue.

To create safety stock, a firm places an order for delivery earlier than when the item is typically needed.[1] The replenishment order therefore arrives ahead of time, giving a cushion against uncertainty. For example, suppose that the average lead time from a supplier is 3 weeks, but a firm orders 5 weeks in advance just to be safe. This policy creates a safety stock equal to a 2-weeks' supply $(5 - 3 = 2)$.

anticipation inventory

Inventory used to absorb uneven rates of demand or supply.

Anticipation Inventory Inventory used to absorb uneven rates of demand or supply, which businesses often face, is referred to as **anticipation inventory**. Predictable, seasonal demand patterns lend themselves to the use of anticipation inventory. Uneven demand can motivate a manufacturer to stockpile anticipation inventory during periods of low demand so that output levels do not have to be increased much when demand peaks. Anticipation inventory also can help when suppliers are threatened with a strike or have severe capacity limitations.

pipeline inventory

Inventory that is created when an order for an item is issued but not yet received.

Pipeline Inventory Inventory that is created when an order for an item is issued but not yet received is called **pipeline inventory**. This form of inventory exists because the firm must commit to enough inventory (on-hand plus in-transit) to cover the lead time for the order. Longer lead times or higher demands per week create more pipeline inventory. As such, the average pipeline inventory between two stocking points can be measured as the average demand during lead time, $\overline{D}_L$, which is the average demand for the item per period ($\overline{d}$) multiplied by the number of periods in the item's lead time (L) to move between the two points, or

$$\text{Pipeline inventory} = \overline{D}_L = \overline{d}L$$

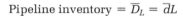

The equation assumes that both $\overline{d}$ and L are constants and that L is not affected by the order or lot size, Q. Changing an item's lot size does not directly affect the average level of the pipeline inventory. Nonetheless, the lot size can *indirectly* affect pipeline inventory if it is related to the lead time. In such a case, pipeline inventory will change depending on the relationship of L to Q. Example 1 shows how this can happen.

Pipeline inventories result from moving items and materials from one location to another. Because trains offer an economical way to transport large quantities of goods, they are a favorite choice to reduce the costs of pipeline inventories.

EXAMPLE 1	Estimating Inventory Levels

MyLab Operations Management

Tutor 1 in MyLab Operations Management provides a new example to practice the estimation of inventory levels.

A plant makes monthly shipments of electric drills to a wholesaler in average lot sizes of 280 drills. The wholesaler's average demand is 70 drills a week, and the lead time from the plant is 3 weeks. The wholesaler must pay for the inventory from the moment the plant makes a shipment. If the wholesaler is willing to increase its purchase quantity to 350 units, the plant will give priority to the wholesaler and guarantee a lead time of only 2 weeks. What is the effect on the wholesaler's cycle and pipeline inventories?

---

[1]When orders are placed at fixed intervals, a second way to create safety stock is used. Each new order placed is larger than the quantity typically needed through the next delivery date.

SOLUTION

The wholesaler's current cycle and pipeline inventories are

$$\text{Cycle inventory} = \frac{Q}{2} = \frac{280}{2} = 140 \text{ drills}$$

$$\text{Pipeline inventory} = \bar{D}_L = \bar{d}L = (70 \text{ drills/week})(3 \text{ weeks}) = 210 \text{ drills}$$

Figure 3 shows the cycle and pipeline inventories if the wholesaler accepts the new proposal.

1. Enter the average lot size, average demand during a period, and the number of periods of lead time:

Average lot size	350
Average demand	70
Lead time	2

2. To compute cycle inventory, simply divide average lot size by 2. To compute pipeline inventory, multiply average demand by lead time:

Cycle inventory	175
Pipeline inventory	140

◄ **FIGURE 3**
Estimating Inventory Levels
Using Tutor 1

DECISION POINT

The effect of the new proposal on cycle inventories is to increase them by 35 units, or 25 percent. The reduction in pipeline inventories, however, is 70 units, or 33 percent. The proposal would reduce the total investment in cycle and pipeline inventories. Also, it is advantageous to have shorter lead times because the wholesaler only has to commit to purchases 2 weeks in advance, rather than 3 weeks.

Inventory Reduction Tactics

Managers are always eager to find cost-effective ways to reduce inventory in supply chains. In this section we discuss the basic tactics (which we call *levers*) for reducing cycle, safety stock, anticipation, and pipeline inventories in supply chains. A primary lever is one that must be activated if inventory is to be reduced. A secondary lever reduces the penalty cost of applying the primary lever and the need for having inventory in the first place.

Cycle Inventory

The primary lever to reduce cycle inventory is simply to reduce the lot sizes of items moving in the supply chain. However, making such reductions in Q without making any other changes can be devastating. For example, setup costs or ordering costs can skyrocket. If these changes occur, two secondary levers can be used:

1. Streamline the methods for placing orders and making setups to reduce ordering and setup costs and allow Q to be reduced. This may involve redesigning the infrastructure for information flows or improving manufacturing processes.

2. Increase repeatability to eliminate the need for changeovers. **Repeatability** is the degree to which the same work can be done again. Repeatability can be increased through high product demand; the use of specialization; the devotion of resources exclusively to a product; the use of the same part in many different products; the use of *flexible automation*; the use of the *one-worker, multiple-machines* concept; or through *group technology*. Increased repeatability may justify new setup methods, reduce transportation costs, and allow quantity discounts from suppliers.

repeatability

The degree to which the same work can be done again.

Safety Stock Inventory

The primary lever to reduce safety stock inventory is to place orders closer to the time when they must be received. However, this approach can lead to unacceptable customer service unless demand, supply, and delivery uncertainties can be minimized. Four secondary levers can be used in this case:

1. Improve demand forecasts so that fewer surprises come from customers. Design the mechanisms to increase collaboration with customers to get advanced warnings for changes in demand levels.

2. Cut the lead times of purchased or produced items to reduce demand uncertainty. For example, local suppliers with short lead times could be selected when possible.

3. Reduce supply uncertainties. Suppliers are likely to be more reliable if production plans are shared with them. Put in place the mechanisms to increase collaboration with suppliers. Surprises from unexpected scrap or rework can be reduced by improving manufacturing processes. Preventive maintenance can minimize unexpected downtime caused by equipment failure.

4. Rely more on equipment and labor buffers, such as *capacity cushions* and cross-trained workers. These buffers are important to businesses in the service sector because they generally cannot inventory their services.

Anticipation Inventory

The primary lever to reduce anticipation inventory is simply to match demand rate with production rate. Secondary levers can be used to even out customer demand in one of the following ways:

1. Add new products with different demand cycles so that a peak in the demand for one product compensates for the seasonal low for another.

2. Provide off-season promotional campaigns.

3. Offer seasonal pricing plans.

Pipeline Inventory

An operations manager has direct control over lead times but not demand rates. Because pipeline inventory is a function of demand during the lead time, the primary lever is to reduce the lead time. Two secondary levers can help managers cut lead times:

1. Find more responsive suppliers and select new carriers for shipments between stocking locations or improve materials handling within the plant. Improving the information system could overcome information delays between a distribution center and retailer.

2. Change Q in those cases where the lead time depends on the lot size.

Inventories in supply chains are managed with the help of inventory control systems. These systems manage the levels of cycle, safety stock, anticipation, and pipeline inventories in a firm. Regardless of whether an item experiences independent or dependent demand, three important questions must be answered: What degree of control should we impose on an item? How much should we order? and When should we place the order? An approach called ABC analysis, which we address in the next section, helps with the first question. Inventory control systems respond to the last two questions. In selecting an inventory control system for a particular application, the nature of the demands imposed on the inventory items is crucial. In this text, we focus on inventory control systems for independent demand items, which is the type of demand the bookstore owner, other retailers, service providers, and distributors face. Even though demand from any one customer is difficult to predict, low demand from some customers for a particular item often is offset by high demand from others. Thus, total demand for any independent demand item may follow a relatively smooth pattern, with some random fluctuations. For items facing dependent demands, such as raw materials and WIP inventories, material requirements planning (MRP) systems are useful.

In the remainder of this text we first address the question of what degree of control to impose on an item, and then answer the question of how much to order. In the last two sections we discuss and compare two inventory control systems: (1) the continuous review system, called a Q system, and (2) the periodic review system, called a P system.

ABC Analysis

stock-keeping unit (SKU)

An individual item or product that has an identifying code and is held in inventory somewhere along the supply chain.

ABC analysis

The process of dividing SKUs into three classes, according to their dollar usage, so that managers can focus on items that have the highest dollar value.

Thousands of items, often referred to as stock-keeping units, are held in inventory by a typical organization, but only a small percentage of them deserve management's closest attention and tightest control. A **stock-keeping unit (SKU)** is an individual item or product that has an identifying code and is held in inventory somewhere along the supply chain. **ABC analysis** is the process of dividing SKUs into three classes according to their dollar usage so that managers can focus on items that have the highest dollar value. This method is the equivalent of creating a *Pareto chart* except that it is applied to inventory rather than to process errors. As Figure 4 shows, class A items typically represent only about 20 percent of the SKUs but account for 80 percent of the dollar usage. Class B items account for another 30 percent of the SKUs but only 15 percent of the dollar usage. Finally, 50 percent of the SKUs fall in class C, representing a mere 5 percent of the dollar usage. The goal of ABC analysis is to identify the class A SKUs so management can closely control their inventory levels.

The analysis begins by multiplying the annual demand rate for an SKU by the dollar value (cost) of one unit of that SKU to determine its dollar usage. After ranking the SKUs on the basis of dollar usage and creating the Pareto chart, the analyst looks for "natural" changes in slope. The dividing lines in Figure 4 between classes are inexact. Class A SKUs could be somewhat higher or lower than 20 percent of all SKUs but normally account for the bulk of the dollar usage.

Class A SKUs are reviewed frequently to reduce the average lot size and to ensure timely deliveries from suppliers. It is important to maintain high inventory turnover for these items. By contrast, class B SKUs require an intermediate level of control. Here, less frequent monitoring of suppliers coupled with adequate safety stocks can provide cost-effective coverage of demands. For class C SKUs, much looser control is appropriate. While a stockout of a class C SKU can be as crucial as for a class A SKU, the inventory holding cost of class C SKUs tends to be low. These features suggest that higher inventory levels can be tolerated and that more safety stock and larger lot sizes may suffice for class C SKUs. See Solved Problem 2 for a detailed example of ABC analysis.

Creating ABC inventory classifications is useless unless inventory records are accurate. Technology can help; many companies are tracking inventory wherever it exists in the supply chain. Chips imbedded in product packaging contain information on the product and send signals that can be accessed by sensitive receivers and transmitted to a central location for processing. There are other, less sophisticated approaches of achieving accuracy that can be used. One way is to assign responsibility to specific employees for issuing and receiving materials and accurately reporting each transaction. Another method is to secure inventory behind locked doors or gates to prevent unauthorized or unreported withdrawals. This method also guards against accidentally storing newly received inventory in the wrong locations, where it can be lost for months. **Cycle counting** can also be used, whereby storeroom personnel physically count a small percentage of the total number of SKUs each day, correcting errors that they find. Class A SKUs are counted most frequently. A final method is to make logic error checks on each transaction reported and fully investigate any discrepancies. The discrepancies can include (1) actual receipts when no receipts are scheduled, (2) disbursements that exceed the current on-hand inventory balance, and (3) receipts with an inaccurate (nonexistent) SKU number.

Now that we have identified the inventory items deserving of most attention, we turn to the decision of how much to order.

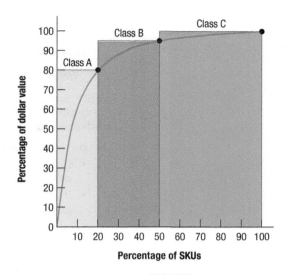

▲ **FIGURE 4**
Typical Chart Using ABC Analysis

cycle counting

An inventory control method, whereby storeroom personnel physically count a small percentage of the total number of items each day, correcting errors that they find.

Economic Order Quantity

Supply chain managers face conflicting pressures to keep inventories low enough to avoid excess inventory holding costs but high enough to reduce ordering and setup costs. *Inventory holding cost* is the sum of the cost of capital and the variable costs of keeping items on hand, such as storage and handling, taxes, insurance, and shrinkage. *Ordering cost* is the cost of preparing a purchase order for a supplier or a production order for the shop, while *setup cost* is the cost of changing over a machine to produce a different item. In this section, we will address the *cycle inventory*, which is that portion of total inventory that varies directly with lot size. A good starting point for balancing these conflicting pressures and determining the best cycle-inventory level for an item is finding the **economic order quantity (EOQ)**, which is the lot size that minimizes total annual cycle-inventory holding and ordering costs. The approach to determining the EOQ is based on the following assumptions:

economic order quantity (EOQ)

The lot size that minimizes total annual inventory holding and ordering costs.

1. The demand rate for the item is constant (e.g., always 10 units per day) and known with certainty.

2. No constraints are placed (such as truck capacity or materials handling limitations) on the size of each lot.

3. The only two relevant costs are the inventory holding cost and the fixed cost per lot for ordering or setup.

4. Decisions for one item can be made independently of decisions for other items. In other words, no advantage is gained in combining several orders going to the same supplier.

5. The lead time is constant (e.g., always 14 days) and known with certainty. The amount received is exactly what was ordered and it arrives all at once rather than piecemeal.

The economic order quantity will be optimal when all five assumptions are satisfied. In reality, few situations are so simple. Nonetheless, the EOQ is often a reasonable approximation of the appropriate lot size, even when several of the assumptions do not quite apply. Here are some guidelines on when to use or modify the EOQ.

■ **Do not use the EOQ**
  • If you use the "make-to-order" strategy and your customer specifies that the entire order be delivered in one shipment
  • If the order size is constrained by capacity limitations such as the size of the firm's ovens, amount of testing equipment, or number of delivery trucks

■ **Modify the EOQ**
  • If significant quantity discounts are given for ordering larger lots
  • If replenishment of the inventory is not instantaneous, which can happen if the items must be used or sold as soon as they are finished without waiting until the entire lot has been completed

■ **Use the EOQ**
  • If you follow a "make-to-stock" strategy and the item has relatively stable demand
  • If your carrying costs per unit and setup or ordering costs are known and relatively stable

The EOQ was never intended to be an optimizing tool. Nonetheless, if you need to determine a reasonable lot size, it can be helpful in many situations.

Calculating the EOQ

We begin by formulating the total cost for any lot size Q for a given SKU. Next, we derive the EOQ, which is the Q that minimizes total annual cycle-inventory cost. Finally, we describe how to convert the EOQ into a companion measure, the elapsed time between orders.

When the EOQ assumptions are satisfied, cycle inventory behaves as shown in Figure 5. A cycle begins with Q units held in inventory, which happens when a new order is received. During the cycle, on-hand inventory is used at a constant rate and, because demand is known with certainty and the lead time is a constant, a new lot can be ordered so that inventory falls to 0 precisely when the new lot is received. Because inventory varies uniformly between Q and 0, the average cycle inventory equals half the lot size, Q.

The annual holding cost for this amount of inventory, which increases linearly with Q, as Figure 6(a) shows, is

Annual holding cost = (Average cycle inventory)(Unit holding cost)

The annual ordering cost is

Annual ordering cost = (Number of orders/Year)(Ordering or setup cost)

The average number of orders per year equals annual demand divided by Q. For example, if 1,200 units must be ordered each year and the average lot size is 100 units, then 12 orders will be

FIGURE 5 ▶
Cycle-Inventory Levels

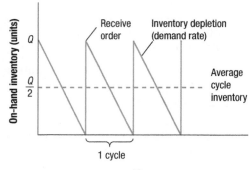

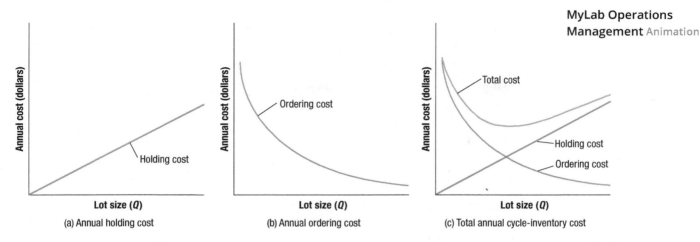

MyLab Operations Management Animation

▲ FIGURE 6
Graphs of Annual Holding, Ordering, and Total Costs

placed during the year. The annual ordering or setup cost decreases nonlinearly as Q increases, as shown in Figure 6(b), because fewer orders are placed.

The total annual cycle-inventory cost,[2] as graphed in Figure 6(c), is the sum of the two cost components:

$$\text{Total cost} = \text{Annual holding cost} + \text{Annual ordering or setup cost}[3]$$

$$C = \frac{Q}{2}(H) + \frac{D}{Q}(S)$$

where
C = total annual cycle-inventory cost
Q = lot size, in units
H = cost of holding one unit in inventory for a year, often expressed as a percentage of the item's value
D = annual demand, in units per year
S = cost of ordering or setting up one lot, in dollars per lot

In Example 2, we show how to calculate the cost of a lot-sizing policy.

EXAMPLE 2   **The Cost of a Lot-Sizing Policy**

A museum of natural history opened a gift shop 2 years ago. Managing inventories has become a problem. Low inventory turnover is squeezing profit margins and causing cash flow problems.

One of the top-selling SKUs in the container group at the museum's gift shop is a bird feeder. Sales are 18 units per week, and the supplier charges $60 per unit. The cost of placing an order with the supplier is $45. Annual holding cost is 25 percent of a feeder's value, and the museum operates 52 weeks per year. Management chose a 390-unit lot size so that new orders could be placed less frequently. What is the annual cycle-inventory cost of the current policy of using a 390-unit lot size? Would a lot size of 468 be better?

MyLab Operations Management
Tutor 2 in MyLab Operations Management provides a new example of the application of ABC analysis.

SOLUTION
We begin by computing the annual demand and holding cost as

$$D = (18 \text{ units/week})(52 \text{ weeks/year}) = 936 \text{ units}$$
$$H = 0.25(\$60/\text{unit}) = \$15$$

---

[2]Expressing the total cost on an annual basis usually is convenient (although not necessary). Any time horizon can be selected as long as D and H cover the same time period. If the total cost is calculated on a monthly basis, D must be monthly demand and H must be the cost of holding a unit for 1 month.

[3]The number of orders actually placed in any year is always a whole number, although the formula allows for the use of fractional values. However, rounding is not needed because what is being calculated is an average of multiple years. Such averages often are nonintegers.

The total annual cycle-inventory cost for the current policy is

$$C = \frac{Q}{2}(H) + \frac{D}{Q}(S)$$

$$= \frac{390}{2}(\$15) + \frac{936}{390}(\$45) = \$2,925 + \$108 = \$3,033$$

The total annual cycle-inventory cost for the alternative lot size is

$$C = \frac{468}{2}(\$15) + \frac{936}{468}(\$45) = \$3,510 + \$90 = \$3,600$$

DECISION POINT
The lot size of 468 units, which is a half-year supply, would be a more expensive option than the current policy. The savings in ordering costs are more than offset by the increase in holding costs. Management should use the total annual cycle-inventory cost function to explore other lot-size alternatives.

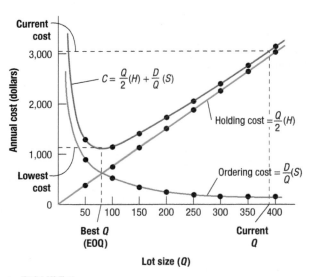

▲ FIGURE 7
Total Annual Cycle-Inventory Cost Function for the Bird Feeder

time between orders (TBO)

The average elapsed time between receiving (or placing) replenishment orders of Q units for a particular lot size.

Figure 7 displays the impact of using several Q values for the bird feeder in Example 2. Eight different lot sizes were evaluated in addition to the current one. Both holding and ordering costs were plotted, but their sum—the total annual cycle-inventory cost curve—is the important feature. The graph shows that the best lot size, or EOQ, is the lowest point on the total annual cost curve, or between 50 and 100 units. Obviously, reducing the current lot-size policy $Q = 390$ can result in significant savings.

A more efficient approach is to use the EOQ formula:

$$EOQ = \sqrt{\frac{2DS}{H}}$$

We use calculus to obtain the EOQ formula from the total annual cycle-inventory cost function. We take the first derivative of the total annual cycle-inventory cost function with respect to Q, set it equal to 0, and solve for Q. As Figure 7 indicates, the EOQ is the order quantity for which annual holding cost equals annual ordering cost. Using this insight, we can also obtain the EOQ formula by equating the formulas for annual ordering cost and annual holding cost and solving for Q. The graph in Figure 7 also reveals that when the annual holding cost for any Q exceeds the annual ordering cost, as with the 390-unit order, we can immediately conclude that Q is too high. A lower Q reduces holding cost and increases ordering cost, bringing them into balance. Similarly, if the annual ordering cost exceeds the annual holding cost, Q should be increased.

Sometimes, inventory policies are based on the time between replenishment orders, rather than on the number of units in the lot size. The **time between orders (TBO)** for a particular lot size is the average elapsed time between receiving (or placing) replenishment orders of Q units. Expressed as a fraction of a year, the TBO is simply Q divided by annual demand. When we use the EOQ and express time in terms of months, the TBO is

$$TBO_{EOQ} = \frac{EOQ}{D}\ (12\ months/year)$$

In Example 3, we show how to calculate TBO for years, months, weeks, and days.

EXAMPLE 3	Finding the EOQ, Total Cost, and TBO

MyLab Operations Management

Tutor 3 in MyLab Operations Management provides a new example to practice the application of the EOQ model.

For the bird feeder in Example 2, calculate the EOQ and its total annual cycle-inventory cost. How frequently will orders be placed if the EOQ is used?

SOLUTION
Using the formulas for EOQ and annual cost, we get

$$EOQ = \sqrt{\frac{2DS}{H}} = \sqrt{\frac{2(936)(45)}{15}} = 74.94,\ or\ 75\ units$$

Parameters

		Economic Order Quantity	75
Current Lot Size (Q)	390		
Demand (D)	936		
Order Cost (S)	$45		
Unit Holding Cost (H)	$15		

Annual Costs		**Annual Costs based on EOQ**	
Orders per Year	2.4	Orders per Year	12.48
Annual Ordering Cost	$108.00	Annual Ordering Cost	$561.60
Annual Holding Cost	$2,925.00	Annual Holding Cost	$562.50
Annual Inventory Cost	$3,033.00	Annual Inventory Cost	$1,124.10

MyLab Operations Management

Active Model 1 in MyLab Operations Management provides additional insight on the EOQ model and its uses.

◀ **FIGURE 8**
Total Annual Cycle-Inventory Costs Based on EOQ Using Tutor 3

Figure 8 shows that the total annual cost is much less than the $3,033 cost of the current policy of placing 390-unit orders.

When the EOQ is used, the TBO can be expressed in various ways for the same time period:

$$\text{TBO}_{EOQ} = \frac{EOQ}{D} = \frac{75}{936} = 0.080 \text{ year}$$

$$\text{TBO}_{EOQ} = \frac{EOQ}{D}(12 \text{ months/year}) = \frac{75}{936}(12) = 0.96 \text{ month}$$

$$\text{TBO}_{EOQ} = \frac{EOQ}{D}(52 \text{ weeks/year}) = \frac{75}{936}(52) = 4.17 \text{ weeks}$$

$$\text{TBO}_{EOQ} = \frac{EOQ}{D}(365 \text{ days/year}) = \frac{75}{936}(365) = 29.25 \text{ days}$$

DECISION POINT
Using the EOQ, about 12 orders per year will be required. Using the current policy of 390 units per order, an average of 2.4 orders will be needed each year (every 5 months). The current policy saves on ordering costs but incurs a much higher cost for carrying the cycle inventory. Although it is easy to see which option is best on the basis of total ordering and holding costs, other factors may affect the final decision. For example, if the supplier would reduce the price per unit for large orders, it may be better to order the larger quantity.

Managerial Insights from the EOQ

Subjecting the EOQ formula to *sensitivity analysis* can yield valuable insights into the management of inventories. Sensitivity analysis is a technique for systematically changing crucial parameters to determine the effects of a change. Table 1 shows the effects on the EOQ when we substitute different values into the numerator or denominator of the formula.

As Table 1 shows, the EOQ provides support for some of the intuition you may have about inventory management. However, the effect of ordering or setup cost changes on inventories is especially important for *lean systems*. This relationship explains why manufacturers are so concerned about reducing setup time and costs; it makes small lot production economic. Actually, lean systems provide an environment conducive to the use of the EOQ. For example, yearly, monthly, daily, or hourly demand rates are known with reasonable certainty in lean systems,

TABLE 1 │ SENSITIVITY ANALYSIS OF THE EOQ

Parameter	EOQ	Parameter Change	EOQ Change	Comments
Demand	$\sqrt{\dfrac{2DS}{H}}$	↑	↑	Increase in lot size is in proportion to the square root of *D*.
Order/Setup Costs	$\sqrt{\dfrac{2DS}{H}}$	↓	↓	Weeks of supply decreases and inventory turnover increases because the lot size decreases.
Holding Costs	$\sqrt{\dfrac{2DS}{H}}$	↓	↑	Larger lots are justified when holding costs decrease.

Retailers typically face independent demands for the products on their shelves. Thousands of customers may shop at a large store, each looking for a different selection of products. The products must be restocked from a distribution center in the region. Here shoppers look for bargains at a JCPenney store in the Glendale Galleria in California.

and the rate of demand is relatively uniform. Lean systems may have few process constraints if the firm practices *constraint management*. In addition, lean systems strive for constant delivery lead times and dependable delivery quantities from suppliers, both of which are assumptions of the EOQ. Consequently, the EOQ as a lot-sizing tool is quite compatible with the principles of lean systems.

We now turn to a discussion of the two most common independent demand inventory control systems: the continuous review (Q) system and the periodic review (P) system.

Continuous Review System

A **continuous review (Q) system**, sometimes called a **reorder point (ROP) system** or *fixed order-quantity system*, tracks the remaining inventory of a SKU each time a withdrawal is made to determine whether it is time to reorder. In practice, these reviews are done frequently (e.g., daily) and often continuously (after each withdrawal). The advent of computers and electronic cash registers linked to inventory records has made continuous reviews easy. At each review, a decision is made about a SKU's inventory position. If it is judged to be too low, the system triggers a new order. The **inventory position (IP)** measures the SKU's ability to satisfy future demand. It includes **scheduled receipts (SR)**, which are orders that have been placed but have not yet been received, plus on-hand inventory (OH) minus backorders (BO). Sometimes, scheduled receipts are called **open orders**. More specifically,

Inventory position = On-hand inventory + Scheduled receipts − Backorders

$$IP = OH + SR − BO$$

When the inventory position reaches a predetermined minimum level, called the **reorder point (R)**, a fixed quantity Q of the SKU is ordered. In a continuous review system, although the order quantity Q is fixed, the time between orders can vary. Hence, Q can be based on the EOQ, a price break quantity (the minimum lot size that qualifies for a quantity discount), a container size (such as a truckload), or some other quantity selected by management.

Selecting the Reorder Point when Demand and Lead Time Are Constant

To demonstrate the concept of a reorder point, suppose that the demand for feeders at the museum gift shop in Example 3 is always 18 per week, the lead time is a constant 2 weeks, and the supplier always ships the exact number ordered on time. With both demand and lead time constant, the museum's buyer can wait until the inventory position drops to 36 units, or (18 units/week) (2 weeks), to place a new order. Thus, in this case, the reorder point, R, equals the *total demand during lead time*, with no added allowance for safety stock.

Figure 9 shows how the system operates when demand and lead time are constant. The downward-sloping line represents the on-hand inventory, which is being depleted at a constant rate. When it reaches the reorder point R (the horizontal line), a new order for Q units is placed. The on-hand inventory continues to drop throughout lead time L until the order is received. At that time, which marks the end of the lead time, on-hand inventory jumps by Q units. A new order arrives just when inventory drops to 0. The TBO is the same for each cycle.

The inventory position, IP, shown in Figure 9 corresponds to the on-hand inventory, except during the lead

continuous review (Q) system

A system designed to track the remaining inventory of a SKU each time a withdrawal is made to determine whether it is time to reorder.

reorder point (ROP) system

See continuous review (Q) system.

inventory position (IP)

The measurement of a SKU's ability to satisfy future demand.

scheduled receipts (SR)

Orders that have been placed but have not yet been received.

open orders

See scheduled receipts (SR).

reorder point (R)

The predetermined minimum level that an inventory position must reach before a fixed quantity Q of the SKU is ordered.

▲ **FIGURE 9**

Q System when Demand and Lead Time Are Constant and Certain

time. Just after a new order is placed, at the start of the lead time, IP increases by Q, as shown by the dashed line. The IP exceeds OH by this same margin throughout the lead time.[4] At the end of the lead time, when the scheduled receipts convert to on-hand inventory, IP = OH once again. The key point here is to compare IP, not OH, with R in deciding whether to reorder. A common error is to ignore scheduled receipts or backorders.

In Example 4, we show how to determine the time to place a new order when both the demand and lead time are constant.

| EXAMPLE 4 | Placing a New Order when Demand and Lead Time are Constant |

Demand for chicken soup at a supermarket is always 25 cases a day and the lead time is always 4 days. The shelves were just restocked with chicken soup, leaving an on-hand inventory of only 10 cases. No backorders currently exist, but there is one open order in the pipeline for 200 cases. What is the inventory position? Should a new order be placed?

SOLUTION

$$R = \text{Total demand during lead time} = (25)(4) = 100 \text{ cases}$$
$$IP = OH + SR - BO$$
$$= 10 + 200 - 0 = 210 \text{ cases}$$

DECISION POINT

Because IP exceeds R (210 versus 100), do not reorder. Inventory is almost depleted, but a new order need not be placed because the scheduled receipt is in the pipeline.

MyLab Operations
Management Animation

▼ FIGURE 10
Q System when Demand Is Uncertain

Selecting the Reorder Point when Demand Is Variable and Lead Time Is Constant

In reality demand is not always predictable. Figure 10 shows how the Q system operates when demand is variable and lead time is constant. The wavy downward-sloping line indicates that demand varies from day to day. Its slope is steeper in the second cycle, which means that the demand rate is higher during this time period. The changing demand rate means that the time between orders changes, so $\text{TBO}_1 \neq \text{TBO}_2 \neq \text{TBO}_3$. Example 5 shows the mechanics of the continuous review system when demand is variable and the lead time is constant.

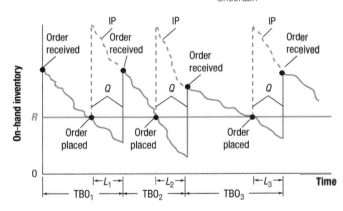

| EXAMPLE 5 | Placing a New Order when Demand Is Variable and Lead Time Is Constant |

A distribution center (DC) in Wisconsin stocks Sony plasma TV sets. The center receives its inventory from a mega warehouse in Kansas with a lead time (L) of 5 days. The DC uses a reorder point (R) of 300 sets and a fixed order quantity (Q) of 250 sets. The current on-hand inventory (OH) at the end of Day 1 is 400 sets, there are no scheduled receipts (SR), and there are no backorders (BO). Assume that all demands and receipts occur at the end of the day. The inventory position is compared to the reorder point after demands and receipts are accounted for. If necessary, an order is placed and the inventory position is updated. Given the demand schedule in the table provided, determine when to order using a (Q) system.

---

[4]A possible exception is the situation when more than one scheduled receipt is open at the same time because of long lead times or larger than average demands during the lead time. Such is the case in Example 5.

SOLUTION

We use the following equation:

Inventory position (IP) = OH + SR − BO

Day	Demand	OH	SR	BO	IP	Q
1	50	400			400 + 0 = 400	
2	60	340			340 + 0 = 340	
3	80	260	**250** after ordering		260 < R before ordering 260 + **250** = 510 after ordering	**250** (due Day 8)
4	40	220	**250**		220 + **250** = 470	
5	75	145	**250**		145 + **250** = 395	
6	55	90	**250**		90 + **250** = 340	
7	95	0	**250 + 250 = 500** after ordering	5	0 + **250** − 5 = 245 < R before ordering 245 + **250** = 495 after ordering	**250** (due Day 12)
8	50	0 + **250** − 50 − 5 = 195	**250**		195 + **250** = 445	
9	45	195 − 45 = 150	**250**		150 + **250** = 400	
10	30	120	**250**		120 + **250** = 370	
11	50	70	**250**		70 + **250** = 320	
12	60	70 − 60 + **250** = 260	**250** after ordering		260 < R before ordering 260 + **250** = 510 after ordering	**250** (due Day 17)
13	40	260 − 40 = 220	**250**		220 + **250** = 470	
14	50	170	**250**		170 + **250** = 420	

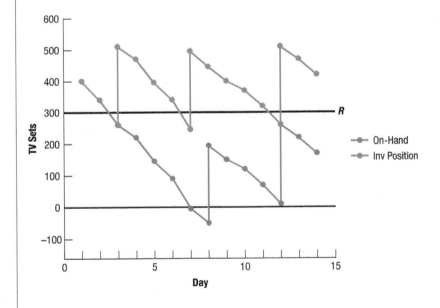

DECISION POINT

The figure shows the relationship between the on-hand quantity of TV sets and the inventory position. The IP at the DC drops below the reorder point of 300 sets for the first time on Day 3, triggering an order for 250 sets. On Day 7, demand exceeded the supply of TVs, generating a backorder of 5 sets. Notice that the calculation for IP accounts for the backorder as well as the fact that there are two scheduled receipts on the books once the new order is placed. This situation occurred because the reorder point was breached one day before the open order for 250 sets was received. On Day 8, the shipment of 250 sets arrives and the backorders are satisfied. Note that the on-hand inventory satisfies the demand for that day, as well as the backorders, from the shipment of 250 sets, leaving only 195 sets for inventory. The demands at the DC are fairly volatile and can cause the reorder point to be breached quite dramatically at times. This often happens with continuous review systems when customers place orders in large quantities, rather than one unit at a time. The customers of the DC could be large retailers who purchase large volumes of TV sets for sales promotions. Another possible reason is that the DC in this example performs all inventory transactions at the end of the day; even if shipments to customers were only one unit at a time, they were treated as one large shipment for purposes of inventory control. With today's technology and the use of product bar codes, the DC could continuously monitor inventory and place replenishment orders just as the reorder point was reached.

As shown in Example 5, because of uncertainty, demands during the lead time are unpredictable and backorders or stockouts can occur. That is why managers add safety stock to hedge against lost sales. Consequently R is higher in Figure 10 than in Figure 9. It also explains why the on-hand inventory usually does not drop to 0 by the time a replenishment order arrives for well-designed continuous review systems. The greater the safety stock and thus the higher reorder point R, the less likely a stockout. In general

$$\text{Reorder point} = \text{Average demand during lead time} + \text{Safety stock}$$
$$= \overline{d}L + \text{safety stock}$$

where

$$\overline{d} = \text{average demand per week or day or month}$$

$$L = \text{constant lead time in weeks or days or months}$$

Because the average demand during lead time is variable, the real decision to be made when selecting R concerns the safety stock level. Deciding on a small or large safety stock is a trade-off between customer service and inventory holding costs. Cost minimization models can be used to find the best safety stock, but they require estimates of stockout and backorder costs, which are usually difficult to make with any precision because it is hard to estimate the effect of lost sales, lost customer confidence, future loyalty of customers, and market share because the customer went to a competitor. The usual approach for determining R is for management—based on judgment—to set a reasonable service-level policy for the inventory and then determine the safety stock level that satisfies this policy. There are three steps to arrive at a reorder point:

1. Choose an appropriate service-level policy.

2. Determine the distribution of demand during lead time.

3. Determine the safety stock and reorder point levels.

Step 1: Service Level Policy Select a **service level**, or **cycle-service level** (the desired probability of not running out of stock in any one ordering cycle), which begins at the time an order is placed and ends when it arrives in stock. The intent is to provide coverage over the **protection interval**, or the period over which safety stock must protect the user from running out of stock. For the Q system, the lead time is the protection interval. For example, in a bookstore the manager may select a 90 percent cycle-service level for a book. In other words, the probability is 90 percent that demand will not exceed the supply during the lead time. The probability of running short *during the protection interval*, creating a stockout or backorder, is only 10 percent $(100 - 90)$ in our example. This stockout risk, which occurs only during the lead time in the Q system, is greater than the overall risk of a stockout because the risk is nonexistent outside the ordering cycle.

Step 2: Distribution of Demand during Lead Time Determine the distribution of demand during lead time, which requires the specification of its mean and standard deviation. To translate a cycle-service level policy into a specific safety stock level, we must know how demand during the lead time is distributed. If demand and lead times vary little around their averages, the safety stock can be small. Conversely, if they vary greatly from one order cycle to the next, the safety stock must be large. Variability is measured by the distribution of demand during lead time. Sometimes, average demand during the lead time and the standard deviation of demand during the lead time are not directly available and must be calculated by combining information on the demand rate with information on the lead time. Suppose that lead time is constant and demand is variable, but records on demand are not collected for a time interval that is exactly the same as the lead time. The same inventory control system may be used to manage thousands of different SKUs, each with a different lead time. For example, if demand is reported *weekly*, these records can be used directly to compute the average and the standard deviation of demand during the lead time if the lead time is exactly 1 week. However, if the lead time is 3 weeks, the computation is more difficult.

We can determine the demand during the lead time distribution by making some reasonable assumptions. Suppose that the average demand, $\overline{d}$, is known along with the standard deviation of demand, σ_d, over some time interval such as days or weeks. Also, suppose that the probability distributions of demand for each time interval are identical and independent of each other. For example, if the time interval is a week, the probability distributions of demand are assumed to be the same each week (identical $\overline{d}$ and σ_d), and the total demand in 1 week does not affect the total demand in another week. Let L be the constant lead time, expressed in the same time units as the demand. Under these assumptions, average demand during the lead time will be the sum of the averages for each of the L identical and independent distributions of demand, or $\overline{d} + \overline{d} + \overline{d} + \ldots = \overline{d}L$. In addition, the variance of the distribution of demand

service level

The desired probability of not running out of stock in any one ordering cycle, which begins at the time an order is placed and ends when it arrives in stock.

cycle-service level

See service level.

protection interval

The period over which safety stock must protect the user from running out of stock.

during lead time will be the sum of the variances of the L identical and independent distributions of demand, or

$$\sigma_d^2 + \sigma_d^2 + \sigma_d^2 + \ldots = \sigma_d^2 L$$

Finally, the standard deviation of the distribution of demand during lead time is

$$\sigma_{dLT} = \sqrt{\sigma_d^2 L} = \sigma_d \sqrt{L}$$

Figure 11 shows how the demand distribution of the lead time is developed from the individual distributions of weekly demands, where $\overline{d} = 75$, $\sigma_d = 15$, and $L = 3$. In this example, average demand during the lead time is $(75)(3) = 225$ units and $\sigma_{dLT} = 15\sqrt{3} = 25.98$.

FIGURE 11 ▶
Development of Distribution of
Demand During Lead Time

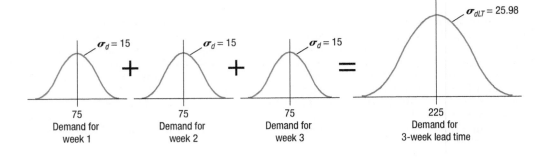

▲ FIGURE 12
Finding Safety Stock with
Normal Probability Distribu-
tion for an 85 Percent Cycle-
Service Level

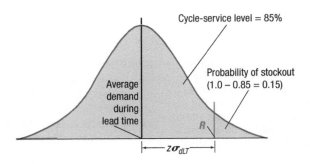

Step 3: Safety Stock and Reorder Point When selecting the safety stock, the inventory planner often assumes that demand during the lead time is normally distributed, as shown in Figure 12.

The average demand during the lead time is the centerline of the graph, with 50 percent of the area under the curve to the left and 50 percent to the right. Thus, if a cycle-service level of 50 percent were chosen, the reorder point R would be the quantity represented by this centerline. Because R equals the average demand during the lead time plus the safety stock, the safety stock is 0 when R equals this average demand. Demand is less than average 50 percent of the time and, thus, having no safety stock will be sufficient only 50 percent of the time.

To provide a service level above 50 percent, the reorder point must be higher than the average demand during the lead time. As Figure 12 shows, that requires moving the reorder point to the right of the centerline so that more than 50 percent of the area under the curve is to the left of R. An 85 percent cycle-service level is achieved in Figure 12 with 85 percent of the area under the curve to the left of R (in blue) and only 15 percent to the right (in pink). We compute the safety stock as follows:

$$\text{Safety stock} = z\sigma_{dLT}$$

where

z = the number of standard deviations needed to achieve the cycle-service level

σ_{dLT} = standard deviation of demand during the lead time

The reorder point becomes

$$R = \overline{d}L + \text{safety stock}$$

The higher the value of z, the higher the safety stock and the cycle-service level should be. If $z = 0$, there is no safety stock, and stockouts will occur during 50 percent of the order cycles. For a cycle-service level of 85 percent, $z = 1.04$. Example 6 shows how to use the appendix on the normal distribution to find the appropriate z value, safety stock, and reorder point.

EXAMPLE 6	Reorder Point for Variable Demand and Constant Lead Time

Let us return to the bird feeder in Example 3. The EOQ is 75 units. Suppose that the average demand is 18 units per week with a standard deviation of 5 units. The lead time is constant at 2 weeks. Determine the safety stock and reorder point if management wants a 90 percent cycle-service level.

SOLUTION

In this case, $\sigma_d = 5$, $\overline{d} = 18$ units, and $L = 2$ weeks, so $\sigma_{dLT} = \sigma_d\sqrt{L} = 5\sqrt{2} = 7.07$. Consult the body of the table in the appendix on the normal distribution for 0.9000, which corresponds to a 90 percent cycle-service level. The closest number is 0.8997, which corresponds to 1.2 in the row heading and 0.08 in the column heading. Adding these values gives a z value of 1.28. With this information, we calculate the safety stock and reorder point as follows:

$$\text{Safety stock} = z\sigma_{dLT} = 1.28(7.07) = 9.05, \text{ or 9 units}$$
$$\text{Reorder point} = \overline{d}L + \text{Safety stock}$$
$$= 2(18) + 9 = 45 \text{ units}$$

DECISION POINT

The Q system for the bird feeder operates as follows: Whenever the inventory position reaches 45 units, order the EOQ of 75 units. Various order quantities and safety stock levels can be used in a Q system. For example, management could specify a different order quantity (because of shipping constraints) or a different safety stock (because of storage limitations).

MyLab Operations Management

Tutor 4 in MyLab Operations Management provides a new example to determine the safety stock and the reorder point for a Q system.

Selecting the Reorder Point when Both Demand and Lead Time Are Variable

In practice, it is often the case that both the demand and the lead time are variable. Unfortunately, the equations for the safety stock and reorder point become more complicated. In the equation for safety stock below we make two simplifying assumptions. First, the demand distribution and the lead time distribution are measured in the same time units. For example, both demand and lead time are measured in weeks. Second, demand and lead time are *independent*. That is, demand per week is not affected by the length of the lead time.

$$\text{Safety stock} = z\sigma_{dLT}$$
$$R = (\text{Average weekly demand} \times \text{Average lead time in weeks}) + \text{Safety stock}$$
$$= \overline{d}\overline{L} + \text{Safety stock}$$

where

$$\overline{d} = \text{Average weekly or daily or monthly demand}$$
$$\overline{L} = \text{Average weekly or daily or monthly lead time}$$
$$\sigma_d = \text{Standard deviation of weekly or daily or monthly demand}$$
$$\sigma_{LT} = \text{Standard deviation of the lead time, and}$$
$$\sigma_{dLT} = \sqrt{\overline{L}\sigma_d^2 + \overline{d}^2\sigma_{LT}^2}$$

Now that we have determined the mean and standard deviation of the distribution of demand during lead time under these more complicated conditions, we can determine the safety stock and then select the reorder point as we did before for the case where the lead time was constant, as shown in Example 7.

EXAMPLE 7	Reorder Point for Variable Demand and Variable Lead Time

The Office Supply Shop estimates that the average demand for a popular ball-point pen is 12,000 pens per week with a standard deviation of 3,000 pens. The current inventory policy calls for replenishment orders of 156,000 pens. The average lead time from the distributor is 5 weeks, with a standard deviation of 2 weeks. If management wants a 95 percent cycle-service level, what should the reorder point be?

SOLUTION

We have $\overline{d} = 12,000$ pens, $\sigma_d = 3,000$ pens, $\overline{L} = 5$ weeks, and $\sigma_{LT} = 2$ weeks.

$$\sigma_{dLT} = \sqrt{\overline{L}\sigma_d^2 + \overline{d}^2\sigma_{LT}^2} = \sqrt{(5)(3,000)^2 + (12,000)^2(2)^2} = 24,919.87 \text{ pens}$$

Consult the body of the appendix on the normal distribution for 0.9500, which corresponds to a 95 percent cycle-service level. That value falls exactly in the middle of the tabular values of 0.9495 (for a z

value of 1.64) and 0.9505 (for a z value of 1.65). Consequently, we will use the more conservative value of 1.65. We calculate the safety stock and reorder point as follows:

$$\text{Safety stock} = z\sigma_{dLT} = (1.65)(24{,}919.87) = 41{,}117.79, \text{ or } 41{,}118 \text{ pens}$$

$$\text{Reorder point} = \overline{dL} + \text{Safety stock} = (12{,}000)(5) + 41{,}118 = 101{,}118 \text{ pens}$$

DECISION POINT

Whenever the stock of ball-point pens drops to 101,118, management should place another replenishment order of 156,000 pens to the distributor.

MyLab Operations Management

Sometimes, the theoretical distributions for demand and lead time are not known. In those cases, we can use simulation to find the distribution of demand during lead time using discrete distributions for demand and lead times. Simulation can also be used to estimate the performance of an inventory system. More discussion, and an example, can be found in MyLab Operations Management.

Systems Based on the Q System

Two systems based on the Q system are the two-bin system and the base-stock system.

visual system

A system that allows employees to place orders when inventory visibly reaches a certain marker.

two-bin system

A visual system version of the Q system in which a SKU's inventory is stored at two different locations.

Two-Bin System The concept of a Q system can be incorporated in a **visual system**, that is, a system that allows employees to place orders when inventory visibly reaches a certain marker. Visual systems are easy to administer because records are not kept on the current inventory position. The historical usage rate can simply be reconstructed from past purchase orders. Visual systems are intended for use with low-value SKUs that have a steady demand, such as nuts and bolts or office supplies. Overstocking is common, but the extra inventory holding cost is minimal because the items have relatively little value.

A visual system version of the Q system is the **two-bin system** in which a SKU's inventory is stored at two different locations. Inventory is first withdrawn from one bin. If the first bin is empty, the second bin provides backup to cover demand until a replenishment order arrives. An empty first bin signals the need to place a new order. Premade order forms placed near the bins let workers send one to purchasing or even directly to the supplier. When the new order arrives, the second bin is restored to its normal level and the rest is put in the first bin. The two-bin system operates like a Q system, with the normal level in the second bin being the reorder point R. The system also may be implemented with just one bin by marking the bin at the reorder point level.

base-stock system

An inventory control system that issues a replenishment order, Q, each time a withdrawal is made, for the same amount of the withdrawal.

Base-Stock System In its simplest form, the **base-stock system** issues a replenishment order, Q, each time a withdrawal is made, for the same amount as the withdrawal. This one-for-one replacement policy maintains the inventory position at a base-stock level equal to expected demand during the lead time plus safety stock. The base-stock level, therefore, is equivalent to the reorder point in a Q system. However, order quantities now vary to keep the inventory position at R at all times. Because this position is the lowest IP possible that will maintain a specified service level, the base-stock system may be used to minimize cycle inventory. More orders are placed, but each order is smaller. This system is appropriate for expensive items, such as replacement engines for jet airplanes. No more inventory is held than the maximum demand expected until a replacement order can be received.

Calculating Total Q System Costs

Total costs for the continuous review (Q) system is the sum of three cost components:

$$\text{Total cost} = \text{Annual cycle inventory holding cost} + \text{annual ordering cost}$$
$$+ \text{ annual safety stock holding cost}$$

$$C = \frac{Q}{2}(H) + \frac{D}{Q}(S) + (H)(\text{Safety stock})$$

The annual cycle-inventory holding cost and annual ordering cost are the same equations we used for computing the total annual cycle-inventory cost in Example 2. The annual cost of holding the safety stock is computed under the assumption that the safety stock is on hand at all times. Referring to Figure 10 in each order cycle, we will sometimes experience a demand greater than the average demand during lead time, and sometimes we will experience less. On average over the year, we can assume the safety stock will be on hand. See Solved Problems 4 and 6 at the end of this text for an example of calculating the total costs for a Q system.

Advantages of the Q System

Primary advantages of Q systems are the following:

1. The review frequency of each SKU may be individualized. Tailoring the review frequency to the SKU can reduce total ordering and holding costs.

2. Fixed lot sizes, if large enough, can result in quantity discounts. The firm's physical limitations, such as its truckload capacities, materials handling methods, and shelf space might also necessitate a fixed lot size.

3. The system requires low levels of safety stock for the amount of uncertainty in demands during the lead time.

Periodic Review System

An alternative inventory control system is the **periodic review (P) system**, sometimes called a *fixed interval reorder system* or *periodic reorder system*, in which an item's inventory position is reviewed periodically rather than continuously. Such a system can simplify delivery scheduling because it establishes a routine. A new order is always placed at the end of each review, and the time between orders (TBO) is fixed at P. Demand is a random variable, so total demand between reviews varies. In a P system, the lot size, Q, may change from one order to the next, but the time between orders is fixed. An example of a periodic review system is that of a soft-drink supplier making weekly rounds of grocery stores. Each week, the supplier reviews the store's inventory of soft drinks and restocks the store with enough items to meet demand and safety stock requirements until the next week.

Under a P system, four of the original EOQ assumptions are maintained: (1) no constraints are placed on the size of the lot, (2) the relevant costs are holding and ordering costs, (3) decisions for one SKU are independent of decisions for other SKUs, and (4) lead times are certain and supply is known. However, demand uncertainty is again allowed for. Figure 13 shows the periodic review system under these assumptions. The downward-sloping line again represents on-hand inventory. When the predetermined time, P, has elapsed since the last review, an order is placed to bring the inventory position, represented by the dashed line, up to the target inventory level, T. The lot size for the first review is Q_1, or the difference between inventory position IP_1 and T. As with the continuous review system, IP and OH differ only during the lead time. When the order arrives at the end of the lead time, OH and IP again are identical. Figure 13 shows that lot sizes vary from one order cycle to the next. Because the inventory position is lower at the second review, a greater quantity is needed to achieve an inventory level of T.

Example 8 shows how to determine the order quantity in a P system.

periodic review (P) system

A system in which an item's inventory position is reviewed periodically rather than continuously.

MyLab Operations Management Animation

▼ **FIGURE 13**
 P System when Demand Is Uncertain

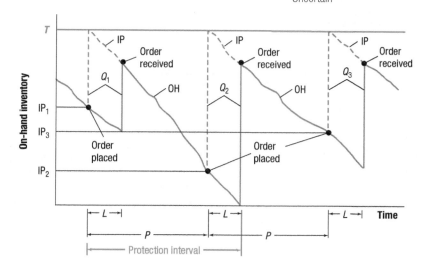

EXAMPLE 8 | Determining How Much to Order in a P System

Return to the distribution center (DC) in Example 5. Suppose that management wants to use a periodic review system for the Sony TV sets. The first review of the inventory is scheduled for the end of Day 2. Assume that all demands and receipts occur at the end of the day. On the scheduled review day, inventory replenishment orders are placed after the demands and receipts have been accounted for. The lead time is 5 days, and management has set $T = 620$ and $P = 6$ days. Given the demand schedule in the table provided, determine the order quantity (Q) using a P system.

SOLUTION

We use the following equations:

$$\text{Inventory Position (IP)} = \text{OH} + \text{SR} - \text{BO}$$

$$\text{Order Quantity (Q)} = T - \text{IP}$$

Day	Demand	OH	SR	BO	IP	Q
1	50	400			400	
2	60	340	**280** after ordering		340 before ordering 340 + **280** = 620 after ordering	620 − 340 = **280** (due Day 7)
3	80	260	**280**		260 + **280** = 540	
4	40	220	**280**		220 + **280** = 500	
5	75	145	**280**		145 + **280** = 425	
6	55	90	**280**		90 + **280** = 370	
7	95	90 + **280** − 95 = 275			275 + 0 = 275	
8	50	225	**395** after ordering		225 + 0 = 225 before ordering 225 + **395** = 620 after ordering	620 − 225 = **395** (due Day 13)
9	45	180	**395**		180 + **395** = 575	
10	30	150	**395**		150 + **395** = 545	
11	50	100	**395**		100 + **395** = 495	
12	60	40	**395**		40 + **395** = 435	
13	40	40 + **395** − 40 = 395			395 + 0 = **395**	
14	50	345	**275** after ordering		345 + 0 = 345 before ordering 345 + **275** = 620 after ordering	620 − 345 = **275** (due Day 19)

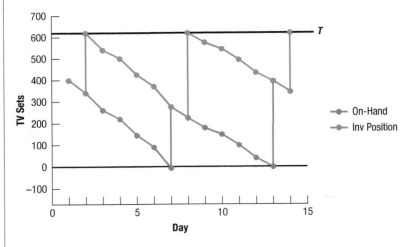

DECISION POINT

The figure shows the relationship between on-hand inventory and the inventory position. The DC did not experience any backorders because on Day 7 the replenishment order arrived in the nick of time. Notice that the order quantities vary in size while the time between orders remains a constant. Compare the operation of the *P* system in this example to the *Q* system in Example 5. The *Q* system requires constant monitoring to determine when the order point is reached. However, the average daily inventory is only 188 sets, compared to 226 sets for the *P* system. Granted, the *Q* system experienced backorders because of some unexpectedly large orders. Nonetheless, it is a general rule that to gain the benefits of periodic ordering, the *P* system requires more inventory for the same level of protection against stockouts or backorders. We will see why this is the case as we develop the parameters for the *P* system.

Selecting the Time Between Reviews

To run a *P* system, managers must make two decisions: the length of time between reviews, *P*, and the target inventory level, *T*. Let us first consider the time between reviews, *P*. It can be any convenient interval, such as each Friday or every other Friday. Another option is to base *P* on the cost trade-offs of the EOQ. In other words, *P* can be set equal to the average time between orders for the economic order quantity, or TBO_{EOQ}. Because demand is variable, some orders will be larger than the EOQ and some will be smaller. However, over an extended period of time, the average lot size should be close to the EOQ. If other models are used to determine the lot size, we divide the lot size chosen by the annual demand, D, and use this ratio as P. It will be expressed as the fraction of a year between orders, which can be converted into months, weeks, or days as needed.

Selecting the Target Inventory Level when Demand Is Variable and Lead Time Is Constant

Now, let us calculate the target inventory level, T, when demand is variable but the lead time is constant. Figure 13 reveals that an order must be large enough to make the inventory position, IP, last beyond the next review, which is P time periods away. The checker must wait P periods to revise, correct, and reestablish the inventory position. Then, a new order is placed, but it does not arrive until after the lead time, L. Therefore, as Figure 13 shows, a protection interval of $P + L$ periods is needed. A fundamental difference between the Q and P systems is the length of time needed for stockout protection. A Q system needs stockout protection only during the lead time because orders can be placed as soon as they are needed and will be received L periods later. A P system, however, needs stockout protection for the longer $P + L$ protection interval because orders are placed only at fixed intervals, and the inventory is not checked until the next designated review time.

As with the Q system, we need to develop the appropriate distribution of demand during the protection interval to specify the system fully. In a P system, we must develop the distribution of demand for $P + L$ time periods. The target inventory level T must equal the expected demand during the protection interval of $P + L$ periods, plus enough safety stock to protect against demand uncertainty over this same protection interval. We assume that lead time is constant and that demand in one period is independent of demand in the next period. Thus, the average demand during the protection interval is $\overline{d}(P + L)$, or

$$T = \overline{d}(P + L) + \text{Safety stock for the protection interval}$$

We compute safety stock for a P system much as we did for the Q system. However, the safety stock must cover demand uncertainty for a longer period of time. When using a normal probability distribution, we multiply the desired standard deviations to implement the cycle-service level, z, by the standard deviation of demand during the protection interval, σ_{P+L}. The value of z is the same as for a Q system with the same cycle-service level. Thus,

$$\text{Safety stock} = z\sigma_{P+L}$$

Based on our earlier logic for calculating σ_{dLT} we know that the standard deviation of the distribution of demand during the protection interval is

$$\sigma_{P+L} = \sigma_d\sqrt{P + L}$$

Because a P system requires safety stock to cover demand uncertainty over a longer time period than a Q system, a P system requires more safety stock; that is, σ_{P+L} exceeds σ_{dLT}. Hence, to gain the convenience of a P system requires that overall inventory levels be somewhat higher than those for a Q system. Example 9 demonstrates the calculation of P and T for the bird feeder example.

Large, fixed-capacity modes of transportation require defined schedules of operation. Such a situation supports the use of periodic review systems. Here ocean vessels await loads of petrochemicals at the Vopak terminal in the Port of Rotterdam.

Horizons WWP/TRVL/Alamy Stock Photo

EXAMPLE 9	Calculating *P* and *T*

Again, let us return to the bird feeder example. Recall that demand for the bird feeder is normally distributed with a mean of 18 units per week and a standard deviation in weekly demand of 5 units. The lead time is 2 weeks, and the business operates 52 weeks per year. The Q system developed in Example 6 called for an EOQ of 75 units and a safety stock of 9 units for a cycle-service level of 90 percent. What is the equivalent P system? Answers are to be rounded to the nearest integer.

MyLab Operations Management

Tutor 5 in MyLab Operations Management provides a new example to determine the review interval and the target inventory for a *P* system.

SOLUTION

We first define D and then P. Here, P is the time between reviews, expressed in weeks because the data are expressed as demand *per week*:

$$D = (18 \text{ units/week})(52 \text{ weeks/year}) = 936 \text{ units}$$

$$P = \frac{EOQ}{D}(52) = \frac{75}{936}(52) = 4.2, \text{ or } 4 \text{ weeks}$$

With $\bar{d} = 18$ units per week, an alternative approach is to calculate P by dividing the EOQ by $\bar{d}$ to get $75/18 = 4.2$, or 4 weeks. Either way, we would review the bird feeder inventory every 4 weeks. We now find the standard deviation of demand over the protection interval ($P + L = 6$):

$$\sigma_{P+L} = \sigma_d\sqrt{P + L} = 5\sqrt{6} = 12.25 \text{ units}$$

Before calculating T, we also need a z value. For a 90 percent cycle-service level, $z = 1.28$ (see the appendix on the normal distribution). The safety stock becomes

$$\text{Safety stock} = z\sigma_{P+L} = 1.28(12.25) = 15.68, \text{ or } 16 \text{ units}$$

We now solve for T:

$$T = \text{Average demand during the protection interval} + \text{Safety stock}$$
$$= \bar{d}(P + L) + \text{Safety stock}$$
$$= (18 \text{ units/week})(6 \text{ weeks}) + 16 \text{ units} = 124 \text{ units}$$

DECISION POINT

Every 4 weeks we would order the number of units needed to bring inventory position IP (counting the new order) up to the target inventory level of 124 units. The P system requires 16 units in safety stock, while the Q system only needs 9 units. If cost were the only criterion, the Q system would be the choice for the bird feeder. As we discuss later, other factors may sway the decision in favor of the P system.

Selecting the Target Inventory Level when Demand and Lead Time Are Variable

A useful approach for finding P and T in practice is simulation. Given discrete probability distributions for demand and lead time, simulation can be used to estimate the demand during the protection interval distribution. The *Demand During the Protection Interval Simulator* in OM Explorer can be used to determine the distribution. Once determined, the distribution can be used to select a value for T, given a desired cycle-service level. More discussion, and an example, can be found in MyLab Operations Management.

MyLab Operations Management

Systems Based on the *P* System

Two systems based on the P system are the single-bin system and the optional replenishment system.

single-bin system

A system of inventory control in which a maximum level is marked on the storage shelf or bin, and the inventor is brought up to the mark periodically.

Single-Bin System   The concept of a P system can be translated into a simple visual system of inventory control. In the **single-bin system**, a maximum level is marked on the storage shelf or bin, and the inventory is brought up to the mark periodically—say, once a week. The single bin may be, for example, a gasoline storage tank at a service station or a storage bin for small parts at a manufacturing plant.

optional replenishment system

A system used to review the inventory position at fixed time intervals and, if the position has dropped to (or below) a predetermined level, to place a variable-sized order to cover expected needs.

Optional Replenishment System   Sometimes called the optional review, min–max, or (s, S) system, the **optional replenishment system** is much like the P system. It is used to review the inventory position at fixed time intervals and, if the position has dropped to (or below) a predetermined level, to place a variable-sized order to cover expected needs. The new order is large enough to bring the inventory position up to a target inventory, similar to T for the P system. However, orders are not placed after a review unless the inventory position has dropped to the predetermined minimum level. The minimum level acts as the reorder point R does in a Q system. If the target is 100 and the minimum level is 60, the minimum order size is 40 (or $100 - 60$). Because continuous reviews need not be made, this system is particularly attractive when both review and ordering costs are high.

Calculating Total *P* System Costs

The total costs for the *P* system are the sum of the same three cost elements for the *Q* system. The differences are in the calculation of the order quantity and the safety stock. As shown in Figure 13, the average order quantity will be the average consumption of inventory during the *P* periods between orders. Consequently, $Q = \bar{d}P$. Total costs for the *P* system are

$$C = \frac{\bar{d}P}{2}(H) + \frac{D}{\bar{d}P}(S) + (H)(\text{Safety stock})$$

See Solved Problem 5 at the end of this text for an example of calculating total *P* system costs.

Advantages of the *P* System

Primary advantages of *P* systems are the following:

1. The system is convenient because replenishments are made at fixed intervals. Fixed replenishment intervals allow for standardized pickup and delivery times. In contrast, individual items are ordered on their own best intervals with the *Q* system, which can differ widely.

2. Orders for multiple items from the same supplier can be combined into a single purchase order. This approach reduces ordering and transportation costs and can result in a price break from the supplier.

3. The inventory position, IP, needs to be known only when a review is made (not continuously, as in a *Q* system). However, this advantage is moot for firms using computerized record-keeping systems, in which a transaction is reported upon each receipt or withdrawal. When inventory records are always current, the system is called a **perpetual inventory system**.

Both the *Q* system and the *P* system have their advantages. Indeed, the advantages for one system become the disadvantages for the other. In conclusion, the choice between *Q* and *P* systems is not clear cut. Which system is better depends on the relative importance of its advantages in various situations.

perpetual inventory system

A system of inventory control in which the inventory records are always current.

LEARNING GOALS IN REVIEW

Learning Goal	Guidelines for Review	MyLab Operations Management Resources
1 Identify the advantages, disadvantages, and costs of holding inventory.	We cover these important aspects of inventories in the section "Inventory Trade-offs". Focus on the pressures for small or large inventories and Figure 1.	**Video:** Inventory Management at Crayola
2 Define the different types of inventory and the roles they play in supply chains.	The section "Types of Inventory," explains each type of inventory and provides an example in Figure 2. Example 1 and Solved Problem 1 show how to estimate inventory levels. Be sure to understand the distinction between independent and dependent inventories.	**OM Explorer Tutor:** 1: Estimating Inventory Levels
3 Explain the tactics for reducing inventories in supply chains.	See the section "Inventory Reduction Tactics," for important approaches to managing inventory levels. The main tools for eliminating unneeded inventories are inventory control systems.	
4 Use ABC analysis to identify the items deserving most attention and tightest inventory control.	The section "ABC Analysis," shows a simple approach to categorizing inventory items for ease of management oversight. Figure 4 has an example. Solved Problem 2 demonstrates the calculations.	**OM Explorer Tutor:** 2: ABC Analysis **POM for Windows:** ABC Analysis

Learning Goal	Guidelines for Review	MyLab Operations Management Resources
5 Calculate the economic order quantity and apply it to various situations.	See the section "Economic Order Quantity," for a complete discussion of the EOQ model. Focus on Figures 5, 6 , and 7 to see how the EOQ model affects inventory levels under the standard assumptions and how the EOQ provides the lowest cost solution. Review Examples 2 and 3 and Solved Problem 3 for help in calculating the total costs of various lot-size choices. Table 1 reveals important managerial insights from the EOQ. See also the Active Model Exercise.	**Active Model:** 1: Economic Order Quantity **OM Explorer Tutor:** 3: Finding EOQ and Total Cost **POM for Windows:** Economic Order Quantity (EOQ) Model **Tutor Exercise:** 1: Finding EOQ; Safety Stock; *R, P, T* at Bison College Bookstore
6 Determine the order quantity and reorder point for a continuous review inventory control system.	The section "Continuous Review System," builds the essence of the Q system from basic principles to more realistic assumptions. Be sure to understand Figures 10 and 12. Examples 4, 5, and 6 and Solved Problems 4 and 6 show how to determine the parameters Q and R under various assumptions.	**OM Explorer Solvers:** Inventory Systems Designer; Demand During Protection Interval Simulator; Q System Simulator **OM Explorer Tutor:** 4: Finding the Safety Stock and R **Tutor Exercise:** 1: Finding EOQ; Safety Stock; *R,P,T* at Bison College Bookstore **Tutorial on Inventory Management Systems:** Using Simulation to Develop Inventory Management Systems **Advanced Problems:** Office Supply Shop Simulation; Floral Shop Simulation; Simquick Simulation Exercise
7 Determine the review interval and target inventory level for a periodic review inventory control system.	We summarize the key concepts in the section "Periodic Review System". Figure 13 shows how a P system operates while Examples 8 and 9 and Solved Problem 5 demonstrate how to calculate the parameters P and T.	**OM Explorer Solver:** Inventory Systems Designer; Demand During Protection Interval Simulator **OM Explorer Tutor:** 5: Calculating P and T **Tutor Exercise:** 1: Finding EOQ; Safety Stock; *R,P,T* at Bison College Bookstore **Tutorial on Inventory Management Systems:** Using Simulation to Develop Inventory Management Systems **Advanced Problem:** Grocery Store Simulation; Simquick Simulation Exercise

Key Equations

Types of Inventory

1. Average cycle inventory: $\dfrac{Q}{2}$

2. Pipeline inventory: $\overline{D}_L = \overline{d}L$

Economic Order Quantity

3. Total annual cycle-inventory cost = Annual holding cost + Annual ordering or setup cost:

$$C = \frac{Q}{2}(H) + \frac{D}{Q}(S)$$

4. Economic order quantity:

$$\text{EOQ} = \sqrt{\frac{2DS}{H}}$$

5. Time between orders, expressed in weeks:

$$\text{TBO}_{\text{EOQ}} = \frac{\text{EOQ}}{D}(52 \text{ weeks/year})$$

Continuous Review System

6. Inventory position = On-hand inventory + Scheduled receipts − Backorders:

$$IP = OH + SR - BO$$

7. Continuous review system:

Protection interval = Lead time (L)

Standard deviation of demand during the lead time (constant L) = $\sigma_{dLT} = \sigma_d\sqrt{L}$

Standard deviation of demand during the lead time (variable L) = $\sigma_{dLT} = \sqrt{\bar{L}\sigma_d^2 + \bar{d}^2\sigma_{LT}^2}$

Safety stock = $z\sigma_{dLT}$

Reorder point R for constant lead time = $\bar{d}L$ + Safety stock

Reorder point R for variable lead time = $\bar{d}\bar{L}$ + Safety stock

Order quantity = EOQ

Replenishment rule: Order EOQ units when IP ≤ R

Total Q system cost: $C = \dfrac{Q}{2}(H) + \dfrac{D}{Q}(S) + (H)(\text{Safety stock})$

Periodic Review System

1. Periodic review system:

Review interval = Time between orders = P

Protection interval = Time between orders + Lead time = $P + L$

Standard deviation of demand during the protection interval $\sigma_{P+L} = \sigma_d\sqrt{P + L}$

Safety stock = $z\sigma_{P+L}$

Target inventory level (T) = Average demand during the protection interval + Safety stock

$$= \bar{d}(P + L) + \text{Safety stock}$$

Order quantity: Target inventory level − Inventory position = $T - IP$

Replenishment rule: Every P time periods, order $T - IP$ units

Total P system cost: $C = \dfrac{\bar{d}P}{2}(H) + \dfrac{D}{\bar{d}P}(S) + (H)(\text{Safety stock})$

Key Terms

ABC analysis
anticipation inventory
base-stock system
continuous review (Q) system
cycle counting
cycle inventory
cycle-service level
dependent demand items
economic order quantity (EOQ)
finished goods (FG)
independent demand items
inventory
inventory holding cost

inventory management
inventory position (IP)
lot size
lot sizing
open orders
optional replenishment system
ordering cost
periodic review (P) system
perpetual inventory system
pipeline inventory
protection interval
quantity discount
raw materials (RM)

reorder point (R)
reorder point (ROP) system
repeatability
safety stock inventory
scheduled receipts (SR)
service level
setup cost
single-bin system
stock-keeping unit (SKU)
time between orders (TBO)
two-bin system
visual system
work-in-process (WIP)

Solved Problem 1

A distribution center experiences an average weekly demand of 50 units for one of its items. The product is valued at $650 per unit. Inbound shipments from the factory warehouse average 350 units. Average lead time (including ordering delays and transit time) is 2 weeks. The distribution center operates 52 weeks per year; it carries a 1-week supply of inventory as safety stock and no anticipation inventory. What is the value of the average aggregate inventory being held by the distribution center?

SOLUTION

Type of Inventory	Calculation of Aggregate Average Inventory	
Cycle	$\dfrac{Q}{2} = \dfrac{350}{2}$	= 175 units
Safety stock	1-week supply	= 50 units
Anticipation	None	
Pipeline	$\bar{d}L$ = (50 units/week) (2 weeks)	= 100 units
	Average aggregate inventory	= 325 units
	Value of aggregate inventory	= $650(325)
		= $211,250

Solved Problem 2

MyLab Operations Management

Tutor 2 in MyLab Operations Management provides a new example of the application of ABC analysis.

Booker's Book Bindery divides SKUs into three classes according to their dollar usage. Calculate the usage values of the following SKUs and determine which is most likely to be classified as class A.

SOLUTION

The annual dollar usage for each SKU is determined by multiplying the annual usage quantity by the value per unit. As shown in Figure 14, the SKUs are then sorted by annual dollar usage, in declining order. Finally, A–B and B–C class lines are drawn roughly, according to the guidelines presented in the text. Here, class A includes only one SKU (signatures), which represents only 1/7, or 14 percent, of the SKUs but accounts for 83 percent of annual dollar usage. Class B includes the next two SKUs, which taken together represent 28 percent of the SKUs and account for 13 percent of annual dollar usage. The final four SKUs, class C, represent over half the number of SKUs but only 4 percent of total annual dollar usage.

SKU Number	Description	Quantity Used per Year	Unit Value ($)
1	Boxes	500	3.00
2	Cardboard (square feet)	18,000	0.02
3	Cover stock	10,000	0.75
4	Glue (gallons)	75	40.00
5	Inside covers	20,000	0.05
6	Reinforcing tape (meters)	3,000	0.15
7	Signatures	150,000	0.45

SKU Number	Description	Quantity Used per Year		Unit Value ($)		Annual Dollar Usage ($)
1	Boxes	500	×	3.00	=	1,500
2	Cardboard (square feet)	18,000	×	0.02	=	360
3	Cover stock	10,000	×	0.75	=	7,500
4	Glue (gallons)	75	×	40.00	=	3,000
5	Inside covers	20,000	×	0.05	=	1,000
6	Reinforcing tape (meters)	3,000	×	0.15	=	450
7	Signatures	150,000	×	0.45	=	67,500
					Total	81,310

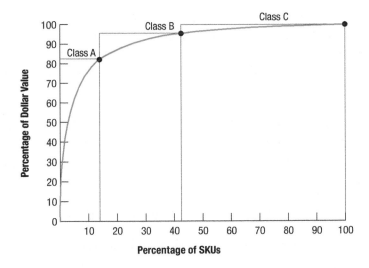

SKU #	Description	Qty Used/Year	Value	Dollar Usage	Pct of Total	Cumulative % of Dollar Value	Cumulative % of SKU	Class
7	Signatures	150,000	$0.45	$67,500	83.0%	83.0%	14.3%	A
3	Cover stock	10,000	$0.75	$7,500	9.2%	92.2%	28.6%	B
4	Glue	75	$40.00	$3,000	3.7%	95.9%	42.9%	B
1	Boxes	500	$3.00	$1,500	1.8%	97.8%	57.1%	C
5	Inside covers	20,000	$0.05	$1,000	1.2%	99.0%	71.4%	C
6	Reinforcing tape	3,000	$0.15	$450	0.6%	99.6%	85.7%	C
2	Cardboard	18,000	$0.02	$360	0.4%	100.0%	100.0%	C
Total				$81,310				

◄ **FIGURE 14**
Annual Dollar Usage for Class A, B, and C SKUs Using Tutor 2

Solved Problem 3

Nelson's Hardware Store stocks a 19.2-volt cordless drill that is a popular seller. Annual demand is 5,000 units, the ordering cost is $15, and the inventory holding cost is $4/unit/year.

a. What is the economic order quantity?

b. What is the total annual cost for this inventory item?

SOLUTION

a. The order quantity is

$$\text{EOQ} = \sqrt{\frac{2DS}{H}} = \sqrt{\frac{2(5,000)(\$15)}{\$4}} = \sqrt{37,500}$$
$$= 193.65, \text{ or } 194 \text{ drills}$$

b. The total annual cost is

$$C = \frac{Q}{2}(H) + \frac{D}{Q}(S) = \frac{194}{2}(\$4) + \frac{5,000}{194}(\$15) = \$774.60$$

Solved Problem 4

MyLab Operations
Manageament Video

A regional distributor purchases discontinued appliances from various suppliers and then sells them on demand to retailers in the region. The distributor operates 5 days per week, 52 weeks per year. Only when it is open for business can orders be received. The following data are estimated for a countertop mixer:

Average daily demand $(\overline{d})$ = 100 mixers

Standard deviation of daily demand (σ_d) = 30 mixers

Lead time (L) = 3 days

Holding cost (H) = \$9.40/unit/year

Ordering cost (S) = \$35/order

Cycle-service level = 92 percent

The distributor uses a continuous review Q system.

a. What order quantity, Q, and reorder point, R, should be used?

b. What is the total annual cost of the system?

c. If on-hand inventory is 40 units, one open order for 440 mixers is pending, and no back-orders exist, should a new order be placed?

SOLUTION

a. Annual demand is

$$D = (5 \text{ days/week})(52 \text{ weeks/year})(100 \text{ mixers/day}) = 26,000 \text{ mixers/year}$$

The order quantity is

$$\text{EOQ} = \sqrt{\frac{2DS}{H}} = \sqrt{\frac{2(26,000)(\$35)}{\$9.40}} = \sqrt{193,167} = 440.02, \text{ or } 440 \text{ mixers}$$

The standard deviation of the distribution of demand during lead time is

$$\sigma_{dLT} = \sigma_d\sqrt{L} = 30\sqrt{3} = 51.96$$

A 92 percent cycle-service level corresponds to $z = 1.41$ (see the appendix on the normal distribution). Therefore,

$$\text{Safety stock} = z\sigma_{dLT} = 1.41(51.96 \text{ mixers}) = 73.26, \text{ or } 73 \text{ mixers}$$
$$\text{Average demand during the lead time} = \overline{d}L = 100(3) = 300 \text{ mixers}$$
$$\text{Reorder point } R = \text{Average demand during the lead time} + \text{Safety stock}$$
$$= 300 \text{ mixers} + 73 \text{ mixers} = 373 \text{ mixers}$$

With a continuous review system, $Q = 440$ and $R = 373$.

b. The total annual cost for the Q systems is

$$C = \frac{Q}{2}(H) + \frac{D}{Q}(S) + (H)(\text{Safety stock})$$

$$C = \frac{440}{2}(\$9.40) + \frac{26,000}{440}(35) + (\$9.40)(73) = \$4,822.38$$

c. Inventory position = On-hand inventory + Scheduled receipts − Backorders

$$\text{IP} = \text{OH} + \text{SR} - \text{BO} = 40 + 440 - 0 = 480 \text{ mixers}$$

Because IP (480) exceeds R (373), do not place a new order.

Solved Problem 5

Suppose that a periodic review (P) system is used at the distributor in Solved Problem 4, but otherwise the data are the same.

a. Calculate the P (in workdays, rounded to the nearest day) that gives approximately the same number of orders per year as the EOQ.

b. What is the target inventory level, T? Compare the P system to the Q system in Solved Problem 4.

c. What is the total annual cost of the P system?

d. It is time to review the item. On-hand inventory is 40 mixers; receipt of 440 mixers is scheduled, and no backorders exist. How much should be reordered?

SOLUTION

a. The time between orders is

$$P = \frac{\text{EOQ}}{D} \,(260 \text{ days/year}) = \frac{440}{26{,}000}\,(260) = 4.4, \text{ or } 4 \text{ days}$$

b. Figure 15 shows that $T = 812$ and safety stock $= (1.41)(79.37) = 111.91$, or about 112 mixers. The corresponding Q system for the countertop mixer requires less safety stock.

c. The total annual cost of the P system is

$$C = \frac{\bar{d}P}{2}\,(H) + \frac{D}{\bar{d}P}\,(S) + (H)(\text{Safety stock})$$

$$C = \frac{(100)(4)}{2}\,(\$9.40) + \frac{26{,}000}{(100)(4)}\,(\$35) + (\$9.40)(1.41)(79.37)$$

$$= \$5{,}207.80$$

d. Inventory position is the amount on hand plus scheduled receipts minus backorders, or

$$\text{IP} = \text{OH} + \text{SR} - \text{BO} = 40 + 440 - 0 = 480 \text{ mixers}$$

The order quantity is the target inventory level minus the inventory position, or

$$Q = T - \text{IP} = 812 \text{ mixers} - 480 \text{ mixers} = 332 \text{ mixers}$$

An order for 332 mixers should be placed.

Continuous Review (Q) System		Periodic Review (P) System		
z	1.41	Time Between Reviews (P)	4.00	Days
Safety Stock	73		☑ Enter manually	
Reorder Point	373	Standard Deviation of Demand During Protection Interval	79.37	
Annual Cost	$4,822.38	Safety Stock	112	
		Average Demand During Protection Interval	700	
		Target Inventory Level (T)	812	
		Annual Cost	$5,207.80	

◀ FIGURE 15
OM Explorer Solver for Inventory Systems

Solved Problem 6

Grey Wolf Lodge is a popular 500-room hotel in the North Woods. Managers need to keep close tabs on all room service items, including a special pine-scented bar soap. The daily demand for the soap is 275 bars, with a standard deviation of 30 bars. Ordering cost is $10 and the inventory holding cost is $0.30/bar/year. The lead time from the supplier is 5 days, with a standard deviation of 1 day. The lodge is open 365 days a year.

a. What is the economic order quantity for the bar of soap?

b. What should the reorder point be for the bar of soap if management wants to have a 99 percent cycle-service level?

c. What is the total annual cost for the bar of soap, assuming a Q system will be used?

SOLUTION

a. We have $D = (275)(365) = 100,375$ bars of soap; $S = \$10$; and $H = \$0.30$. The EOQ for the bar of soap is

$$\text{EOQ} = \sqrt{\frac{2DS}{H}} = \sqrt{\frac{2(100,375)(\$10)}{\$0.30}} = \sqrt{6,691,666.7}$$

$$= 2,586.83, \text{ or } 2,587 \text{ bars}$$

b. We have $\bar{d} = 275$ bars/day, $\sigma_d = 30$ bars, $\bar{L} = 5$ days, and $\sigma_{LT} = 1$ day.

$$\sigma_{dLT} = \sqrt{\bar{L}\sigma_d^2 + \bar{d}^2\sigma_{LT}^2} = \sqrt{(5)(30)^2 + (275)^2(1)^2} = 283.06 \text{ bars}$$

Consult the body of the appendix on the normal distribution for 0.9900, which corresponds to a 99 percent cycle-service level. The closest value is 0.9901, which corresponds to a z value of 2.33. We calculate the safety stock and reorder point as follows:

$$\text{Safety stock} = z\sigma_{dLT} = (2.33)(283.06) = 659.53, \text{ or } 660 \text{ bars}$$

$$\text{Reorder point} = \bar{d}L + \text{Safety stock} = (275)(5) + 600 = 2,035 \text{ bars}$$

c. The total annual cost for the Q system is

$$C = \frac{Q}{2}(H) + \frac{D}{Q}(S) + (H)(\text{Safety stock})$$

$$= \frac{2,587}{2}(\$0.30) + \frac{100,375}{2,587}(\$10) + (\$0.30)(660) = \$974.05$$

Discussion Questions

1. What is the relationship between inventory and the nine competitive priorities Suppose that two competing manufacturers, Company H and Company L, are similar except that Company H has much higher investments in raw materials, work-in-process, and finished goods inventory than Company L. In which of the nine competitive priorities will Company H have an advantage?

2. Suppose that a large discount retailer with a lot of purchasing power in a supply chain requires that all suppliers incorporate a new information system that will reduce the cost of placing orders between the retailer and its suppliers as well as between the suppliers and their suppliers. Suppose also that order quantities and lead times are related; the smaller the order quantity the shorter the lead time from suppliers. Assume that all members of the supply chain use a continuous review system and EOQ order quantities. Explain the implications of the new information system for the supply chain in general and the inventory systems of the supply chain members in particular.

3. Will organizations ever get to the point where they will no longer need inventories? Why or why not?

Problems

The OM Explorer and POM for Windows software is available to all students. Go to **http://www.pearsonhighered.com/krajewski** to download these computer packages. If you purchased MyLab Operations Management you also have access to Active Models software and significant help in doing the following problems. Check with your instructor on how best to use these resources. In many cases, the instructor wants you to understand how to do the calculations by hand. At the least, the software provides a check on your calculations. When calculations are particularly complex and the goal is interpreting the results in making decisions, the software replaces entirely the manual calculations.

Types of Inventory

1. A part is produced in lots of 1,000 units. It is assembled from two components worth $50 total. The value added in production (for labor and variable overhead) is $60 per unit, bringing total costs per completed unit to $110. The average lead time for the part is 6 weeks and annual demand is 3,800 units, based on 50 business weeks per year.

   a. How many units of the part are held, on average, in cycle inventory? What is the dollar value of this inventory?

   b. How many units of the part are held, on average, in pipeline inventory? What is the dollar value of this inventory? (*Hint:* Assume that the typical part in pipeline inventory is 50 percent completed. Thus, half the labor and variable overhead cost has been added, bringing the unit cost to $80, or $50 + $60/2).

2. Prince Electronics, a manufacturer of consumer electronic goods, has five distribution centers in different regions of the country. For one of its products, a high-speed modem priced at $350 per unit, the average weekly demand at *each* distribution center is 75 units.

   Average shipment size to each distribution center is 400 units, and average lead time for delivery is 2 weeks. Each distribution center carries 2 weeks' supply as safety stock but holds no anticipation inventory.

   a. On average, how many dollars of pipeline inventory will be in transit to each distribution center?

   b. How much total inventory (cycle, safety, and pipeline) does Prince hold for all five distribution centers?

3. Terminator, Inc. manufactures a motorcycle part in lots of 250 units. The raw materials cost for the part is $150, and the value added in manufacturing 1 unit from its components is $300, for a total cost per completed unit of $450. The lead time to make the part is 3 weeks, and the annual demand is 4,000 units. Assume 50 working weeks per year.

   a. How many units of the part are held, on average, as cycle inventory? What is its value?

   b. How many units of the part are held, on average, as pipeline inventory? What is its value?

Inventory Reduction Tactics

4. Ruby-Star Incorporated is considering two different vendors for one of its top-selling products, which has an average weekly demand of 50 units and is valued at $75 per unit. Inbound shipments from vendor 1 will average 350 units with an average lead time (including ordering delays and transit time) of 2 weeks. Inbound shipments from vendor 2 will average 500 units with an average lead time of 1 week. Ruby-Star operates 52 weeks per year; it carries a 2-week supply of inventory as safety stock and no anticipation inventory.

   a. What would be the average aggregate inventory value of this product if Ruby-Star used vendor 1 exclusively?

   b. What would be the average aggregate inventory value of this product if Ruby-Star used vendor 2 exclusively?

   c. How would your analysis change if average weekly demand increased to 100 units per week?

5. Haley Photocopying purchases paper from an out-of-state vendor. Average weekly demand for paper is 150 cartons per week for which Haley pays $15 per carton. Inbound shipments from the vendor average 1,000 cartons with an average lead time of 3 weeks. Haley operates 52 weeks per year; it carries a 4-week supply of inventory as safety stock and no anticipation inventory. The vendor has recently announced that they will be building a facility near Haley Photocopying that will reduce lead time to 1 week. Further, they will be able to reduce shipments to 200 cartons. Haley believes that they will be able to reduce safety stock to a 1-week supply. What impact will these changes make to Haley's average inventory level and its average aggregate inventory value?

ABC Analysis

6. Oakwood Hospital is considering using ABC analysis to classify laboratory SKUs into three categories: those that will be delivered daily from their supplier (Class A items), those that will be controlled using a continuous review system (B items), and those that will be held in a two-bin system (C items). The following table shows the annual dollar usage for a sample of eight SKUs. Rank the SKUs, and assign them to their appropriate category.

SKU Code	Dollar Value	Annual Usage
1	$0.01	1,200
2	$0.03	120,000
3	$0.45	100
4	$1.00	44,000
5	$4.50	900
6	$0.90	350
7	$0.30	70,000
8	$1.50	200

7. Southern Markets, Inc. is considering the use of ABC analysis to focus on the most critical SKUs in its inventory. Currently, there are approximately 20,000 different SKUs with a total dollar usage of $10,000,000 per year.

   a. What would you expect to be the number of SKUs and the total annual dollar usage for A items, B items, and C items at Southern Markets, Inc.?

   b. The following table provides a random sample of the unit values and annual demands of eight SKUs. Categorize these SKUs as A, B, and C items.

SKU Code	Unit Value	Demand (Units)
A104	$2.10	2,500
D205	$2.50	30
X104	$0.85	350
U404	$0.25	250
L205	$4.75	20

SKU Code	Unit Value	Demand (Units)
S104	$0.02	4,000
X205	$0.35	1,020
L104	$4.25	50

8. New Wave Shelving's inventory manager would like to start using an ABC inventory classification system. The following table shows the annual inventory usage of all the 19 component items that the company holds. Assign them to their appropriate category.

SKU #	Description	Quantity Used per Year	Dollar Value per Unit
a-1	Steel panel	500	$ 25.00
a-2	Steel bumper	750	$ 135.00
a-3	Steel clamp	3,500	$ 5.00
a-4	Steel brace	200	$ 20.00
b-1	Copper coil	1,250	$ 260.00
b-2	Copper panel	1,250	$ 50.00
b-3	Copper brace 1	250	$ 75.00
b-4	Copper brace 2	150	$ 125.00
c-1	Rubber bumper	8,500	$ 0.75
c-2	Rubber foot	6,500	$ 0.75
c-3	Rubber seal 1	1,500	$ 1.00
c-4	Rubber seal 2	3,500	$ 1.00
c-5	Rubber seal 3	1,200	$ 2.25
d-1	Plastic fastener kit	1,500	$ 3.50
d-2	Plastic handle	2,000	$ 0.75
d-3	Plastic panel	1,000	$ 6.50
d-4	Plastic bumper	2,000	$ 1.25
d-5	Plastic coil	450	$ 6.00
d-6	Plastic foot	6,000	$ 0.25

Economic Order Quantity

9. Yellow Press, Inc. buys paper in 1,500-pound rolls for printing. Annual demand is 2,500 rolls. The cost per roll is $800, and the annual holding cost is 15 percent of the cost. Each order costs $50 to process.

   a. How many rolls should Yellow Press, Inc. order at a time?

   b. What is the time between orders?

10. Babble, Inc. buys 400 blank cassette tapes per month for use in producing foreign language courseware.

The ordering cost is $12.50. Holding cost is $0.12 per cassette per year.

   a. How many tapes should Babble, Inc. order at a time?

   b. What is the time between orders?

11. At Dot Com, a large retailer of popular books, demand is constant at 32,000 books per year. The cost of placing an order to replenish stock is $10, and the annual cost of holding is $4 per book. Stock is received 5 working

days after an order has been placed. No backordering is allowed. Assume 300 working days a year.

a. What is Dot Com's optimal order quantity?

b. What is the optimal number of orders per year?

c. What is the optimal interval (in working days) between orders?

d. What is demand during the lead time?

e. What is the reorder point?

f. What is the inventory position immediately after an order has been placed?

12. Leaky Pipe, a local retailer of plumbing supplies, faces demand for one of its SKUs at a constant rate of 30,000 units per year. It costs Leaky Pipe $10 to process an order to replenish stock and $1 per unit per year to carry the item in stock. Stock is received 4 working days after an order is placed. No backordering is allowed. Assume 300 working days a year.

a. What is Leaky Pipe's optimal order quantity?

b. What is the optimal number of orders per year?

c. What is the optimal interval (in working days) between orders?

d. What is the demand during the lead time?

e. What is the reorder point?

f. What is the inventory position immediately after an order has been placed?

Continuous Review System

13. Sam's Cat Hotel operates 52 weeks per year, 6 days per week, and uses a continuous review inventory system. It purchases kitty litter for $11.70 per bag. The following information is available about these bags.

Demand = 90 bags/week

Order cost = $54/order

Annual holding cost = 27 percent of cost

Desired cycle-service level = 80 percent

Lead time = 3 weeks (18 working days)

Standard deviation of *weekly* demand = 15 bags

Current on-hand inventory is 320 bags, with no open orders or backorders.

a. What is the EOQ? What would be the average time between orders (in weeks)?

b. What should R be?

c. An inventory withdrawal of 10 bags was just made. Is it time to reorder?

d. The store currently uses a lot size of 500 bags (i.e., $Q = 500$). What is the annual holding cost of this policy? Annual ordering cost? Without calculating the EOQ, how can you conclude from these two calculations that the current lot size is too large?

e. What would be the annual cost saved by shifting from the 500-bag lot size to the EOQ?

14. Consider again the kitty litter ordering policy for Sam's Cat Hotel in Problem 13.

a. Suppose that the weekly demand forecast of 90 bags is incorrect and actual demand averages only 60 bags per week. How much higher will total costs be, owing to the distorted EOQ caused by this forecast error?

b. Suppose that actual demand is 60 bags but that ordering costs are cut to only $6 by using the Internet to automate order placing. However, the buyer does not tell anyone, and the EOQ is not adjusted to reflect this reduction in S. How much higher will total costs be, compared to what they could be if the EOQ were adjusted?

15. In a Q system, the demand rate for strawberry ice cream is normally distributed, with an average of 300 pints *per week*. The lead time is 9 weeks. The standard deviation of *weekly* demand is 15 pints.

a. What is the standard deviation of demand during the 9-week lead time?

b. What is the average demand during the 9-week lead time?

c. What reorder point results in a cycle-service level of 99 percent?

16. Petromax Enterprises uses a continuous review inventory control system for one of its SKUs. The following information is available on the item. The firm operates 50 weeks in a year.

Demand = 50,000 units/year

Ordering cost = $35/order

Holding cost = $2/unit/year

Average lead time = 3 weeks

Standard deviation of weekly demand = 125 units

a. What is the economic order quantity for this item?

b. If Petromax wants to provide a 90 percent cycle-service level, what should be the safety stock and the reorder point?

17. In a continuous review inventory system, the lead time for door knobs is 5 weeks. The standard deviation of demand during the lead time is 85 units. The desired cycle-service level is 99 percent. The supplier of door knobs streamlined its operations and now quotes a 1-week lead time. How much can safety stock be reduced without reducing the 99 percent cycle-service level?

18. In a two-bin inventory system, the demand for 3-inch lag bolts during the 2-week lead time is normally distributed, with an average of 53 units per week. The standard deviation of weekly demand is 5 units.

a. What is the probability of demand exceeding the reorder point when the normal level in the second bin is set at 130 units?

b. What is the probability of demand exceeding the 130 units in the second bin if it takes 3 weeks to receive a replenishment order?

19. You are in charge of inventory control of a highly successful product retailed by your firm. Weekly demand for this item varies, with an average of 200 units and a standard deviation of 16 units. It is purchased from a wholesaler at a cost of $12.50 per unit. You are using a continuous review system to control this inventory. The supply lead time is 4 weeks. Placing an order costs $50, and the inventory carrying rate per year is 20 percent of the item's cost. Your firm operates 5 days per week, 50 weeks per year.

   a. What is the optimal ordering quantity for this item?

   b. How many units of the item should be maintained as safety stock for 99 percent protection against stock-outs during an order cycle?

   c. If supply lead time can be reduced to 2 weeks, what is the percent reduction in the number of units maintained as safety stock for the same 99 percent stock-out protection?

   d. If through appropriate sales promotions, the demand variability is reduced so that the standard deviation of weekly demand is 8 units instead of 16, what is the percent reduction (compared to that in part [b]) in the number of units maintained as safety stock for the same 99 percent stockout protection?

20. Your firm uses a continuous review system and operates 52 weeks per year. One of the SKUs has the following characteristics.

   Demand (D) = 20,000 units/year

   Ordering cost (S) = $40/order

   Holding cost (H) = $2unit/year

   Lead time (L) = 2 weeks

   Cycle-service level = 95 percent

   Demand is normally distributed, with a standard deviation of *weekly* demand of 100 units.

   Current on-hand inventory is 1,040 units, with no scheduled receipts and no backorders.

   a. Calculate the item's EOQ. What is the average time, in weeks, between orders?

   b. Find the safety stock and reorder point that provide a 95 percent cycle-service level.

   c. For these policies, what are the annual costs of (i) holding the cycle inventory and (ii) placing orders?

   d. A withdrawal of 15 units just occurred. Is it time to reorder? If so, how much should be ordered?

21. A company begins a review of ordering policies for its continuous review system by checking the current policies for a sample of SKUs. Following are the characteristics of one item.

   Demand (D) = 64 units/week (Assume 52 weeks per year)

   Ordering or setup cost (S) = $50/order

   Holding cost (H) = $13/unit/year

   Lead time (L) = 2 weeks

   Standard deviation of *weekly* demand = 12 units

   Cycle-service level = 88 percent

   a. What is the EOQ for this item?

   b. What is the desired safety stock?

   c. What is the reorder point?

   d. What are the cost implications if the current policy for this item is $Q = 200$ and $R = 180$?

22. Osprey Sports stocks everything that a musky fisherman could want in the Great North Woods. A particular musky lure has been very popular with local fishermen as well as those who buy lures on the Internet from Osprey Sports. The cost to place orders with the supplier is $30/order; the demand averages 4 lures per day, with a standard deviation of 1 lure; and the inventory holding cost is $1.00/lure/year. The lead time from the supplier is 10 days, with a standard deviation of 3 days. It is important to maintain a 97 percent cycle-service level to properly balance service with inventory holding costs. Osprey Sports is open 350 days a year to allow the owners the opportunity to fish for muskies during the prime season. The owners want to use a continuous review inventory system for this item.

   a. What order quantity should be used?

   b. What reorder point should be used?

   c. What is the total annual cost for this inventory system?

23. The Farmer's Wife is a country store specializing in knick-knacks suitable for a farmhouse décor. One item experiencing a considerable buying frenzy is a miniature Holstein cow. Average weekly demand is 30 cows, with a standard deviation of 5 cows. The cost to place a replenishment order is $15 and the holding cost is $0.75/cow/year. The supplier, however, is in China. The lead time for new orders is 8 weeks, with a standard deviation of 2 weeks. The Farmer's Wife, which is open only 50 weeks a year, wants to develop a continuous review inventory system for this item with a cycle-service level of 90 percent.

   a. Specify the continuous review system for the cows. Explain how it would work in practice.

   b. What is the total annual cost for the system you developed?

24. Muscle Bound is a chain of fitness stores located in **D** many large shopping centers. Recently, an internal memo from the CEO to all operations personnel complained about the budget overruns at Muscle Bound's central warehouse. In particular, she said that inventories were too high and that the budget will be cut dramatically and proportionately equal for all items in stock. Consequently, warehouse management set up a pilot study to see what effect the budget cuts would have on customer service. They chose 5-pound barbells, which are a high-volume SKU and consume considerable warehouse space. Daily demand for the barbells is 1,000 units, with a standard deviation of 150 units. Ordering costs are $40 per order. Holding costs are $2/unit/year. The supplier is located in the Philippines; consequently, the lead time is 35 days with a standard deviation of 5 days. Muscle Bound stores operate 313 days a year (no Sundays).

D = **Difficult Problem**

Suppose that the barbells are allocated a budget of $16,000 for total annual costs. If Muscle Bound uses a continuous review system for the barbells and cannot change the ordering costs and holding costs or the distributions of demand or lead time, what is the best cycle-service level management can expect from their system?

25. The Georgia Lighting Center stocks more than 3,000 **D** lighting fixtures, including chandeliers, swags, wall lamps, and track lights. The store sells at retail, operates 6 days per week, and advertises itself as the "brightest spot in town." One expensive fixture is selling at an average rate of 5 units per day. The reorder policy is $Q = 40$ and $R = 15$. A new order is placed on the day the reorder point is reached. The lead time is 3 business days. For example, an order placed on Monday will be delivered on Thursday. Simulate the performance of this Q system for the next 3 weeks (18 workdays). Any stockouts result in lost sales (rather than backorders). The beginning inventory is 19 units, and no receipts are scheduled. Table 2 simulates the first week of operation. Extend Table 2 to simulate operations for the next 2 weeks if demand for the next 12 business days is 7, 4, 2, 7, 3, 6, 10, 0, 5, 10, 4, and 7.

a. What is the average daily ending inventory over the 18 days? How many stockouts occurred?

b. Using the same beginning inventory and daily demand data, simulate the inventory performance of the same item assuming a $Q = 30$, $R = 20$ system is used. Calculate the average inventory level and number of stockouts and compare with part (a).

TABLE 2 | FIRST WEEK OF OPERATION

Workday	Beginning Inventory	Orders Received	Daily Demand	Ending Inventory	Inventory Position	Order Quantity
1. Monday	19	—	5	14	14	40
2. Tuesday	14	—	3	11	51	—
3. Wednesday	11	—	4	7	47	—
4. Thursday	7	40	1	46	46	—
5. Friday	46	—	10	36	36	—
6. Saturday	36	—	9	27	27	—

D = Difficult Problem

Periodic Review System

26. Nationwide Auto Parts uses a periodic review inventory control system for one of its stock items. The review interval is 6 weeks, and the lead time for receiving the materials ordered from its wholesaler is 3 weeks. Weekly demand is normally distributed, with a mean of 100 units and a standard deviation of 20 units.

a. What is the average and the standard deviation of demand during the protection interval?

b. What should be the target inventory level if the firm desires 97.5 percent stockout protection?

c. If 350 units were in stock at the time of a periodic review, how many units should be ordered?

27. In a P system, the lead time for a box of weed-killer is 2 weeks and the review period is 1 week. Demand during the protection interval averages 218 boxes, with a standard deviation of 40 boxes.

a. What is the cycle-service level when the target inventory is set at 300 boxes?

b. In the fall season, demand for weed-killer decreases but also becomes more highly variable. Assume that during the fall season, demand during the protection interval is expected to decrease to 180 boxes, but with a standard deviation of 50 boxes. What would be the cycle-service level if management keeps the target inventory level set at 300 boxes?

28. Suppose that Sam's Cat Hotel in Problem 13 uses a P system instead of a Q system. The average daily demand is $\bar{d} = 90/6 = 15$ bags and the standard deviation of

$daily$ demand is $\sigma_d = \dfrac{\sigma_{week}}{\sqrt{6}} = (15/\sqrt{6}) = 6.124$ bags.

a. What P (in working days) and T should be used to approximate the cost trade-offs of the EOQ?

b. How much more safety stock is needed than with a Q system?

c. It is time for the periodic review. How much kitty litter should be ordered?

29. Your firm uses a periodic review system for all SKUs classified, using ABC analysis, as B or C items. Further, it uses a continuous review system for all SKUs classified as A items. The demand for a specific SKU, currently classified as an A item, has been dropping. You have been asked to evaluate the impact of moving the item from continuous review to periodic review. Assume your firm operates 52 weeks per year; the item's current characteristics are:

Demand $(D) = 15,080$ units/year

Ordering cost $(S) = \$125.00$/order

Holding cost $(H) = \$3.00$/unit/year

Lead time $(L) = 5$ weeks

Cycle-service level = 95 percent

Demand is normally distributed, with a standard deviation of weekly demand of 64 units.

a. Calculate the item's EOQ.

b. Use the EOQ to define the parameters of an appropriate continuous review and periodic review system for this item.

c. Which system requires more safety stock and by how much?

30. Using the same information as in Problem 21, develop the best policies for a periodic review system.

a. What value of P gives the same approximate number of orders per year as the EOQ? Round to the nearest week.

b. What safety stock and target inventory level provide an 88 percent cycle-service level?

31. Wood County Hospital consumes 1,000 boxes of bandages per week. The price of bandages is $35 per box, and the hospital operates 52 weeks per year. The cost of processing an order is $15, and the cost of holding one box for a year is 15 percent of the value of the material.

a. The hospital orders bandages in lot sizes of 900 boxes. What *extra* cost does the hospital incur, which it could save by using the EOQ method?

b. Demand is normally distributed, with a standard deviation of weekly demand of 100 boxes. The lead time is 2 weeks. What safety stock is necessary if the hospital uses a continuous review system and a 97 percent cycle-service level is desired? What should be the reorder point?

c. If the hospital uses a periodic review system, with $P = 2$ weeks, what should be the target inventory level, T?

32. A golf specialty wholesaler operates 50 weeks per year. Management is trying to determine an inventory policy for its 1-irons, which have the following characteristics:

Demand (D) = 2,000 units/year

Demand is normally distributed

Standard deviation of *weekly* demand = 3 units

Ordering cost = $40/order

Annual holding cost (H) = $5/units

Desired cycle-service level = 90 percent

Lead time (L) = 4 weeks

a. If the company uses a periodic review system, what should P and T be? Round P to the nearest week.

b. If the company uses a continuous review system, what should R be?

Active Model Exercise

Active Model 1, "Economic Order Quantity," appears in MyLab Operations Management. It allows you to evaluate the sensitivity of the EOQ and associated costs to changes in the demand and cost parameters.

QUESTIONS

1. What is the EOQ and what is the lowest total cost?

2. What is the annual cost of holding inventory at the EOQ and the annual cost of ordering inventory at the EOQ?

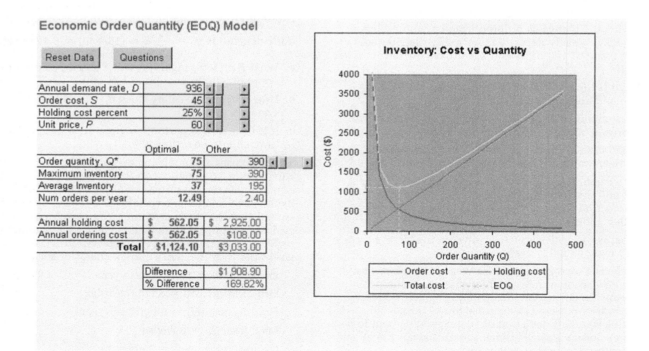

3. From the graph, what can you conclude about the relationship between the lowest total cost and the costs of ordering and holding inventory?

4. How much does the total cost increase if the store manager orders twice as many bird feeders as the EOQ? How much does the total cost increase if the store manager orders half as many bird feeders as the EOQ?

5. What happens to the EOQ and the total cost when demand is doubled? What happens to the EOQ and the total cost when unit price is doubled?

6. Scroll through the lower order cost values and describe the changes to the graph. What happens to the EOQ?

7. Comment on the sensitivity of the EOQ model to errors in demand or cost estimates.

VIDEO CASE   Inventory Management at Crayola

Managing inventory at Crayola is a fine balancing act. With the back-to-school period driving 42 percent of company demand for crayons, markers, paints, modeling compounds, and other products, production starts in February so enough finished goods are in the 800,000-square-foot warehouse in time to supply 3,600 Walmarts, 1,400 Targets, and thousands of other retailers in the United States for the fall school-supply rush.

Crayola must supply customers with nearly 1,500 products, which requires an average inventory investment of $110 million. Finished goods inventory, shown here, must be stored in advance of seasonal demand peaks, such as the back-to-school period, which accounts for 42 percent of annual demand.

This means demand forecasts for raw materials in the master production schedule must be developed months before any of the finished products move to those retail customers. Lead times range from 60 days for domestic raw materials sources to upwards of 90 days for finished goods from suppliers outside the United States. As production ramps up for the back-to-school season well before the first day of classes, Crayola plans inventory levels for the entire year so that production remains reasonably steady. While the back-to-school season represents the lion's share of annual sales, holiday sales account for 35 percent of revenues, and the rest comes from spring sales. Crayola has over 1,500 SKUs, with close to 225 top sellers, so accurate forecasts are essential.

Historical sales patterns as well as orders generated by its U.S. sales divisions located in Easton, Pennsylvania (headquarters), Bentonville, Arkansas (near Walmart's headquarters), and Minneapolis, Minnesota (near Target's headquarters) help managers attain the accuracy needed. Marketing cobranding for the latest movies and comic books plays a role in creating the forecast for new SKUs and bundles, which must be coordinated to hit retailers the same time the movies and comics debut or the company risks missing the market and ending up with inventory that can't easily be sold.

Crayola's inventory holding costs run about 25 percent, and its average inventory value is $110 million. The company must ensure there is warehouse space for finished goods as well as raw materials used in production. Pigments, clays, and packaging materials are moved from the warehouse and positioned close to the production lines, using a Kanban system to pull raw materials inventory as needed. Rail tanker cars from Louisiana and Pennsylvania carrying paraffin wax are delivered twice a week for crayon production. Since the rail cars feed directly into production, any disruption in delivery has the potential for shutting down production. Bad weather is a particular risk in this part of the company's supply chain since it can prevent the transport of goods during hurricanes or snowstorms.

Crayola attempts to source as many raw materials from domestic sources as possible. Cartons, clay, ink, labels, and corrugated boxes come from the mid-Atlantic region of the United States, while those plastic components Crayola does not manufacture onsite, such as nibs for markers, are sourced from Asia and can take up to 120 days to ship through the Panama Canal to the Port of Newark. Materials used in kits and bundles come from Korea, China, Vietnam, and Brazil, and face similar shipping logistics.

When considering work-in-process inventories at Crayola, paints, markers, modeling clays, and many of the crayons coming off the production line are boxed into trays for use downstream in creating kits and bundles. These items are considered WIP items, even though the individual units are finished goods (i.e., a crayon or marker is completely manufactured once it comes off the line). The same is true for marker barrels, paint pots, and other plastics. Specialized equipment is used to make these items, which feed downstream production.

Recently, Crayola's leadership expected that actual demand for its popular Marker Maker© toy product might come in higher than the original forecast. As a countermeasure, Crayola established duplicate capacities in China and the United States to meet the aggregate potential demand. In China, the company produced the original forecast and delivered to customers as planned. However, when the actual demand was 26 percent over the original forecast, Crayola could meet the surge in demand because it had positioned the long lead time ink bottles in its Pennsylvania plants and was able to mold the plastic parts using marker components from its core marker product. By utilizing existing machine capacity in its plants, reducing the lead time of ink bottles by making them in Pennsylvania, and by duplicating tooling, Crayola was able to ensure that its customers and consumers were satisfied during the holiday season.

QUESTIONS

1. Consider the pressures for small versus large inventories. Which situation does Crayola seem to fit, and why?

2. Explain how both independent and dependent demand items are present at Crayola.

3. The Marker Maker© product recently experienced an unexpected surge in demand and the supply chain's agility was credited with helping to meet the crisis. We have discussed four ways to classify operational inventories by how they are created. Regarding the ways managers can use these inventories to satisfy demand, explain how Crayola can achieve the flexibility to adjust to unexpected demand surges.

EXPERIENTIAL LEARNING 1 | Swift Electronic Supply, Inc.

It was a typical fall afternoon in Southern California, with thousands of tourists headed to the beaches to have fun. About 40 miles away, however, Steven Holland, the CEO of Swift Electronic Supply, Inc., faced a severe problem with Swift's inventory management.

An Intel veteran, Steven Holland worked in the electronic components distribution industry for more than 20 years. Seven years ago, he founded Swift Electronic Supply, Inc., an electronic distributor. After several successful years, the company is now troubled with eroding profit margins. Recent economic downturns further worsened the situation. Factors such as the growth of B2B e-commerce, the globalization of markets, the increased popularity of value-added services, and ongoing consolidations among electronic distributors affect the future of Swift.

To reverse these influences, Holland talked to a prestigious local university. After consultation, Holland found the most effective way to increase profitability is to cut inventory costs. As a starting point, he studied in detail a representative product, dynamic random access memory (DRAM), as the basis for his plan.

Industry and Company Preview

Owing to a boom in the telecommunications industry and the information technology revolution, electronics distributors experienced double-digit annual growth over the last decade. To cut the cost of direct purchasing forces, large component manufacturers such as Intel, Cisco, and Texas Instruments

decided to outsource their procurement so that they could focus on product development and manufacturing. Therefore, independent electronic distributors like Swift started offering procurement services to these companies.

Swift serves component manufacturers in California and Arizona. Working as the intermediary between its customers and overseas original equipment manufacturers (OEMs), Swift's business model is quite simple. Forecasting customer demand, Swift places orders to a number of OEMs, stocks those products, breaks the quantities down, and delivers the products to its end customers.

Recently, due to more intense competition and declines in demand, Swift offered more flexible delivery schedules and was willing to accommodate small order quantities. However, customers can always shift to Swift's competitors should Swift not fulfill their orders. Steven Holland was in a dilemma: The intangible costs of losing customers can be enormous; however, maintaining high levels of inventory can also be costly.

DRAM

Holland turned his attention to DRAM as a representative product. Previously, the company ordered a large amount every time it felt it was necessary. Holland's assistant developed a table (Table 3) that has 2 months of demand history. From Holland's experience, the demand for DRAM is relatively stable in the company's product line and it had no sales seasonality. The sales staff agrees that conditions in the current year will not be different from those of

TABLE 3 | HISTORICAL DEMAND DATA FOR THE DRAM (UNITS)

Day	Demand	Day	Demand	Day	Demand
1	869	21	663	41	959
2	902	22	1,146	42	703
3	1,109	23	1,016	43	823
4	947	24	1,166	44	862
5	968	25	829	45	966
6	917	26	723	46	1,042
7	1,069	27	749	47	889
8	1,086	28	766	48	1,002
9	1,066	29	996	49	763
10	929	30	1,122	50	932
11	1,022	31	962	51	1,052
12	959	32	829	52	1,062
13	756	33	862	53	989
14	882	34	793	54	1,029
15	829	35	1,039	55	823
16	726	36	1,009	56	942
17	666	37	979	57	986
18	879	38	976	58	736
19	1,086	39	856	59	1,009
20	992	40	1,036	60	852

past years, and historical demand will be a good indicator of what to expect in the future.

The primary manufacturers of DRAM are those in Southeast Asia. Currently, Swift can purchase one unit of 128M DRAM for $10. After negotiation with a reputable supplier, Holland managed to sign a long-term agreement, which kept the price at $10 and allowed Swift to place orders at any time. The supplier also supplies other items in Swift's inventory. In addition, it takes the supplier of the DRAM 2 days to deliver the goods to Swift's warehouse using air carriers.

When Swift does not have enough inventory to fill a customer's order, the sales are lost; that is, Swift is not able to backorder the shortage because its customers fill their requirements through competitors. The customers will accept partial shipments, however.

It costs Swift $200 to place an order with the suppliers. This amount covers the corresponding internal ordering costs and the costs of delivering the products to the company. Holland estimates that the cost of lost sales amounts to $2 per unit of DRAM. This rough estimate includes the loss of profits, as well as the intangible damage to customer goodwill.

To simplify its inventory management system, Swift has a policy of maintaining a cycle-service level of 95 percent. The holding cost per day per unit is estimated to be 0.5 percent of the cost of goods, regardless of the product. Inventory holding costs are calculated on the basis of the ending inventory each day. The current balance is 1,700 units of DRAM in stock.

The daily purchasing routine is as follows. Orders are placed at the *beginning* of the day, before Swift is open for customer business. The orders arrive at the beginning of the day, 2 days later, and can be used for sales that day. For example, an order placed at the beginning of day 1 will arrive at Swift before Swift is open for business on day 3. The actual daily demand is always recorded at the *end* of the day, after Swift has closed for customer business. All cost computations are done at the end of the day after the total demand has been recorded.

Simulation

Holland believes that simulation is a useful approach to assess various inventory control alternatives. The historical data from Table 3 could be used to develop attractive inventory policies. The table was developed to record various costs and evaluate different alternatives. An example showing some recent DRAM inventory decisions is shown in Table 4.

1. Design a new inventory system for Swift Electronic Supply, Inc. using the data provided.

2. Provide the rationale for your system, which should include the decision rules you would follow to determine how much to order and when.

3. Simulate the use of your inventory system and record the costs. Develop a table such as Table 4 to record your results. Your instructor will provide actual demands on a day-to-day basis during the simulation.

TABLE 4 | EXAMPLE SIMULATION

Day	1	2	3	4	5	6	7	8	9	10
Beginning inventory position	1,700	831	1,500	391	3,000	3,232	2,315			
Number ordered	1,500		3,000	1,200			1,900			
Daily demand	869	902	1,109	947	968	917	1,069			
Day-ending inventory	831	−71	391	−556	2,032	2,315	1,246			
Ordering costs ($200 per order)	200		200	200			200			
Holding costs ($0.05 per piece per day)	41.55	0.00	19.55	0.00	101.60	115.75	62.30			
Shortage costs ($2 per piece)	0	142	0	1,112	0	0	0			
Total cost for day	241.55	142.00	219.55	1,312.00	101.60	115.75	262.30			
Cumulative cost from last day	0.00	241.55	383.55	603.10	1,915.10	2,016.70	2,132.45			
Cumulative costs to date	241.55	383.55	603.10	1,915.10	2,016.70	2,132.45	2,394.75			

CASE | Parts Emporium

Parts Emporium, Inc. is a wholesale distributor of automobile parts formed by two disenchanted auto mechanics, Dan Block and Ed Spriggs. Originally located in Block's garage, the firm showed slow but steady growth for 7 years before it relocated to an old, abandoned meat-packing warehouse on Chicago's South Side. With increased space for inventory storage, the company was able to begin offering an expanded line of auto parts. This increased selection, combined with the trend toward longer car ownership, led to an explosive growth of the business. Fifteen years later, Parts Emporium was the largest independent distributor of auto parts in the north central region.

Recently, Parts Emporium relocated to a sparkling new office and warehouse complex off Interstate 55 in suburban Chicago. The warehouse space alone occupied more than 100,000 square feet. Although only a handful of new products have been added since the warehouse was constructed, its utilization increased from 65 percent to more than 90 percent of capacity. During this same period, however, sales growth stagnated. These conditions motivated Block and Spriggs to hire the first manager from outside the company in the firm's history.

It is June 6, Sue McCaskey's first day in the newly created position of materials manager for Parts Emporium. A recent graduate of a prominent business school, McCaskey is eagerly awaiting her first real-world problem. At approximately 8:30 A.M., it arrives in the form of status reports on inventory and orders shipped. At the top of an extensive computer printout is a handwritten note from Joe Donnell, the purchasing manager: "Attached you will find the inventory and customer service performance data. Rest assured that the individual inventory levels are accurate because we took a complete physical inventory count at the end of last week. Unfortunately, we do not keep compiled records in some of the areas as you requested. However, you are welcome to do so yourself. Welcome aboard!"

A little upset that aggregate information is not available, McCaskey decides to randomly select a small sample of approximately 100 items and compile inventory and customer service characteristics to get a feel for the "total picture." The results of this experiment reveal to her why Parts Emporium decided to create the position she now fills. It seems that the inventory is in all the wrong places. Although an *average* of approximately 60 days of inventory is on hand, the firm's customer service is inadequate. Parts Emporium tries to backorder the customer orders not immediately filled from stock, but some 10 percent of demand is being lost to competing distributorships. Because stockouts are costly, relative to inventory holding costs, McCaskey believes that a cycle-service level of at least 95 percent should be achieved.

McCaskey knows that although her influence to initiate changes will be limited, she must produce positive results immediately. Thus, she decides to concentrate on two products from the extensive product line: the EG151 exhaust gasket and the DB032 drive belt. If she can demonstrate significant gains from proper inventory management for just two products, perhaps Block and Spriggs will give her the backing needed to change the total inventory management system.

The EG151 exhaust gasket is purchased from an overseas supplier, Haipei, Inc. Actual demand for the first 21 weeks of this year is shown in the following table:

Week	Actual Demand	Week	Actual Demand
1	104	12	97
2	103	13	99
3	107	14	102
4	105	15	99
5	102	16	103
6	102	17	101
7	101	18	101
8	104	19	104
9	100	20	108
10	100	21	97
11	103		

A quick review of past orders, shown in another document, indicates that a lot size of 150 units is being used and that the lead time from Haipei is

fairly constant at 2 weeks. Currently, at the end of week 21, no inventory is on hand, 11 units are backordered, and the company is awaiting a scheduled receipt of 150 units.

The DB032 drive belt is purchased from the Bendox Corporation of Grand Rapids, Michigan. Actual demand so far this year is shown in the following table:

Week	Actual Demand	Week	Actual Demand
11	18	17	50
12	33	18	53
13	53	19	54
14	54	20	49
15	51	21	52
16	53		

Because this product is new, data are available only since its introduction in week 11. Currently, 324 units are on hand, with no backorders and no scheduled receipts. A lot size of 1,000 units is being used, with the lead time fairly constant at 3 weeks.

The wholesale prices that Parts Emporium charges its customers are $12.99 for the EG151 exhaust gasket and $8.89 for the DB032 drive belt. Because no quantity discounts are offered on these two highly profitable items, gross margins based on current purchasing practices are 32 percent of the wholesale price for the exhaust gasket and 48 percent of the wholesale price for the drive belt.

Parts Emporium estimates its cost to hold inventory at 21 percent of its inventory investment. This percentage recognizes the opportunity cost of tying money up in inventory and the variable costs of taxes, insurance, and shrinkage. The annual report notes other warehousing expenditures for utilities and maintenance and debt service on the 100,000-square-foot warehouse, which was built for $1.5 million. However, McCaskey reasons that these warehousing costs can be ignored because they will not change for the range of inventory policies that she is considering.

Out-of-pocket costs for Parts Emporium to place an order with suppliers are estimated to be $20 per order for exhaust gaskets and $10 per order for drive belts. On the outbound side, the company can charge a delivery fee. Although most customers pick up their parts at Parts Emporium, some orders are delivered to customers. To provide this service, Parts Emporium contracts with a local company for a flat fee of $21.40 per order, which is added to the customer's bill. McCaskey is unsure whether to increase the ordering costs for Parts Emporium to include delivery charges.

QUESTIONS

1. Put yourself in Sue McCaskey's position and prepare a detailed report to Dan Block and Ed Spriggs on managing the inventory of the EG151 exhaust gasket and the DB032 drive belt. Be sure to present a proper inventory system and r cognize all relevant costs.

2. By how much do your recommendations for these two items reduce annual cycle inventory, stockout, and ordering costs?

Selected References

Inventory Management

Arnold, Tony J. R., Stephen Chapman, and Lloyd M. Clive. Introduction to Materials Management, 7th ed. Upper Saddle River, NJ: Prentice Hall, 2012.

Axsäter, Sven. Inventory Control, 2nd ed. New York: Springer Science + Business Media, LLC, 2006.

Bastow, B. J. "Metrics in the Material World." APICS—The Performance Advantage (May 2005), pp. 49–52.

Benton, W. C. Purchasing and Supply Chain Management, 3rd ed. New York: McGraw-Hill, 2013.

Callioni, Gianpaolo, Xavier de Montgros, Regine Slagmulder, Luk N. Van Wassenhove, and Linda Wright. "Inventory-Driven Costs." Harvard Business Review (March 2005), pp. 135–141.

Cannon, Alan R., and Richard E. Crandall. "The Way Things Never Were." APICS—The Performance Advantage (January 2004), pp. 32–35.

Gaur, V., S. Kesavan, and A. Raman. "Retail Inventory: Managing the Canary in the Coal Mine." California Management Review, vol. 56, no. 2 (2014), pp. 55–76.

Hartvigsen, David. SimQuick: Process Simulation with Excel, 2nd ed. Upper Saddle River, NJ: Prentice Hall, 2004.

Operations Management Body of Knowledge. Falls Church, VA: American Production and Inventory Control Society, 2009.

Timme, Stephen G., and Christine Williams-Timme. "The Real Cost of Holding." Supply Chain Management Review (July/August 2003), pp. 30–37.

Walters, Donald. Inventory Control and Management, 2nd ed. West Sussex, England: John Wiley and Sons, Ltd, 2003.

Glossary

ABC analysis The process of dividing SKUs into three classes, according to their dollar usage, so that managers can focus on items that have the highest dollar value.

anticipation inventory Inventory used to absorb uneven rates of demand or supply. Any product that is manufactured from one or more components.

base-stock system An inventory control system that issues a replenishment order, Q, each time a withdrawal is made, for the same amount of the withdrawal.

continuous review (Q) system A system designed to track the remaining inventory of a SKU each time a withdrawal is made to determine whether it is time to reorder.

cycle counting An inventory control method, whereby storeroom personnel physically count a small percentage of the total number of items each day, correcting errors that they find.

cycle inventory The portion of total inventory that varies directly with lot size.

cycle-service level See service level.

dependent demand items Items whose required quantity varies with the production plans for other items held in the firm's inventory.

economic order quantity (EOQ) The lot size that minimizes total annual inventory holding and ordering costs.

finished goods (FG) The items in manufacturing plants, warehouses, and retail outlets that are sold to the firm's customers.

independent demand items Items for which demand is influenced by market conditions and is not related to the inventory decisions for any other item held in stock or produced.

inventory A stock of materials used to satisfy customer demand or to support the production of services or goods.

inventory holding cost The sum of the cost of capital and the variable costs of keeping items on hand, such as storage and handling, taxes, insurance, and shrinkage.

inventory management The planning and controlling of inventories to meet the competitive priorities of the organization.

inventory position (IP) The measurement of a SKU's ability to satisfy future demand.

lot size The quantity of an inventory item that management either buys from a supplier or manufactures using internal processes.

open orders See scheduled receipts (SR).

optional replenishment system A system used to review the inventory position at fixed time intervals and, if the position has dropped to (or below) a predetermined level, to place a variable-sized order to cover expected needs.

ordering cost The cost of preparing a purchase order for a supplier or a production order for manufacturing.

periodic review (P) system A system in which an item's inventory position is reviewed periodically rather than continuously.

perpetual inventory system A system of inventory control in which the inventory records are always current.

pipeline inventory Inventory that is created when an order for an item is issued but not yet received.

protection interval The period over which safety stock must protect the user from running out of stock.

quantity discount A drop in the price per unit when an order is sufficiently large.

raw materials (RM) The inventories needed for the production of services or goods.

reorder point (R) The predetermined minimum level that an inventory position must reach before a fixed quantity Q of the SKU is ordered.

reorder point (ROP) system See continuous review (Q) system.

repeatability The degree to which the same work can be done again.

safety stock inventory Surplus inventory that a company holds to protect against uncertainties in demand, lead time, and supply changes.

scheduled receipts (SR) Orders that have been placed but have not yet been received.

service level The desired probability of not running out of stock in any one ordering cycle, which begins at the time an order is placed and ends when it arrives in stock.

setup cost The cost involved in changing over a machine or workspace to produce a different item.

single-bin system A system of inventory control in which a maximum level is marked on the storage shelf or bin, and the inventor is brought up to the mark periodically.

stock-keeping unit (SKU) An individual item or product that has an identifying code and is held in inventory somewhere along the supply chain.

time between orders (TBO) The average elapsed time between receiving (or placing) replenishment orders of Q units for a particular lot size.

two-bin system A visual system version of the Q system in which a SKU's inventory is stored at two different locations.

visual system A system that allows employees to place orders when inventory visibly reaches a certain marker.

work-in-process (WIP) Items, such as components or assemblies, needed to produce a final product in manufacturing or service operations.

WAITING LINES

Anyone who has ever waited at a stoplight, at McDonald's, or at the registrar's office has experienced the dynamics of waiting lines. Perhaps one of the best examples of effective management of waiting lines is that of Walt Disney World. One day the park may have only 25,000 customers, but on another day the numbers may top 90,000. Careful analysis of process flows, technology for people-mover (materials handling) equipment, capacity, and layout keeps the waiting times for attractions to acceptable levels.

A **waiting line** is one or more "customers" waiting for service. The customers can be people or inanimate objects, such as machines requiring maintenance, sales orders waiting for shipping, or inventory items waiting to be used. A waiting line forms because of a temporary imbalance between the demand for service and the capacity of the system to provide the service. In most real-life waiting-line problems, the demand rate varies; that is, customers arrive at unpredictable intervals. Most often, the rate of producing the service also varies, depending on customer needs. Suppose that bank customers arrive at an average rate of 15 per hour throughout the day and that the bank can process an average of 20 customers per hour. Why would a waiting line ever develop? The answers are that the customer arrival rate varies throughout the day and the time required to process a customer can vary. During the noon hour, 30 customers may arrive at the bank. Some of them may have complicated transactions requiring above-average process times. The waiting line may grow to 15 customers for a period of time before it eventually disappears. Even though the bank manager provided for more than enough capacity on average, waiting lines can still develop.

In a similar fashion, waiting lines can develop even if the time to process a customer is constant. For example, a subway train is computer controlled to arrive at stations along its route. Each train is programmed to arrive at a station, say, every 15 minutes. Even with the constant service time, waiting lines develop while riders wait for the next train or cannot get on a train because of the size of the crowd at a busy time of the day. Consequently, variability in the rate of demand determines the sizes of the waiting lines in this case. In general, if no variability in the demand or service rate occurs and enough capacity is provided, no waiting lines form.

waiting line

One or more "customers" waiting for service.

LEARNING GOALS *After reading this text, you should be able to:*

1. Identify the structure of waiting lines in real situations.
2. Use the single-server, multiple-server, and finite-source models to analyze operations and estimate the operating characteristics of a process.
3. Describe the situations where simulation should be used for waiting-line analysis and the nature of the information that can be obtained.
4. Explain how waiting-line models can be used to make managerial decisions.

From Supplement B of *Operations Management: Processes and Supply Chains*, Twelfth Edition. Lee J. Krajewski, Manoj K. Malhotra, Larry P. Ritzman. Copyright © 2019 by Pearson Education, Inc. All rights reserved.

Waiting-line theory applies to service as well as manufacturing firms, relating customer arrival and service-system processing characteristics to service-system output characteristics. In our discussion, we use the term *service* broadly—the act of doing work for a customer. The service system might be hair cutting at a hair salon, satisfying customer complaints, or processing a production order of parts on a certain machine. Other examples of customers and services include lines of theatergoers waiting to purchase tickets, trucks waiting to be unloaded at a warehouse, machines waiting to be repaired by a maintenance crew, and patients waiting to be examined by a physician. Regardless of the situation, waiting-line problems have several common elements.

The analysis of waiting lines is of concern to managers because it affects process design, capacity planning, process performance, and ultimately, supply chain performance. In this text we discuss why waiting lines form, the uses of waiting-line models in operations management, and the structure of waiting-line models. We also discuss the decisions managers address with these models. Waiting lines can also be analyzed using computer simulation. Software such as SimQuick or Excel spreadsheets can be used to analyze the problems in this text.

Structure of Waiting-Line Problems

Analyzing waiting-line problems begins with a description of the situation's basic elements. Each specific situation will have different characteristics, but four elements are common to all situations:

1. An input, or **customer population**, that generates potential customers

2. A waiting line of customers

3. The **service facility**, consisting of a person (or crew), a machine (or group of machines), or both, necessary to perform the service for the customer

4. A **priority rule**, which selects the next customer to be served by the service facility.

Figure 1 shows these basic elements. The triangles, circles, and squares are intended to show a diversity of customers with different needs. The **service system** describes the number of lines and the arrangement of the facilities. After the service has been performed, the served customers leave the system.

Customer Population

A customer population is the source of input to the service system. If the potential number of new customers for the service system is appreciably affected by the number of customers already in the system, the input source is said to be *finite*. For example, suppose that a maintenance crew is assigned responsibility for the repair of 10 machines. The customer population for the maintenance crew is 10 machines in working order. The population generates customers for the maintenance crew as a function of the failure rates for the machines. As more machines fail and enter the service system, either waiting for service or for being repaired, the customer population becomes smaller or the rate at which it can generate another customer falls. Consequently, the customer population is said to be finite.

customer population

An input that generates potential customers.

service facility

A person (or crew), a machine (or group of machines), or both, necessary to perform the service for the customer.

priority rule

A rule that selects the next customer to be served by the service facility.

service system

The number of lines and the arrangement of the facilities.

FIGURE 1 ▶
Basic Elements of Waiting-Line Models

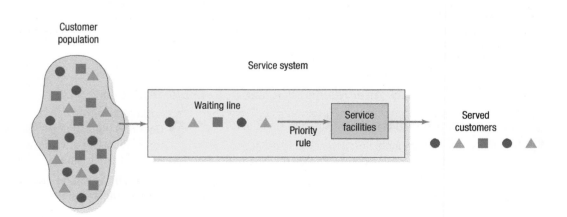

Alternatively, an *infinite* customer population is one in which the number of customers in the system does not affect the rate at which the population generates new customers. For example, consider a mail-order operation for which the customer population consists of shoppers who have received a catalog of products sold by the company. Because the customer population is so large and only a small fraction of the shoppers place orders at any one time, the number of new orders it generates is not appreciably affected by the number of orders waiting for service or being processed by the service system. In this case, the customer population is said to be infinite.

Customers in waiting lines may be *patient* or *impatient*, which has nothing to do with the colorful language a customer may use while waiting in line for a long time on a hot day. In the context of waiting-line problems, a patient customer is one who enters the system and remains there until being served; an impatient customer is one who either decides not to enter the system (balks) or leaves the system before being served (reneges). For the methods used in this text, we make the simplifying assumption that all customers are patient.

The Service System

The service system may be described by the number of lines and the arrangement of facilities.

Number of Lines Waiting lines may be designed to be a *single line* or *multiple lines.* Figure 2 shows an example of each arrangement. Generally, single lines are utilized at airline counters, inside banks, and at some fast-food restaurants whereas multiple lines are utilized in grocery stores, at drive-in bank operations, and in discount stores. When multiple servers are available and each one can handle general transactions, the single-line arrangement keeps servers uniformly busy and gives customers a sense of fairness. Customers believe that they are being served on the basis of when they arrived and not on how well they guessed their waiting time when selecting a particular line. The multiple-line design is best when some of the servers provide a limited set of services. In this arrangement, customers select the services they need and wait in the line where that service is provided, such as at a grocery store that provides special lines for customers paying with cash or having fewer than 10 items.

Sometimes customers are not organized neatly into "lines." Machines that need repair on the production floor of a factory may be left in place, and the maintenance crew comes to them. Nonetheless, we can think of such machines as forming a single line or multiple lines, depending on the number of repair crews and their specialties. Likewise, passengers who telephone for a taxi also form a line even though they may wait at different locations.

Sometimes customers are not organized neatly into lines. Here cars, other vehicles, and people are caught in a messy traffic in Mumbai, one of India's largest cities.

Arrangement of Service Facilities Service facilities consist of the personnel and equipment necessary to perform the service for the customer. Service facility arrangement is described by the number of channels and phases. A **channel** is one or more facilities required to perform a given service. A **phase** is a single step in providing the service. Some services require a single phase, while others require a sequence of phases. Consequently, a service facility uses some combination of channels and phases. Managers should choose an arrangement based on customer volume and the nature of services provided. Figure 3 shows examples of the five basic types of service facility arrangements.

In the *single-channel, single-phase* system, all services demanded by a customer can be performed by a single-server facility. Customers form a single line and go through the service facility one at a time. Examples are a drive-through car wash and a machine that must process several batches of parts.

The *single-channel, multiple-phase* arrangement is used when the services are best performed in sequence by more than one facility, yet customer volume or other constraints limit the design to one channel. Customers form a single line and proceed sequentially from one service facility to the next. An example of this arrangement is a McDonald's drive-through, where the first facility takes the order, the second takes the money, and the third provides the food.

The *multiple-channel, single-phase* arrangement is used when demand is large enough to warrant providing the same service at more than one facility or when the services offered by the

channel

One or more facilities required to perform a given service.

phase

A single step in providing a service.

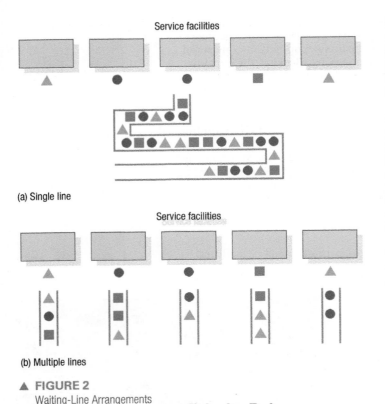

(a) Single line

(b) Multiple lines

▲ **FIGURE 2**
Waiting-Line Arrangements

facilities are different. Customers form one or more lines, depending on the design. In the single-line design, the first available server serves customers, just as it is usually done in the lobby of a bank. If each channel has its own waiting line, customers wait until the server for their line can serve them, as at a bank's drive-through facilities.

The *multiple-channel, multiple-phase* arrangement occurs when customers can be served by one of the first-phase facilities but then require service from a second-phase facility, and so on. In some cases, customers cannot switch channels after service has begun; in others they can. An example of this arrangement is a laundromat. Washing machines are the first-phase facilities, and dryers are the second-phase facilities. Some of the washing machines and dryers may be designed for extra-large loads, thereby providing the customer a choice of channels.

The most complex waiting-line problem involves customers who have unique sequences of required services; consequently, service cannot be described neatly in phases. A *mixed* arrangement is used in such a case. In the mixed arrangement, waiting lines can develop in front of each facility, as in a medical center, where a patient goes to an exam room for a nurse to take his or her blood pressure and weight, goes back to the waiting room until the doctor can see him or her, and after consultation proceeds to the laboratory to give a blood sample, radiology to have an X-ray taken, or the pharmacy for prescribed drugs, depending on specific needs.

Priority Rule

The priority rule determines which customer to serve next. Most service systems that you encounter use the first-come, first-served (FCFS) rule. The customer at the head of the waiting line has the highest priority, and the customer who arrived last has the lowest priority. Other priority disciplines might take the customer with the earliest promised due date (EDD) or the customer with the shortest expected processing time (SPT).[1]

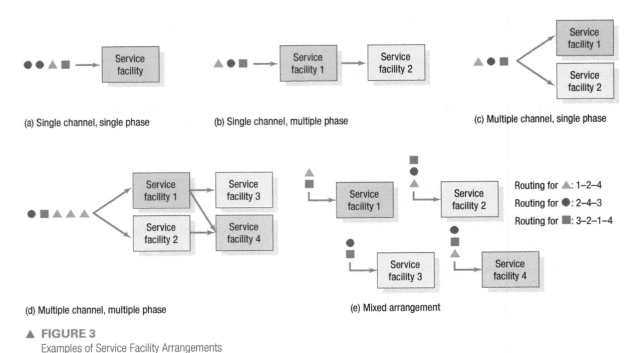

(a) Single channel, single phase

(b) Single channel, multiple phase

(c) Multiple channel, single phase

(d) Multiple channel, multiple phase

(e) Mixed arrangement

Routing for ▲: 1–2–4
Routing for ●: 2–4–3
Routing for ■: 3–2–1–4

▲ **FIGURE 3**
Examples of Service Facility Arrangements

[1]We focus on FCFS in this supplement.

A **preemptive discipline** is a rule that allows a customer of higher priority to interrupt the service of another customer. For example, in a hospital emergency room, patients with the most life-threatening injuries receive treatment first, regardless of their order of arrival. Modeling of systems having complex priority disciplines is usually done using computer simulation.

Probability Distributions

The sources of variation in waiting-line problems come from the random arrivals of customers and the variations in service times. Each of these sources can be described with a probability distribution.

Arrival Distribution

Customers arrive at service facilities randomly. The variability of customer arrivals often can be described by a Poisson distribution, which specifies the probability that n customers will arrive in T time periods:

$$P_n = \frac{(\lambda T)^n}{n!} e^{-\lambda T} \text{ for } n = 0, 1, 2, \ldots$$

where

P_n = probability of n arrivals in T time periods

λ = average number of customer arrivals per period

e = 2.7183

The mean of the Poisson distribution is λT, and the variance also is λT, The Poisson distribution is a discrete distribution; that is, the probabilities are for a specific number of arrivals per unit of time.

EXAMPLE 1	Calculating the Probability of Customer Arrivals

Management is redesigning the customer service process in a large department store. Accommodating four customers is important. Customers arrive at the desk at the rate of two customers per hour. What is the probability that four customers will arrive during any hour?

SOLUTION
In this case $\lambda = 2$ customers per hour, $T = 1$ hour, and $n = 4$ customers. The probability that four customers will arrive in any hour is

$$P_4 = \frac{[2(1)]^4}{4!} e^{-2(1)} = \frac{16}{24} e^{-2} = \mathbf{0.090}$$

DECISION POINT
The manager of the customer service desk can use this information to determine the space requirements for the desk and waiting area. There is a relatively small probability that four customers will arrive in any hour. Consequently, seating capacity for two or three customers should be more than adequate unless the time to service each customer is lengthy. Further analysis on service times is warranted.

Another way to specify the arrival distribution is to do it in terms of customer **interarrival times**—that is, the time between customer arrivals. If the customer population generates customers according to a Poisson distribution, the *exponential distribution* describes the probability that the next customer will arrive, or that service to a customer will conclude, in the next T time periods.

Service Time Distribution

The exponential distribution describes the probability that the service time of the customer at a particular facility will be no more than T time periods. The probability can be calculated by using the formula

$$P(t \leq T) = 1 - e^{-\mu T}$$

where

μ = average number of customers completing service per period

t = service time of the customer

T = target service time

The mean of the service time distribution is $1/\mu$, and the variance is $(1/\mu)^2$. As T increases, the probability that the customer's service time will be less than T approaches 1.0.

For simplicity, let us look at a single-channel, single-phase arrangement.

EXAMPLE 2	Calculating the Service Time Probability

The management of the large department store in Example 1 must determine whether more training is needed for the customer service clerk. The clerk at the customer service desk can serve an average of three customers per hour. What is the probability that a customer will require 10 minutes or less of service?

SOLUTION

We must have all the data in the same time units. Because $\mu = 3$ customers per hour, we convert minutes of time to hours, or $T = 10$ minutes $= 10/60$ hour $= 0.167$ hour. Then

$$P(t \leq T) = 1 - e^{-\mu T}$$
$$P(t \leq 0.167 \text{ hour}) = 1 - e^{-3(0.167)} = 1 - 0.61 = \mathbf{0.39}$$

DECISION POINT

The probability that the customer will require only 10 minutes or less is not high, which leaves the possibility that customers may experience lengthy delays. Management should consider additional training for the clerk so as to reduce the time it takes to process a customer request.

Some characteristics of the exponential distribution do not always conform to an actual situation. The exponential distribution model is based on the assumption that each service time is independent of those that preceded it. In real life, however, productivity may improve as human servers learn about the work. Another assumption underlying the model is that very small, as well as very large, service times are possible. However, real-life situations often require a fixed-length start-up time, some cutoff on total service time, or nearly constant service time.

Using Waiting-Line Models to Analyze Operations

Operations managers can use waiting-line models to balance the gains that might be made by increasing the efficiency of the service system against the costs of doing so. In addition, managers should consider the costs of *not* making improvements to the system: Long waiting lines or long waiting times may cause customers to balk or renege. Managers should therefore be concerned about the following operating characteristics of the system.

1. *Line Length.* The number of customers in the waiting line reflects one of two conditions. Short lines could mean either good customer service or too much capacity. Similarly, long lines could indicate either low server efficiency or the need to increase capacity.

2. *Number of Customers in System.* The number of customers in line and being served also relates to service efficiency and capacity. A large number of customers in the system causes congestion and may result in customer dissatisfaction, unless more capacity is added.

3. *Waiting Time in Line.* Long lines do not always mean long waiting times. If the service rate is fast, a long line can be served efficiently. However, when waiting time seems long, customers perceive the quality of service to be poor. Managers may try to change the arrival rate of customers or design the system to make long wait times seem shorter than they really are. For example, at Walt Disney World, customers in line for an attraction are entertained by videos and also are informed about expected waiting times, which seems to help them endure the wait.

4. *Total Time in System.* The total elapsed time from entry into the system until exit from the system may indicate problems with customers, server efficiency, or capacity. If some

customers are spending too much time in the service system, it may be necessary to change the priority discipline, increase productivity, or adjust capacity in some way.

5. *Service Facility Utilization.* The collective utilization of service facilities reflects the percentage of time that they are busy. Management's goal is to maintain high utilization and profitability without adversely affecting the other operating characteristics.

The best method for analyzing a waiting-line problem is to relate the five operating characteristics and their alternatives to dollars. However, placing a dollar figure on certain characteristics (such as the waiting time of a shopper in a grocery store) is difficult. In such cases, an analyst must weigh the cost of implementing the alternative under consideration against a subjective assessment of the cost of *not* making the change.

We now present three models and some examples showing how waiting-line models can help operations managers make decisions. We analyze problems requiring the single-server, multiple-server, and finite-source models, all of which are single-phase. References to more advanced models are cited at the end of this text.

Single-Server Model

The simplest waiting-line model involves a single server and a single line of customers, commonly referred to as a single-channel, single-phase system. To further specify the single-server model, we make the following assumptions:

1. The customer population is infinite and all customers are patient.

2. The customers arrive according to a Poisson distribution, with a mean arrival rate of λ.

3. The service distribution is exponential, with a mean service rate of μ.

4. The mean service rate exceeds the mean arrival rate.

5. Customers are served on a first-come, first-served basis.

6. The length of the waiting line is unlimited.

Teenagers waiting in line to enter the Line Friends cafe and shop in Shanghai, China.

With these assumptions, we can apply various formulas to describe the operating characteristics of the system:

ρ = Average utilization of the system

$$= \frac{\lambda}{\mu}$$

P_n = Probability that n customers are in the system

$$= (1 - \rho)\rho^n$$

P_0 = Probability that zero customers are in the system

$$= 1 - \rho$$

L = Average number of customers in the service system

$$= \frac{\lambda}{\mu - \lambda}$$

L_q = Average number of customers in the waiting line

$$= \rho L$$

W = Average time spent in the system, including service

$$= \frac{1}{\mu - \lambda}$$

W_q = Average waiting time in line

$$= \rho W$$

EXAMPLE 3	Calculating the Operating Characteristics of a Single-Channel, Single-Phase System with the Single-Server Model

MyLab Operations Management

Active Model 1 in MyLab Operations Management provides additional insight on the single-server model and its uses for this problem.

The manager of a grocery store in the retirement community of Sunnyville is interested in providing good service to the senior citizens who shop in her store. Currently, the store has a separate checkout counter for senior citizens. On average, 30 senior citizens per hour arrive at the counter, according to a Poisson distribution, and are served at an average rate of 35 customers per hour, with exponential service times. Find the following operating characteristics:

a. Probability of zero customers in the system

b. Average utilization of the checkout clerk

c. Average number of customers in the system

d. Average number of customers in line

e. Average time spent in the system

f. Average waiting time in line

SOLUTION

The checkout counter can be modeled as a single-channel, single-phase system. Figure 4 shows the results from the *Waiting-Lines* Solver from OM Explorer. Manual calculations of the equations for the *single-server model* are demonstrated in the Solved Problem at the end of the text.

FIGURE 4 ▶

Waiting-Lines Solver for Single-Channel, Single-Phase System

			(Number of servers *s* assumed to be 1 in single-serve model)
Servers			
Arrival Rate (λ)		30	
Service Rate (μ)		35	

Probability of zero customers in the system (P_0)		0.1429
Probability of [exactly ▼] 0 customers in the system		0.1429
Average utilization of the server (ρ)		0.8571
Average number of customers in the system (*L*)		6.0000
Average number of customers in line (L_q)		5.1429
Average waiting/service time in the system (*W*)		0.2000
Average waiting time in line (W_q)		0.1714

Both the average waiting time in the system (*W*) and the average time spent waiting in line (W_q) are expressed in hours. To convert the results to minutes, simply multiply by 60 minutes/hour. For example, $W = 0.20(60) = $ **12.00** minutes, and $W_q = 0.1714(60) = $ **10.28** minutes.

EXAMPLE 4	Analyzing Service Rates with the Single-Server Model

MyLab Operations Management

Tutor 1 in MyLab Operations Management provides a new example to practice the single-server model.

The manager of the Sunnyville grocery in Example 3 wants answers to the following questions:

a. What service rate would be required so that customers averaged only 8 minutes in the system?

b. For that service rate, what is the probability of having more than four customers in the system?

c. What service rate would be required to have only a 10 percent chance of exceeding four customers in the system?

SOLUTION

The *Waiting-Lines* Solver from OM Explorer could be used iteratively to answer the questions. Here we show how to solve the problem manually.

a. We use the equation for the average time in the system and solve for μ.

$$W = \frac{1}{\mu - \lambda}$$

$$8 \text{ minutes} = 0.133 \text{ hour} = \frac{1}{\mu - 30}$$

$$0.133\mu - 0.133(30) = 1$$

$$\mu = \textbf{37.52} \text{ customers/hour}$$

b. The probability of more than four customers in the system equals 1 minus the probability of four or fewer customers in the system.

$$P = 1 - \sum_{n=0}^{4} P_n$$

$$= 1 \sum_{n=0}^{4} (1 - \rho)\rho^n$$

and

$$\rho = \frac{30}{37.52} = 0.80$$

Then,

$$P = 1 - 0.2(1 + 0.8 + 0.8^2 + 0.8^3 + 0.8^4)$$

$$= 1 - 0.672 = \mathbf{0.328}$$

Therefore, there is a nearly 33 percent chance that more than four customers will be in the system.

c. We use the same logic as in part (b), except that μ is now a decision variable. The easiest way to proceed is to find the correct average utilization first, and then solve for the service rate.

$$P = 1 - (1 - \rho)(1 + \rho + \rho^2 + \rho^3 + \rho^4)$$

$$= 1 - (1 + \rho + \rho^2 + \rho^3 + \rho^4) + \rho(1 + \rho + \rho^2 + \rho^3 + \rho^4)$$

$$= 1 - 1 - \rho - \rho^2 - \rho^3 - \rho^4 + \rho + \rho^2 + \rho^3 + \rho^4 + \rho^5$$

$$= \rho^5$$

or

$$\rho = P^{1/5}$$

If $P = 0.10$,

$$\rho = (0.10)^{1/5} = 0.63$$

Therefore, for a utilization rate of 63 percent, the probability of more than four customers in the system is 10 percent. For $\lambda = 30$, the mean service rate must be

$$\frac{30}{\mu} = 0.63$$

$$\mu = \mathbf{47.62} \text{ customers/hour}$$

DECISION POINT
The service rate would only have to increase modestly to achieve the 8-minute target. However, the probability of having more than four customers in the system is too high. The manager must now find a way to increase the service rate from 35 per hour to approximately 48 per hour. She can increase the service rate in several different ways, ranging from employing a high school student to help bag the groceries to installing self-checkout stations.

Multiple-Server Model

With the multiple-server model, customers form a single line and choose one of s servers when one is available. The service system has only one phase; consequently, we are focusing our discussion on multiple-channel, single-phase systems. We make the following assumptions in addition to those for the single-server model: There are s identical servers, and the service distribution for each server is exponential, with a mean service time of $1/\mu$. It should always be the case that $s\mu$ exceeds λ.

Cars line up at the Triborough Bridge toll, New York City. This is an example of a multiple-channel, single-phase system where some channels are devoted to special services.

| EXAMPLE 5 | Estimating Idle Time and Hourly Operating Costs with the Multiple-Server Model |

The management of the American Parcel Service terminal in Verona, Wisconsin, is concerned about the amount of time the company's trucks are idle (not delivering on the road), which the company defines as waiting to be unloaded and being unloaded at the terminal. The terminal operates with four unloading bays. Each bay requires a crew of two employees, and each crew costs $30 per hour. The estimated cost of an idle truck is $50 per hour. Trucks arrive at an average rate of three per hour, according to a Poisson distribution. On average, a crew can unload a semitrailer rig in one hour, with exponential service times. What is the total hourly cost of operating the system?

SOLUTION

The *multiple-server model* for $s = 4$, $\mu = 1$, and $\lambda = 3$ is appropriate. To find the total cost of labor and idle trucks, we must calculate the average number of trucks in the system at all times.

Figure 5 shows the results for the American Parcel Service problem using the *Waiting-Lines* Solver from OM Explorer. The results show that the four-bay design will be utilized 75 percent of the time and that the average number of trucks either being serviced or waiting in line is 4.53 trucks. That is, on average at any point in time, we have 4.53 idle trucks. We can now calculate the hourly costs of labor and idle trucks:

Labor cost:	$30(s) = $30(4) = $120.00
Idle truck cost:	$50(L) = $50(4.53) = $226.50
	Total hourly cost = **346.50**

FIGURE 5 ▶
Waiting-Lines Solver for Multiple-Server Model

Servers	4
Arrival Rate (λ)	3
Service Rate (μ)	1

Probability of zero customers in the system (P_0)		0.0377
Probability of exactly 0 customers in the system		0.0377
Average utilization of the servers (p)		0.7500
Average number of customers in the system (L)		4.5283
Average number of customers in line (L_q)		1.5283
Average waiting/service time in the system (W)		1.5094
Average waiting time in line (W_q)		0.5094

DECISION POINT

Management must now assess whether $346.50 per day for this operation is acceptable. Attempting to reduce costs by eliminating crews will only increase the waiting time of the trucks, which is more expensive per hour than the crews. However, the service rate can be increased through better work methods; for example, L can be reduced and daily operating costs will be less.

Little's Law

Little's law

Relates the number of customers in a waiting-line system to the arrival rate and the waiting time of customers.

One of the most practical and fundamental laws in waiting-line theory is **Little's law**, which relates the number of customers in a waiting-line system to the arrival rate and the waiting time of customers. Using the same notation we used for the single-server model, Little's law can be expressed as $L = \lambda W$ or $L_q = \lambda W_q$. However, this relationship holds for a wide variety of arrival processes, service-time distributions, and numbers of servers. The practical advantage of Little's law is that you only need to know two of the parameters to estimate the third. For example, consider the manager of a motor vehicle licensing facility who receives many complaints about the time people must spend either having their licenses renewed or getting new license plates. It would be difficult to obtain data on the times individual customers spend at the facility. However, the manager can have an assistant monitor the number of people who arrive at the facility each hour and compute the average (λ). The manager also could periodically count the number of people in the sitting area and at the stations being served and compute the average (L). Using Little's law, the manager can then estimate W, the average time each customer spent in the facility. For example, if 40 customers arrive per hour and the average number of customers being served or waiting is 30, the average time each customer spends in the facility can be computed as

$$\text{Average time in the facility} = W = \frac{L\text{ customers}}{\lambda\text{ customers/hour}} = \frac{30}{40} = 0.75 \text{ hour, or } \mathbf{45} \text{ minutes}$$

If the time a customer spends at the facility is unreasonable, the manager can focus on either adding capacity or improving the work methods to reduce the time spent serving the customers.

Likewise, Little's law can be used for manufacturing processes. Suppose that a production manager knows the average time a unit of product spends at a manufacturing process (W) and the average number of units per hour that arrive at the process (λ). The production manager can then estimate the average work-in-process (L) using Little's law. *Work in process* (WIP) consists of items, such as components or assemblies, needed to produce a final product in manufacturing. For example, if the average time a gear case used for an outboard marine motor spends at a machine center is 3 hours, and an average of five gear cases arrive at the machine center per hour, the average number of gear cases waiting and being processed (or work in process) at the machine center can be calculated as

$$\text{Work-in-process} = L = \lambda W = (5 \text{ gear cases/hour})(3 \text{ hours}) = \mathbf{15} \text{ gear cases}$$

Knowing the relationship between the arrival rate, the lead time, and the work in process, the manager has a basis for measuring the effects of process improvements on the work in process at the facility. For example, adding some capacity to a bottleneck in the process can reduce the average lead time of the product at the process, thereby reducing the work-in-process inventory.

Even though Little's law is applicable in many situations in both service and manufacturing environments, it is not applicable in situations where the customer population is finite, which we address next.

Finite-Source Model

We now consider a situation in which all but one of the assumptions of the single-server model are appropriate. In this case, the customer population is finite, having only N potential customers. If N is greater than 30 customers, the single-server model with the assumption of an infinite customer population is adequate. Otherwise, the finite-source model is the one to use.

EXAMPLE 6	Analyzing Maintenance Costs with the Finite-Source Model

The Worthington Gear Company installed a bank of 10 robots about 3 years ago. The robots greatly increased the firm's labor productivity, but recently attention has focused on maintenance. The firm does no preventive maintenance on the robots because of the variability in the breakdown distribution. Each machine has an exponential breakdown (or interarrival) distribution with an average time between failures of 200 hours. Each machine hour lost to downtime costs $30, which means that the firm has to react quickly to machine failure. The firm employs one maintenance person, who needs 10 hours on average to fix a robot. Actual maintenance times are exponentially distributed. The wage rate is $10 per hour for the maintenance person, who can be put to work productively elsewhere when not fixing robots. Determine the daily cost of labor and robot downtime.

MyLab Operations Management

Tutor 3 in MyLab Operations Management provides a new example to practice the finite-source model.

SOLUTION

The *finite-source model* is appropriate for this analysis because the customer population consists of only 10 machines and the other assumptions are satisfied. Here, $\lambda = 1/200$, or 0.005 break-down per hour, and $\mu = 1/10 = 0.10$ robot per hour. To calculate the cost of labor and robot downtime, we need to estimate the average utilization of the maintenance person and L, the average number of robots in the maintenance system at any time. Either OM Explorer or POM for Windows can be used to help with the calculations. Figure 6 shows the results for the Worthington Gear Problem using the *Waiting-Lines* Solver from OM Explorer. The results show that the maintenance person is utilized only **46.2** percent of the time, and the average number of robots waiting in line or being repaired is **0.76** robot. However, a failed robot will spend an average of **16.43** hours in the repair system, of which 6.43 hours of that time is spent waiting for service. While an individual robot may spend more than 2 days with the maintenance person, the maintenance person has a lot of idle time with a utilization rate of only **42.6** percent. That is why there is only an average of 0.76 robot being maintained at any point of time.

MyLab Operations Management

Active Model 3 in MyLab Operations Management provides additional insight on the finite-source model and its uses for this problem.

FIGURE 6 ▶

Waiting-Lines Solver for
Finite-Source Model

Customers	10
Arrival Rate (λ)	0.005
Service Rate (μ)	0.1

Probability of zero customers in the system (P_0)	0.5380
Probability of [fewer than ▼] 0 customers in the system	#N/A
Average utilization of the server (p)	0.4620
Average number of customers in the system (L)	0.7593
Average number of customers in line (L_q)	0.2972
Average waiting/service time in the system (W)	16.4330
Average waiting time in line (W_q)	6.4330

The daily cost of labor and robot downtime is

Labor cost: ($10/hour)(8 hours/day)(0.462 utilization) = $36.96

Idle robot cost: (0.76 robot)($30/robot hour)(8 hours/day) = 182.40

Total daily cost = **$219.36**

DECISION POINT

The labor cost for robot repair is only 20 percent of the idle cost of the robots. Management might consider having a second repair person on call in the event two or more robots are waiting for repair at the same time.

Waiting Lines and Simulation

For each of the problems we analyzed with the waiting-line models, the arrivals had a Poisson distribution (or exponential interarrival times), the service times had an exponential distribution, the service facilities had a simple arrangement, the waiting line was unlimited, and the priority discipline was first-come, first-served. Waiting-line theory has been used to develop other models in which these criteria are not met, but these models are complex. For example, POM for Windows includes a finite system-size model in which limits can be placed on the size of the system (waiting line and server capacity). It also has several models that relax assumptions on the service time distribution. Nonetheless, many times the nature of the customer population, the constraints on the line, the priority rule, the service-time distribution, and the arrangement of the facilities are such that waiting-line theory is no longer useful. In these cases, simulation often is used. Here we illustrate process simulation with the SimQuick software (also provided in MyLab Operations Management).

Passengers go through a TSA security checkpoint screening at Logan International Airport, Boston, Massachusetts. The airport security process is a multi-channel, multiphase system.

SimQuick

SimQuick is an easy-to-use package that is simply an Excel spreadsheet with some macros. Models can be created for a variety of simple processes, such as waiting lines, inventory control, and projects. Here, we consider the passenger security process at one terminal of a medium-sized airport between the hours of 8 A.M. and 10 A.M. The process works as follows. Passengers arriving at the security area immediately enter a single line. After waiting in line, each passenger goes through one of two inspection stations, which involves walking through a metal detector and running any carry-on baggage through a scanner. After completing this inspection, 10 percent of the passengers are randomly selected for an additional inspection, which involves a pat-down and a more thorough search of the person's carry-on baggage. Two stations handle this additional inspection, and selected passengers go through only one of them. Management is interested in examining the effect of increasing the percentage of passengers who undergo the second inspection. In particular, they want to compare the waiting times for the second inspection when 10 percent, then 15 percent, and then 20 percent of the passengers are randomly selected for this inspection. Management also wants to know how opening a third station for the second inspection would affect these waiting times.

A first step in simulating this process with SimQuick is to draw a flowchart of the process using SimQuick's building blocks. SimQuick has five building blocks that can be combined in a wide variety of ways. Four of these types are used to model this process. An *entrance* is used to model the arrival of passengers at the security process. A *buffer* is used to model each of the two waiting lines, one before each type of inspection, as well as the passengers that have finished the process. Each of the four inspection stations is modeled with a *workstation*. Finally, the random selection of passengers for the second inspection is modeled with a *decision point*. Figure 7 shows the flowchart.

Information describing each building block is entered into SimQuick tables. In this model, three key types of information are entered: (1) when people arrive at the entrance, (2) how long inspections take at the four stations, and (3) what percentage of passengers are randomly selected for the additional inspection. All of this information must be entered into SimQuick in the form of statistical distributions. The first two types of information are determined by observing the real process from 8 A.M. and 10 A.M. The third type of information is a policy decision (10 percent, 15 percent, or 20 percent).

The original model is run 30 times, simulating the arrival of passengers during the hours from 8 A.M. to 10 A.M. Statistics are collected by SimQuick and summarized. Figure 8 provides some key results for the model of the present process as output by SimQuick (many other statistics are collected, but not displayed here).

The numbers shown are averages across the 30 simulations. The number 237.23 is the average number of passengers that enter line 1 during the simulated 2 hours. The two mean inventory statistics tell us, on average, 5.97 simulated passengers were standing in line 1 and 0.10 standing in line 2. The two statistics on *cycle time*, interpreted here as the time a passenger spends in one or more SimQuick building blocks, tell us that the simulated passengers in line 1 waited an average of 3.12 minutes, while those in line 2 waited 0.53 minutes. The final inventory statistic tells us that, on average, 224.57 simulated passengers passed through the security process in the simulated 2 hours. The next step is to change the percentage of simulated passengers selected for the second inspection to 15 percent, and then to 20 percent, and rerun the model. Of course, these process changes will increase the average waiting time for the second inspection, but by how much? The final step is to rerun these simulations with one more workstation and see its effect on the waiting time for the second inspection. All the details for this model (as well as many others) appear in the book *SimQuick: Process Simulation with Excel*, which is included, along with the SimQuick software, in MyLab Operations Management.

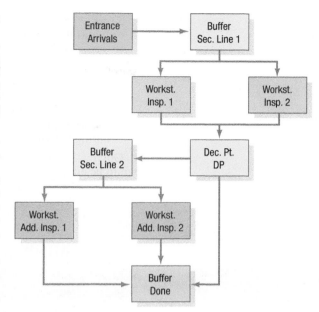

▲ **FIGURE 7**
Flowchart of Passenger Security Process

Element Types	Element Names	Statistics	Overall Means
Entrance(s)	Door	Objects entering process	237.23
Buffer(s)	Line 1	Mean inventory	5.97
		Mean cycle time	3.12
	Line 2	Mean inventory	0.10
		Mean cycle time	0.53
	Done	Final inventory	224.57

▲ **FIGURE 8**
Simulation Results of Passenger Security Process

MyLab Operations Management

Decision Areas for Management

After analyzing a waiting-line problem, management can improve the service system by making changes in one or more of the following areas.

1. *Arrival Rates.* Management often can affect the rate of customer arrivals, λ, through advertising, special promotions, or differential pricing. For example, hotels in the Caribbean will reduce their room rates during the hot, rainy season to attract more customers and increase their utilization.

2. *Number of Service Facilities.* By increasing the number of service facilities, such as tool cribs, toll booths, or bank tellers, or by dedicating some facilities in a phase to a unique set of services, management can increase system capacity.

3. *Number of Phases.* Managers can decide to allocate service tasks to sequential phases if they determine that two sequential service facilities may be more efficient than one. For instance, in assembly lines a decision concerns the number of phases or workers needed along the assembly line. Determining the number of workers needed on the line also involves assigning a certain set of work elements to each one. Changing the facility arrangement can increase the service rate, μ, of each facility and the capacity of the system.

4. *Number of Servers per Facility.* Managers can influence the service rate by assigning more than one person to a service facility.

5. *Server Efficiency.* By adjusting the capital-to-labor ratio, devising improved work methods, or instituting incentive programs, management can increase the efficiency of servers assigned to a service facility. Such changes are reflected in μ.

6. *Priority Rule.* Managers set the priority rule to be used, decide whether to have a different priority rule for each service facility, and decide whether to allow preemption (and, if so, under what conditions). Such decisions affect the waiting times of the customers and the utilization of the servers.

7. *Line Arrangement.* Managers can influence customer waiting times and server utilization by deciding whether to have a single line or a line for each facility in a given phase of service.

Obviously, these factors are interrelated. An adjustment in the customer arrival rate might have to be accompanied by an increase in the service rate, λ, in some way. Decisions about the number of facilities, the number of phases, and waiting-line arrangements also are related.

LEARNING GOALS IN REVIEW

Learning Goal	Guidelines for Review	MyLab Operations Management Resources
1 Identify the structure of waiting lines in real situations.	The section "Structure of Waiting-Line Problems," defines the four elements of every waiting-line problem. Figures 1, 2, and 3 depict these elements and various service facility arrangements.	
2 Use the single-server, multiple-server, and finite-source models to analyze operations and estimate the operating characteristics of a process.	See the section "Using Waiting-Line Models to Analyze Operations," for a description and demonstration of these three models. Examples 3, 4, and the Solved Problem at the end of the text apply the single-server model. Example 5 shows the multiple-server model and Example 6 applies the finite-source model. In addition, Examples 3 through 6 show how to obtain estimates for the important operating characteristics of processes using waiting-line models.	**Active Model Exercises:** 1: Single-Server Waiting-Line Model; 2: Multi-Server Model with Costs; 3: Finite Source Model with Costs **OM Explorer Solvers:** Single-Server Waiting-Line Model; Multi-Server Model; Finite Source Model **OM Explorer Tutors:** 1: Single-Server Waiting-Line Model; 2: Multi-Server Model; 3: Finite Source Model **POM for Windows:** 1: Single-Server Waiting-Line Model; 2: Multi-Server Model with Costs; 3: Finite Source Model with Costs; 4: Finite System-Size Model
3 Describe the situations where simulation should be used for waiting-line analysis and the nature of the information that can be obtained.	The section "Waiting Lines and Simulation," explains when simulation must be used and discusses an example that demonstrates the nature of the managerial information that can be obtained from that analysis.	**Online Text:** SimQuick: Process Simulation with Excel, 2e
4 Explain how waiting-line models can be used to make managerial decisions.	The section "Decision Areas for Management," describes seven decision areas that can be analyzed with waiting-line models.	

Key Equations

Structure of Waiting-Line Problems

1. Customer arrival Poisson distribution:

$$P_n = \frac{(\lambda T)^n}{n!} e^{-\lambda T}$$

2. Service time exponential distribution:

$$P(t \le T) = 1 - e^{-\mu T}$$

Using Waiting-Line Models to Analyze Operations ————

3. Average utilization of the system:

$$\rho = \frac{\lambda}{\mu}$$

4. Probability that n customers are in the system:

$$P_n = (1 - \rho)\rho^n$$

5. Probability that zero customers are in the system:

$$P_0 = 1 - \rho$$

6. Average number of customers in the service system:

$$L = \frac{\lambda}{\mu - \lambda}$$

7. Average number of customers in the waiting line:

$$L_q = \rho L$$

8. Average time spent in the system, including service:

$$W = \frac{1}{\mu - \lambda}$$

9. Average waiting time in line:

$$W_q = \rho W$$

10. Little's law:

$$L = \lambda W$$

Key Terms ————

channel	phase	service system
customer population	preemptive discipline	waiting line
interarrival times	priority rule	
Little's law	service facility	

Solved Problem ————

A photographer takes passport pictures at an average rate of 20 pictures per hour. The photographer must wait until the customer smiles, so the time to take a picture is exponentially distributed. Customers arrive at a Poisson-distributed average rate of 19 customers per hour.

MyLab Operations Management Video

a. What is the utilization of the photographer?

b. How much time will the average customer spend with the photographer?

SOLUTION

a. The assumptions in the problem statement are consistent with a single-server model. Utilization is

$$\rho = \frac{\lambda}{\mu} = \frac{19}{20} = \mathbf{0.95}$$

b. The average customer time spent with the photographer is

$$W = \frac{1}{\mu - \lambda} = \frac{1}{20 - 19} = \mathbf{1 \ hour}$$

Problems

The OM Explorer and POM for Windows software is available to all students. Go to **http://www.pearsonhighered.com/krajewski** to download these computer packages. If you purchased MyLab Operations Management, you also have access to Active Models software and significant help in doing the following problems. Check with your instructor on how best to use these resources. In many cases, the instructor wants you to understand how to do the calculations by hand. At the least, the software provides a check on your calculations. When calculations are particularly complex and the goal is interpreting the results in making decisions, the software entirely replaces the manual calculations.

Structure of Waiting-Line Problems

1. Wingard Credit Union is redesigning the entryway into its bank of ATM machines. Management is trying to conceptually understand the interarrival of individuals, which has been described to them as following a Poisson distribution. If on an average, two customers arrive per minute randomly during busy times, calculate the probability that during a specific minute, no customers arrive. Calculate the probability that between one and four customers arrive.

2. Wingard Credit Union (from problem 1) is also interested in understanding how long customers spend in front of the ATMs. Customer service times follow an Exponential distribution, with an average customer taking 1.5 minutes to complete a transaction. Calculate the probability that a customer will take less than half a minute. Additionally, calculate the probability that a customer will take more than 3 minutes.

Using Waiting-Line Models to Analyze Operations

3. The Solomon, Smith, and Samson law firm produces many legal documents that must be word processed for clients and the firm. Requests average eight pages of documents per hour, and they arrive according to a Poisson distribution. The secretary can word process 10 pages per hour on average according to an exponential distribution.

   a. What is the average utilization rate of the secretary?

   b. What is the probability that more than four pages are waiting or being word processed?

   c. What is the average number of pages waiting to be word processed?

4. Benny's Arcade has six video game machines. The average time between machine failures is 50 hours. Jimmy, the maintenance engineer, can repair a machine in 15 hours on average. The machines have an exponential failure distribution, and Jimmy has an exponential service-time distribution.

   a. What is Jimmy's utilization?

   b. What is the average number of machines out of service, that is, waiting to be repaired or being repaired?

   c. What is the average time a machine is out of service?

5. Moore, Aiken, and Payne is a critical care dental clinic serving the emergency needs of the general public on a first-come, first-served basis. The clinic has five dental chairs, three of which are currently staffed by a dentist. Patients in distress arrive at the rate of five per hour, according to a Poisson distribution, and do not balk or renege. The average time required for an emergency treatment is 30 minutes, according to an exponential distribution. Use POM for Windows or OM Explorer to answer the following questions:

   a. If the clinic manager would like to ensure that patients do not spend more than 15 minutes on average waiting to see the dentist, are three dentists

   on staff adequate? If not, how many more dentists are required?

   b. From the current state of three dentists on staff, what is the change in each of the following operating characteristics when a fourth dentist is placed on staff:

   - Average utilization
   - Average number of customers in line
   - Average number of customers in the system

   c. From the current state of three dentists on staff, what is the change in each of the following operating characteristics when a fifth dentist is placed on staff:

   - Average utilization
   - Average number of customers in line
   - Average number of customers in the system

6. Fantastic Styling Salon is run by three stylists, Jenny Perez, Jill Sloan, and Jerry Tiller, each capable of serving four customers per hour, on average. Use POM for Windows or OM Explorer to answer the following questions:

   During busy periods of the day, when nine customers on average arrive per hour, all three stylists are on staff.

   a. If all customers wait in a common line for the next available stylist, how long would a customer wait in line, on average, before being served?

   b. Suppose that each customer wants to be served by a specific stylist, 1/3 want Perez, 1/3 want Sloan, 1/3 want Tiller. How long would a customer wait in line, on average, before being served?

   During less busy periods of the day, when six customers on average arrive per hour, only Perez and Sloan are on staff.

   c. If all customers wait in a common line for the next available stylist, how long would a customer wait in line, on average, before being served?

d. Suppose that each customer wants to be served by a specific stylist, 60 percent want Perez and 40 percent want Sloan. How long would a customer wait in line, on average, before being served by Perez? By Sloan? Overall?

7. You are the manager of a local bank where three tellers provide services to customers. On average, each teller takes 3 minutes to serve a customer. Customers arrive, on average, at a rate of 50 per hour. Having recently received complaints from some customers that they waited a long time before being served, your boss asks you to evaluate the service system. Specifically, you must provide answers to the following questions:

a. What is the average utilization of the three-teller service system?

b. What is the probability that no customers are being served by a teller or are waiting in line?

c. What is the average number of customers waiting in line?

d. On average, how long does a customer wait in line before being served?

e. On average, how many customers would be at a teller's station and in line?

8. Pasquist Water Company (PWC) operates a 24-hour facility designed to efficiently fill water-hauling tanker trucks. Trucks arrive randomly to the facility and wait in line to access a wellhead pump. Since trucks vary in size and the filling operation is manually performed by the truck driver, the time to fill a truck is also random.

a. If the manager of PWC uses the multiple-server model to calculate the operating characteristics of the facility's waiting line, list three assumptions she must make regarding the behavior of waiting trucks and the truck arrival process.

b. Suppose an average of 336 trucks arrive each day, there are four wellhead pumps, and each pump can serve an average of four trucks per hour.

- What is the probability that exactly 10 trucks will arrive between 1:00 P.M. and 2:00 P.M. on any given day?

- How likely is it that once a truck is in position at a wellhead, the filling time will be less than 15 minutes?

c. Contrast and comment on the performance differences between:

- One waiting line feeding all four stations.

- One waiting line feeding two wellhead pumps and a second waiting line feeding two other wellhead pumps. Assume that drivers cannot see each line and must choose randomly between them. Further, assume that once a choice is made, the driver cannot back out of the line.

9. The supervisor at the Precision Machine Shop wants to determine the staffing policy that minimizes total operating costs. The average arrival rate at the tool crib, where tools are dispensed to the workers, is eight machinists per hour. Each machinist's pay is $20 per hour. The supervisor can staff the crib either with a junior attendant who is paid $5 per hour and can process 10 arrivals per hour or with a senior attendant who is paid $12 per hour and can process 16 arrivals

per hour. Which attendant should be selected, and what would be the total estimated hourly cost?

10. The daughter of the owner of a local hamburger restaurant is preparing to open a new fast-food restaurant called Hasty Burgers. Based on the arrival rates at her father's outlets, she expects customers to arrive at the drive-up window according to a Poisson distribution, with a mean of 20 customers per hour. The service rate is flexible; however, the service times are expected to follow an exponential distribution. The drive-in window is a single-server operation.

a. What service rate is needed to keep the average number of customers in the service system (waiting line and being served) to four?

b. For the service rate in part (a), what is the probability that more than four customers are in line and being served?

c. For the service rate in part (a), what is the average waiting time in line for each customer? Does this average seem satisfactory for a fast-food business?

11. The manager of a branch office of Banco Mexicali observed that during peak hours an average of 20 customers arrives per hour and that there is an average of four customers in the branch office at any time. How long does the average customer spend waiting in line and being serviced?

12. Paula Caplin is manager of a major electronics repair facility owned by Fisher Electronics. Recently, top management expressed concern over the growth in the number of repair jobs in process at the facility. The average arrival rate is 120 jobs per day. The average job spends four days at the facility.

a. What is the current work-in-process level at the facility?

b. Suppose that top management has put a limit of one-half the current level of work in process. What goal must Paula establish, and how might she accomplish it?

13. Failsafe Textiles employs three highly skilled maintenance workers who are responsible for repairing the numerous industrial robots used in its manufacturing process. A worker can fix one robot every 8 hours on average, with an exponential distribution. An average of one robot fails every 3 hours, according to a Poisson distribution. Each down robot costs the company $100.00 per hour in lost production. A new maintenance worker costs the company $80.00 per hour in salary, benefits, and equipment. Should the manager hire any new personnel? If so, how many people? What would you recommend to the manager, based on your analysis?

14. The College of Business and Public Administration at Benton University has a copy machine on each floor for faculty use. Heavy use of the five copy machines causes frequent failures. Maintenance records show that a machine fails every 2.5 days (or $\lambda = 0.40$ failure/day). The college has a maintenance contract with the authorized dealer of the copy machines. Because the copy machines fail so frequently, the dealer has assigned one person to the college to repair them. The person can repair an average of 2.5 machines per day. Using the finite-source model, answer the following questions:

a. What is the average utilization of the maintenance person?

b. On average, how many copy machines are being repaired or waiting to be repaired?

c. What is the average time spent by a copy machine in the repair system (waiting and being repaired)?

15. The manager of Vintage Time Video Machine Parlor is responsible for ensuring that all six of his machines are in good condition. Machines frequently need attention but can normally be returned to service quickly. On an average, each machine requires attention five times each hour. The manager averages 4 minutes per repair.

    a. What percentage of each hour is the manager fixing machines?

    b. On an average, how many machines are broken down and waiting for repair?

    c. On an average, how many minutes in an hour are machines waiting for repair or being repaired?

16. Two nurses at Northwood Hospital's Cardiac Care Unit are assigned to care for eight patients. Nurses are responsible for administering medication, taking vital signs, and responding to frequent calls for assistance that can come either from the patient, or the equipment monitoring the patient's current condition. On an average, each patient requires attention three times each hour. Nurses average 6 minutes per patient visit.

    a. What is the average utilization of the nursing staff?

    b. On an average, how many patients are waiting for a nurse?

    c. By how much would adding a third nurse reduce the patient waiting time?

17. You are in charge of a quarry that supplies sand and stone aggregates to your company's construction sites. Empty trucks from construction sites arrive at the quarry's huge piles of sand and stone aggregates and wait in line to enter the station, which can load either sand or aggregate. At the station, they are filled with material, weighed, checked out, and proceed to a construction site. Currently, nine empty trucks arrive per hour, on average. Once a truck has entered a loading station, it takes 6 minutes for it to be filled, weighed, and checked out. Concerned that trucks are spending too much time waiting and being filled, you are evaluating two alternatives to reduce the average time the trucks spend in the system. The first alternative is to add side boards to the trucks (so that more material could be loaded) and to add a helper at the loading station (so that filling time could be reduced) at a total cost of $50,000. The arrival rate of trucks would change to six per hour, and the filling time would be reduced to 4 minutes. The second alternative is to add another loading station identical to the current one at a cost of $80,000. The trucks would wait in a common line and the truck at the front of the line would move to the next available station.

    Which alternative would you recommend if you want to reduce the current average time the trucks spend in the system, including service?

Selected References

Buell, R., and M. Norton. "Think Customers Hate Waiting? Not so Fast." Harvard Business Review, vol. 89, no. 5 (2011), pp. 34.

Cooper, Robert B. Introduction to Queuing Theory, 3rd ed. Washington, DC: George Washington University, 1990.

Hartvigsen, David. SimQuick: Process Simulation with Excel, 2nd ed. Upper Saddle River, NJ: Prentice Hall, 2004.

Hillier, F. S., and G. S. Lieberman. Introduction to Operations Research, 9th ed. New York: McGraw-Hill, 2009.

Little, J. D. C. "A Proof for the Queuing Formula: $L = \lambda M$." Operations Research, vol. 9, (1961), pp. 383–387.

Morse, P. M. Queues, Inventories and Maintenance. New York: Dover Publications, 2004.

Glossary

channel One or more facilities required to perform a given service.

customer population An input that generates potential customers.

interarrival times The time between customer arrivals.

Little's law Relates the number of customers in a waiting-line system to the arrival rate and the waiting time of customers.

phase A single step in providing a service.

preemptive discipline A rule that allows a customer of higher priority to interrupt the service of another customer.

priority rule A rule that selects the next customer to be served by the service facility.

service facility A person (or crew), a machine (or group of machines), or both, necessary to perform the service for the customer.

service system The number of lines and the arrangement of the facilities.

waiting line One or more "customers" waiting for service.

NORMAL DISTRIBUTION

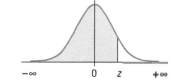

z	.00	.01	.02	.03	.04	.05	.06	.07	.08	.09
.0	.5000	.5040	.5080	.5120	.5160	.5199	.5239	.5279	.5319	.5359
.1	.5398	.5438	.5478	.5517	.5557	.5596	.5636	.5675	.5714	.5753
.2	.5793	.5832	.5871	.5910	.5948	.5987	.6026	.6064	.6103	.6141
.3	.6179	.6217	.6255	.6293	.6331	.6368	.6406	.6443	.6480	.6517
.4	.6554	.6591	.6628	.6664	.6700	.6736	.6772	.6808	.6844	.6879
.5	.6915	.6950	.6985	.7019	.7054	.7088	.7123	.7157	.7190	.7224
.6	.7257	.7291	.7324	.7357	.7389	.7422	.7454	.7486	.7517	.7549
.7	.7580	.7611	.7642	.7673	.7704	.7734	.7764	.7794	.7823	.7852
.8	.7881	.7910	.7939	.7967	.7995	.8023	.8051	.8078	.8106	.8133
.9	.8159	.8186	.8212	.8238	.8264	.8289	.8315	.8340	.8365	.8389
1.0	.8413	.8438	.8461	.8485	.8508	.8531	.8554	.8577	.8599	.8621
1.1	.8643	.8665	.8686	.8708	.8729	.8749	.8770	.8790	.8810	.8830
1.2	.8849	.8869	.8888	.8907	.8925	.8944	.8962	.8980	.8997	.9015
1.3	.9032	.9049	.9066	.9082	.9099	.9115	.9131	.9147	.9162	.9177
1.4	.9192	.9207	.9222	.9236	.9251	.9265	.9279	.9292	.9306	.9319
1.5	.9332	.9345	.9357	.9370	.9382	.9394	.9406	.9418	.9429	.9441
1.6	.9452	.9463	.9474	.9484	.9495	.9505	.9515	.9525	.9535	.9545
1.7	.9554	.9564	.9573	.9582	.9591	.9599	.9608	.9616	.9625	.9633
1.8	.9641	.9649	.9656	.9664	.9671	.9678	.9686	.9693	.9699	.9706
1.9	.9713	.9719	.9726	.9732	.9738	.9744	.9750	.9756	.9761	.9767
2.0	.9772	.9778	.9783	.9788	.9793	.9798	.9803	.9808	.9812	.9817
2.1	.9821	.9826	.9830	.9834	.9838	.9842	.9846	.9850	.9854	.9857
2.2	.9861	.9864	.9868	.9871	.9875	.9878	.9881	.9884	.9887	.9890
2.3	.9893	.9896	.9898	.9901	.9904	.9906	.9909	.9911	.9913	.9916
2.4	.9918	.9920	.9922	.9925	.9927	.9929	.9931	.9932	.9934	.9936
2.5	.9938	.9940	.9941	.9943	.9945	.9946	.9948	.9949	.9951	.9952
2.6	.9953	.9955	.9956	.9957	.9959	.9960	.9961	.9962	.9963	.9964
2.7	.9965	.9966	.9967	.9968	.9969	.9970	.9971	.9972	.9973	.9974
2.8	.9974	.9975	.9976	.9977	.9977	.9978	.9979	.9979	.9980	.9981
2.9	.9981	.9982	.9982	.9983	.9984	.9984	.9985	.9985	.9986	.9986
3.0	.9987	.9987	.9987	.9988	.9988	.9989	.9989	.9989	.9990	.9990
3.1	.9990	.9991	.9991	.9991	.9992	.9992	.9992	.9992	.9993	.9993
3.2	.9993	.9993	.9994	.9994	.9994	.9994	.9994	.9995	.9995	.9995
3.3	.9995	.9995	.9995	.9996	.9996	.9996	.9996	.9996	.9996	.9997
3.4	.9997	.9997	.9997	.9997	.9997	.9997	.9997	.9997	.9997	.9998

From Appendix of *Operations Management: Processes and Supply Chains*, Twelfth Edition. Lee J. Krajewski, Manoj K. Malhotra, Larry P. Ritzman. Copyright © 2019 by Pearson Education, Inc. All rights reserved.

Index